ON WRITING WELL

Books by William Zinsser

Any Old Place with You
Seen Any Good Movies Lately?
The City Dwellers
Weekend Guests
The Haircurl Papers
Pop Goes America
The Paradise Bit
The Lunacy Boom
On Writing Well
Writing with a Word Processor
Willie and Dwike
Writing to Learn
Spring Training

Editor

Extraordinary Lives: The Art and Craft
of American Biography
Inventing the Truth: The Art and Craft of Memoir
Spiritual Quests: The Art and Craft of Religious Writing
Paths of Resistance: The Art and Craft of the Political Novel
Worlds of Childhood: The Art and Craft
of Writing for Children

WILLIAM ZINSSER

ON WRITING WELL

AN INFORMAL GUIDE TO WRITING NONFICTION

FOURTH EDITION

Revised, Updated and Expanded

 HarperPerennial
A Division of HarperCollins*Publishers*

Designed by Cassandra J. Pappas

Library of Congress Cataloging-in-Publication Data

Zinsser, William Knowlton.

   On writing well: an informal guide to writing nonfiction /
William Zinsser.—4th ed., rev., updated, and exp., 1st Perennial
Library ed.
     p. cm.
   Includes bibliographical references.
   ISBN 0-06-055272-7—ISBN 0-06-096831-1 (pbk.)
    1. English language—Rhetoric. 2. Exposition (Rhetoric)
I. Title.
PE1429.Z5 1990
808'.042—dc20   90-80384

BOMC offers recordings and compact discs, cassettes
and records. For information and catalog write to
BOMR, Camp Hill, PA 17012.

Contents

16. Business Writing   147
17. Sports   159
18. Criticism   172
19. Humor   187
20. Writing About Yourself   208

PART III: ATTITUDES

21. Writing with a Word Processor   223
22. Trust Your Material   235
23. A Writer's Decisions   245
24. Write as Well as You Can   265

    Sources   275
    Index   279

Introduction

This book was written in 1976 and expanded in 1980 and 1986. Now, in 1990, it has been expanded again and has also had a major overhaul. I won't go so far as to say that with this Fourth Edition I've finally got it right. But I can say that it's the book I would like to have written in the first place.

I didn't write it earlier because I didn't know enough; I've continued to learn new things about writing and teaching writing. Much has also happened in the field itself. The advent of the word processor has given writers a whole new way to write, rewrite, edit and organize their work. Better yet, women have achieved recognition as important writers in every area of nonfiction. *On Writing Well* was still lopsidedly male, and I was impatient to fix it. One fix led to another, and I ended up writing two new chapters, adding many new sections, and making a number of revisions, updatings and cuts.

Originally the book grew out of a course that I created and taught at Yale, starting in 1971. I gave the course a plain title—"Nonfiction Workshop"—because I had a plain purpose: to try to help Yale undergraduates to write about the world they lived in. I taught out of my own experience: thirteen years as a writer and editor on the *New York Herald Tribune* and eleven more as a free-lance writer for magazines. I had been lucky in my apprenticeship: the *Herald Tribune* was an education in high standards. The older editors who made us rewrite what we had written—and rewritten—were custodians of a craft; writing well was a point of honor. That notion of nonfiction writing as honorable work was what I now wanted to pass along myself.

In 1976 I put what I had been teaching into a book and assumed that it said everything I wanted to say. But then I began to visit schools and colleges and to talk with teachers and students. They raised many questions that hadn't occurred to me before, and I found that there was more to say after all. I wrote a Second Edition, which dealt with the questions that had been asked most often. I also expanded the chapter on humor, having since taught a course at Yale in humor writing, and wrote a new chapter on business writing, having since taught some workshops at American corporations which told me that they couldn't understand their own memos any more. The new edition of *On Writing Well* took on a robust new life—reason enough to leave well enough alone.

But unexpected events continued to help me in my own writing that I thought might help other writers; a Third Edition would have to be written. At least it could be written on a word processor, and I began with a chapter on how that machine helps writers to write—and, more important, to rewrite. Rewriting is the essence of writing, as this book has always insisted, but nowhere had I explained the process—what writers should look for when they revisit their first draft. Another new chapter, "Trust Your Material," grew out of a lesson that had taken me by surprise during a writing project of my own: that truth needs no adornment and that writers who overexplain their material are doing considerable damage.

Another new chapter, on nonfiction as the new American literature, grew out of an anger I had noticed among writers and teachers and had long felt myself. *On Writing Well* is grounded in the belief that nonfiction is where much of the best writing of the day is being done. Yet writers and teachers of writing kept telling me that they are made to feel guilty if they prefer it to fiction. I wanted to assure them that no such guilt is necessary and to place nonfiction in its rich historical context. Finally, I wrote a new concluding chapter—very much a personal statement—called "Write as Well as You Can," which states my belief that writers must set the highest standards for their work and then defend it against editors whose standards may not be as high. With this summarizing credo I felt that I had said my final word.

Suddenly, however, 1990 arrived. *On Writing Well* was a child of the '70s. Was the child ready for the new decade? I knew that its principles were still valid: it still worked as a teaching book. But did it represent the different person I had become and the different society America had become? I took a fresh look and got a jolt. Much of the nonfiction that I admire today is written by women; yet the examples of good writing that I had put in the book were mostly by men. How that happened was easy to see in retrospect. When I first started teaching, the writers I cited as models were the ones who had influenced me when *I* was learning the craft: H. L. Mencken, E. B. White, Joseph Mitchell, Virgil Thomson, Red Smith and many others. When the course became a book I just took those men along. I also now saw (with a little help from women readers) that the book was littered with male pronouns. "He," "him" and "his" were used throughout to refer to "the writer" and "the reader." Both in content and in tone *On Writing Well* was not representative of nonfiction writing today or of how I thought about it.

I hacked at the pronouns first, getting rid of more than a hundred examples of sexist usage. Where the male pronoun remains, I feel that it's the only clean solution. (For a fuller explanation of what I did, and why, see pages 117–120.) Then I added passages by women writers in many areas of nonfiction, from Diane Ackerman in science to Eudora Welty in memoir.

What the newly arrived women bring to the book is far more than the sum of who they are. They bring a new range of sensibilities and concerns. Janice Kaplan, for instance, writing about sports, goes to the heart of the gains—both in performance and in public attitude—that have revolutionized the status of women athletes. Molly Haskell, writing about movies, wonders at the compulsion of so many of today's male film-makers to make films about their idealized boyhood. Would a male critic also have found it odd? Kennedy Fraser, writing about memoir, reveals the healing power that women writers hold for other women when they dare to use such personal forms as journals, diaries and letters.

Next I took a fresh look at the men writers in *On Writing Well.* Some who had been in previous editions no longer served my purposes, and they were gently eased overboard. But many others came to mind—writers I wanted to have along on the trip to illustrate forms and subjects I had added, such as memoir (John Mortimer, Leonard Woolf) and mathematics (S. M. Ulam), or to approach an old form from a new direction: writers such as Garrison Keillor and Tom Wolfe. In the case of two old favorites who have been with me from the beginning, Alan Moorehead and Lewis Thomas, I rewrote their sections to make a new point.

I also wrote two new chapters. One, "Writing About Yourself," deals with a loss in American life that I have come to feel strongly about. A blanket of timidity has settled over the country, paralyzing writers of all ages. Students feel that they have to write what the teacher wants; writers feel that they have to write what the editor wants. None of them will give themselves permission to write what *they* want to write—to use their own lives as material. This erosion of self-esteem is a national writing problem and a national teaching problem, and Chapter 20 tries to address it. On one level it's a chapter about memoir, one of nonfiction's most appealing forms. But on a deeper level it's a plea to writers of all ages to believe in their individuality and in the validity of their everyday experience. The plea is echoed in several subsequent passages that talk about integrity, initiative and risk.

The other new chapter, "A Writer's Decisions," is an attempt to make specific the general advice that has gone before: to provide in condensed form a handbook to *On Writing Well* as a whole. Strictly pedagogical, it analyzes the decisions that went into one of my own articles, about a trip to Timbuktu. My hope was to demonstrate that all writing boils down to a succession of big and small decisions, that no decision is too small to be worth wrestling with, and that every writing problem contains within itself the decision that will solve it.

On Writing Well is a highly subjective book—one man's opinions and prejudices—and every new edition has been more subjective than its predecessor. That's no accident. Since 1976 I've talked with or heard from thousands of writers, editors, teachers and students all across America. Their affection for the book has been a nourishment to me, and their letters have taken me into their own writing and teaching concerns. If this Fourth Edition is the most personal and the most trusting of its readers, it's because so many people have put some part of themselves into it.

NEW YORK
September 1990

PART I

Principles

1

The Transaction

About ten years ago a school in Connecticut held "a day devoted to the arts," and I was asked if I would come and talk about writing as a vocation. When I arrived I found that a second speaker had been invited—Dr. Brock (as I'll call him), a surgeon who had recently begun to write and had sold some stories to national magazines. He was going to talk about writing as an avocation. That made us a panel, and we sat down to face a crowd of student newspaper editors, English teachers and parents, all eager to learn the secrets of our glamorous work.

Dr. Brock was dressed in a bright red jacket, looking vaguely bohemian, as authors are supposed to look, and the first question went to him. What was it like to be a writer?

He said it was tremendous fun. Coming home from an arduous day at the hospital, he would go straight to his yellow pad and write his tensions away. The words just flowed. It was easy.

I then said that writing wasn't easy and it wasn't fun. It was hard and lonely, and the words seldom just flowed.

Next Dr. Brock was asked if it was important to rewrite. Absolutely not, he said. "Let it all hang out," and whatever form the sentences take will reflect the writer at his most natural.

I then said that rewriting is the essence of writing. I pointed out that professional writers rewrite their sentences repeatedly and then rewrite what they have rewritten. I mentioned that E. B. White and James Thurber rewrote their pieces eight or nine times.

"What do you do on days when it isn't going well?" Dr. Brock was asked. He said he just stopped writing and put the work aside for a day when it would go better.

I then said that the professional writer must establish a daily schedule and stick to it. I said that writing is a craft, not an art, and that the man who runs away from his craft because he lacks inspiration is fooling himself. He is also going broke.

"What if you're feeling depressed or unhappy?" a student asked. "Won't that affect your writing?"

Probably it will, Dr. Brock replied. Go fishing. Take a walk.

Probably it won't, I said. If your job is to write every day, you learn to do it like any other job.

A student asked if we found it useful to circulate in the literary world. Dr. Brock said that he was greatly enjoying his new life as a man of letters, and he told several stories of being taken to lunch by his publisher and his agent at chic Manhattan restaurants where writers and editors gather. I said that professional writers are solitary drudges who seldom see other writers.

"Do you put symbolism in your writing?" a student asked me.

"Not if I can help it," I replied. I have an unbroken record of missing the deeper meaning in any story, play or movie, and as for dance and mime, I have never had even a remote notion of what is being conveyed.

"I *love* symbols!" Dr. Brock exclaimed, and he described with gusto the joys of weaving them through his work.

So the morning went, and it was a revelation to all of us. At the end Dr. Brock told me he was enormously interested in my answers—it had never occurred to him that writing could be hard. I told him I was just as interested in *his* answers—it had never occurred to me that writing could be easy. (Maybe I should take up surgery on the side.)

As for the students, anyone might think we left them bewildered. But in fact we probably gave them a broader glimpse of the writing process than if only one of us had talked. For of course there isn't any "right" way to do such intensely personal work. There are all kinds of writers and all kinds of methods, and any method that helps people to say what they want to say is the right method for them.

Some people write by day, others by night. Some people need silence, others turn on the radio. Some write by hand, some by typewriter or word processor, some by talking into a tape recorder. Some people write their first draft in one long burst and then revise; others can't write the second paragraph until they have fiddled endlessly with the first.

But all of them are vulnerable and all of them are tense. They are driven by a compulsion to put some part of themselves on paper, and yet they don't just write what comes naturally. They sit down to commit an act of literature, and the self who emerges on paper is a far stiffer person than the one who sat down. The problem is to find the real man or woman behind all the tension.

For ultimately the product that any writer has to sell is not the subject being written about, but who he or she is. I often find myself reading with interest about a topic I never thought would interest me—some unusual scientific quest, for instance. What holds me is the enthusiasm of the writer for his field. How was he drawn into it? What emotional baggage did he bring along? How did it change his life? It's not necessary to want to spend a year alone at Walden Pond to become deeply involved with a writer who did.

This is the personal transaction that's at the heart of good nonfiction writing. Out of it come two of the most important qualities that this book will go in search of: humanity and warmth. Good writing has an aliveness that keeps the reader reading from one paragraph to the next, and it's not a question of gimmicks to "personalize" the author. It's a question of using the English language in a way that will achieve the greatest strength and the least clutter.

Can such principles be taught? Maybe not. But most of them can be learned.

2
Simplicity

Clutter is the disease of American writing. We are a society strangling in unnecessary words, circular constructions, pompous frills and meaningless jargon.

Who can understand the viscous language of everyday American commerce and enterprise: the business letter, the interoffice memo, the corporation report, the notice from the bank explaining its latest "simplified" statement? What member of an insurance or medical plan can decipher the brochure that describes what the costs and benefits are? What father or mother can put together a child's toy—on Christmas Eve or any other eve—from the instructions on the box? Our national tendency is to inflate and thereby sound important. The airline pilot who announces that he is presently anticipating experiencing considerable precipitation wouldn't dream of saying that it may rain. The sentence is too simple—there must be something wrong with it.

But the secret of good writing is to strip every sentence to its cleanest components. Every word that serves no function, every long word that could be a short word, every adverb that carries the same meaning that's already in the verb, every passive construction that leaves the reader unsure of who is doing what—these are the thousand and one adulterants that weaken the strength of a sentence. And they usually occur, ironically, in proportion to education and rank.

During the late 1960s the president of a major university wrote a letter to mollify the alumni after a spell of campus unrest. "You are probably aware," he began, "that we have been experiencing very considerable potentially explosive expressions of dissatisfaction on issues only partially related." He meant that the students had been hassling them about different things. I was far more upset by the president's English than by the students' potentially explosive expressions of dissatisfaction. I would have preferred the presidential approach taken by Franklin D. Roosevelt when he tried to convert into English his own government's memos, such as this blackout order of 1942:

> Such preparations shall be made as will completely obscure all Federal buildings and non-Federal buildings occupied by the Federal government during an air raid for any period of time from visibility by reason of internal or external illumination.

"Tell them," Roosevelt said, "that in buildings where they have to keep the work going to put something across the windows."

Simplify, simplify. Thoreau said it, as we are so often reminded, and no American writer more consistently practiced what he preached. Open *Walden* to any page and you will find a man saying in a plain and orderly way what is on his mind:

> I went to the woods because I wished to live deliberately, to front only the essential facts of life, and see if I could not learn what it had to teach, and not, when I came to die, discover that I had not lived. I did not wish to live what was not life, living is so dear; nor did I wish to practice resignation, unless it was quite necessary. I wanted to live deep and suck out all the marrow of life, to live so sturdily and Spartan-like

as to put to rout all that was not life, to cut a broad swath and shave close, to drive life into a corner, and reduce it to its lowest terms, and, if it proved to be mean, why then to get the whole and genuine meanness of it, and publish its meanness to the world; or if it were sublime, to know it by experience, and be able to give a true account of it.

How can the rest of us achieve such enviable freedom from clutter? The answer is to clear our heads of clutter. Clear thinking becomes clear writing; one can't exist without the other. It's impossible for a muddy thinker to write good English. You may get away with it for a paragraph or two, but soon the reader will be lost, and there's no sin so grave, for the reader will not easily be lured back.

Who is this elusive creature, the reader? The reader is someone with an attention span of about sixty seconds—a person assailed by forces competing for the minutes that might otherwise be spent on a magazine or a book. At one time these forces weren't so numerous or so possessive: newspapers, radio, spouse, home, children. Today they also include a "home entertainment center" (TV, VCR, video camera, tapes and CDs), pets, a fitness program, a lawn and a garden and all the gadgets that have been bought to keep them spruce, and that most potent of competitors, sleep. The person snoozing in a chair, holding a magazine or a book, is a person who was being given too much unnecessary trouble by the writer.

It won't do to say that the reader is too dumb or too lazy to keep pace with the train of thought. If the reader is lost, it's usually because the writer hasn't been careful enough. The carelessness can take any number of forms. Perhaps a sentence is so excessively cluttered that the reader, hacking through the verbiage, simply doesn't know what it means. Perhaps a sentence has been so shoddily constructed that the reader could read it in any of several ways. Perhaps the writer has switched

is too dumb or too lazy to keep pace with the ~~writer's~~ train
of thought. My sympathies are ~~entirely~~ with him.) ~~He's not~~
~~so dumb.~~ (If the reader is lost, it is generally because the
writer ~~of the article~~ has not been careful enough to keep
him on the ~~proper~~ path.

This carelessness can take any number of ~~different~~ forms.
Perhaps a sentence is so excessively ~~long and~~ cluttered that
the reader, hacking his way through ~~all~~ the verbiage, simply
doesn't know what *it* ~~the writer~~ means. Perhaps a sentence has
been so shoddily constructed that the reader could read it in
any of *several* ~~two or three different~~ ways. ~~He thinks he knows what~~
~~the writer is trying to say, but he's not sure.~~ Perhaps the
writer has switched pronouns in mid-sentence, or ~~perhaps he~~
has switched tenses, so the reader loses track of who is
talking ~~to whom~~ or ~~exactly~~ when the action took place. Perhaps Sentence B is not a logical sequel to Sentence A -- the
writer, in whose head the connection is ~~perfectly~~ clear, has
not *bothered to provide* ~~given enough thought to providing~~ the missing link. Perhaps the writer has used an important word incorrectly by not
taking the trouble to look it up ~~and make sure.~~ He may think
that "sanguine" and "sanguinary" mean the same thing, but)
~~I can assure you that~~ (the difference is a bloody big one ~~to the~~
~~reader.~~ *The reader* ~~He~~ can only ~~try to~~ infer ~~what~~ (speaking of big differences) what the writer is trying to imply.

Faced with *these* ~~such a variety of~~ obstacles, the reader
is at first a remarkably tenacious bird. He ~~tends to~~ blame*s*
himself, ~~He~~ obviously missed something, ~~he thinks,~~ and he goes
back over the mystifying sentence, or over the whole paragraph,

piecing it out like an ancient rune, making guesses and moving
on. But he won't do this for long. ~~He will soon run out of patience.~~ The writer is making him work too hard ~~-- harder than he should have to work --~~ and the reader will look for
~~a writer~~ one who is better at his craft.

The writer must therefore constantly ask himself: What am
I trying to say ~~in this sentence?~~ Surprisingly often, he
doesn't know. ~~And~~ Then he must look at what he has ~~just~~
written and ask: Have I said it? Is it clear to someone
encountering ~~who is coming upon~~ the subject for the first time? If it's
not, ~~clear,~~ it is because some fuzz has worked its way into the
machinery. The clear writer is a person ~~who is~~ clear-headed
enough to see this stuff for what it is: fuzz.

I don't mean ~~to suggest~~ that some people are born
clear-headed and are therefore natural writers, whereas
others ~~other people~~ are naturally fuzzy and will ~~therefore~~ never write
well. Thinking clearly is ~~an entirely~~ conscious act that the
writer must force ~~keep forcing~~ upon himself, just as if he were
embarking ~~starting out~~ on any other ~~kind of~~ project that requires ~~calls for~~ logic:
adding up a laundry list or doing an algebra problem ~~or playing chess.~~ Good writing doesn't ~~just~~ come naturally, though most
people obviously think it does ~~it's as easy as walking.~~ The professional

Two pages of the final manuscript of this chapter from the First Edition
of *On Writing Well.* Although they look like a first draft, they had
already been rewritten and retyped—like almost every other page—
four or five times. With each rewrite I try to make what I have written
tighter, stronger and more precise, eliminating every element that is
not doing useful work. Then I go over it once more, reading it aloud,
and am always amazed at how much clutter can still be cut. In this
Fourth Edition I've eliminated the sexist pronoun "he" to denote "the
writer" and "the reader."

pronouns in midsentence, or has switched tenses, so the reader loses track of who is talking or when the action took place. Perhaps Sentence B is not a logical sequel to Sentence A—the writer, in whose head the connection is clear, hasn't bothered to provide the missing link. Perhaps the writer has used an important word incorrectly by not taking the trouble to look it up. The writer may think that "sanguine" and "sanguinary" mean the same thing, but the difference is a bloody big one. The reader can only infer (speaking of big differences) what the writer is trying to imply.

Faced with such obstacles, readers are at first remarkably tenacious. They blame themselves—they obviously missed something, and they go back over the mystifying sentence, or over the whole paragraph, piecing it out like an ancient rune, making guesses and moving on. But they won't do this for long. The writer is making them work too hard, and they will look for one who is better at the craft.

Writers must therefore constantly ask: What am I trying to say? Surprisingly often they don't know. Then they must look at what they have written and ask: Have I said it? Is it clear to someone encountering the subject for the first time? If it's not, that's because some fuzz has worked its way into the machinery. The clear writer is someone clearheaded enough to see this stuff for what it is: fuzz.

I don't mean that some people are born clearheaded and are therefore natural writers, whereas others are naturally fuzzy and will never write well. Thinking clearly is a conscious act that writers must force upon themselves, just as if they were embarking on any other project that requires logic: adding up a laundry list or doing an algebra problem. Good writing doesn't come naturally, though most people obviously think it does. The professional writer is constantly being bearded by strangers who say they'd like to "try a little writing some-time"—meaning when they retire from their real profession, like insurance or real estate. Or they say, "I could write a book about that." I doubt it.

Writing is hard work. A clear sentence is no accident. Very few sentences come out right the first time, or even the third time. Remember this as a consolation in moments of despair. If you find that writing is hard, it's because it *is* hard. It's one of the hardest things that people do.

3

Clutter

Fighting clutter is like fighting weeds—the writer is always slightly behind. New varieties sprout overnight, and by noon they are part of American speech. Consider what Nixon's aide John Dean accomplished in just one day of testimony on TV during the Watergate hearings. The next day everyone in America was saying "at this point in time" instead of "now."

Consider all the prepositions that are draped onto verbs that don't need any help. We no longer head committees. We head them up. We don't face problems anymore. We face up to them when we can free up a few minutes. A small detail, you may say—not worth bothering about. It *is* worth bothering about. The game is won or lost on hundreds of small details. Writing improves in direct ratio to the number of things we can keep out of it that shouldn't be there. "Up" in "free up" shouldn't be there. Can we picture anything being freed *up*? To write clean English you must examine every word you put on paper. You'll find a surprising number of words that don't serve any purpose.

Take the adjective "personal," as in "a personal friend of mine," "his personal feeling" or "her personal physician." It's typical of the words that can be eliminated nine times out of ten. The personal friend has come into the language to distinguish him from the business friend, thereby debasing both language and friendship. Someone's feeling *is* his personal feeling—that's what "his" means. As for the personal physician, he is that man summoned to the dressing room of a stricken actress so that she won't have to be treated by the impersonal physician assigned to the theater. Someday I'd like to see him identified as "her doctor." Physicians are physicians, friends are friends. The rest is clutter.

Clutter is the laborious phrase that has pushed out the short word that means the same thing. Even before John Dean, people had stopped saying "now." They were saying "at the present time," or "currently," or "presently" (which means "soon"). Yet the idea can always be expressed by "now" to mean the immediate moment ("Now I can see him"), or by "today" to mean the historical present ("Today prices are high"), or simply by a form of the verb "to be" ("It is raining"). There's no need to say, "At the present time we are experiencing precipitation."

Speaking of which, we are experiencing considerable difficulty getting *that* word out of the language. Even your dentist will ask if you are experiencing any pain. If he had one of his own children in the chair he would say, "Does it hurt?" He would, in short, be himself. By using a more pompous phrase in his professional role he not only sounds more important, he blunts the painful edge of truth. It's the language of the airline stewardess demonstrating the oxygen mask that will drop down if the plane should somehow run out of air. "In the unlikely possibility that the aircraft should experience such an eventuality," she begins—a phrase so oxygen-depriving in itself that we are prepared for any disaster, and even gasping death shall lose its sting. As for her request to "kindly extinguish all smoking materials," I often wonder what materials are smoking. It's a terrifying sentence.

Clutter is the ponderous euphemism that turns a slum into a depressed socioeconomic area, a salesman into a marketing representative, garbage collectors into waste-disposal personnel and the town dump into the volume reduction unit. I think of Bill Mauldin's cartoon showing two hoboes riding a freight train. One of them says, "I started as a simple bum, but now I'm hard-core unemployed."

Clutter is the official language used by the American corporation—in its news releases and its annual report—to hide its mistakes. When one big company recently announced that it was "decentralizing its organizational structure into major profit-centered businesses" and that "corporate staff services will be realigned under two senior vice-presidents," it meant that it had had a lousy year.

Clutter is the language of the interoffice memo ("The trend to mosaic communication is reducing the meaningfulness of concern about whether or not demographic segments differ in their tolerance of periodicity") and the language of computers ("Congruent command paradigms explicitly represent the semantic oppositions in the definitions of the commands to which they refer").

Clutter is the language of the Pentagon throwing dust in the eyes of the populace by calling an invasion a "reinforced protective reaction strike" and by justifying its vast budgets on the need for "credible second-strike capability" and "counterforce deterrence." How can we grasp such vaporous double-talk? As George Orwell pointed out in "Politics and the English Language," an essay written in 1946 but cited frequently during the Vietnam and Cambodia years of Johnson and Nixon, "In our time, political speech and writing are largely the defense of the indefensible. . . . Thus political language has to consist largely of euphemism, question-begging and sheer cloudy vagueness." Orwell's warning that clutter is not just a nuisance but a deadly tool has come true in the recent decades of American military adventurism in Southeast Asia, Central America and other parts of the world.

Verbal camouflage reached new heights of invention during

General Alexander Haig's tenure as secretary of state in the
Reagan administration. Before Haig, nobody had ever thought
of saying "at this juncture of maturization" to mean "now." He
told the American people that he saw "improved pluralization"
in El Salvador, that terrorism could be fought with "meaningful
sanctionary teeth" and that intermediate nuclear missiles were
"at the vortex of cruciality." As for any worries that the public
might harbor about such matters, his message—reduced to one-
syllable words—was "leave it to Al." What he actually said was,
"We must push this to a lower decibel of public fixation. I don't
think there's much of a learning curve to be achieved in this
area of content."

I could go on quoting examples from various fields—every
profession has its growing arsenal of jargon to fire at the layman
and hurl him back from its walls. But the list would be depressing and the lesson tedious. The point of raising it now is to serve
notice that clutter is the enemy, whatever form it takes. It slows
the reader and makes the writer seem pretentious.

Beware, then, of the long word that is no better than the short
word: "numerous" (many), "facilitate" (ease), "individual" (man
or woman), "remainder" (rest), "initial" (first), "implement"
(do), "sufficient" (enough), "attempt" (try), "referred to as"
(called), and hundreds more. Beware, too, of all the slippery
new fad words for which the language already has equivalents:
overview and quantify, paradigm and parameter, optimize and
maximize, prioritize and potentialize. They are all weeds that
will smother what you write. Don't dialogue with someone you
can talk to. Don't interface with anybody.

Nor are all the weeds so obvious. Just as insidious are the little
growths of ordinary words with which we explain how we pro-
pose to go about our explaining, or which inflate a simple preposition or conjunction into a whole windy phrase.

"I might add," "It should be pointed out," "It is interesting
to note that"—how many sentences begin with these dreary

clauses announcing what the writer is going to do next? If you might add, add it. If it should be pointed out, point it out. If it is interesting to note, *make* it interesting. Being told that something is interesting is the surest way of tempting the reader to find it dull; are we not all stupefied by what follows when someone says, "This will interest you"? As for the inflated prepositions and conjunctions, they are the countless phrases like "with the possible exception of" (except), "due to the fact that" (because), "he totally lacked the ability to" (he couldn't), "until such time as" (until), "for the purpose of" (for).

Is there any way to recognize clutter at a glance? Here's a device that my students at Yale found helpful. I would put brackets around any component in a piece of writing that wasn't doing useful work. Often it was just one word that got bracketed: the unnecessary preposition that is appended to a verb ("order up"), or the adverb that carries the same meaning as the verb ("smile happily"), or the adjective that states a known fact ("tall skyscraper"). Often my brackets surrounded the little qualifiers that weaken any sentence they inhabit ("a bit," "sort of"), or the announcements like "I'm tempted to say," or the phrases like "in a sense" that don't mean anything at all. Sometimes my brackets surrounded an entire sentence— the one that essentially repeats what the previous sentence said, or that says something that readers don't need to know or can figure out for themselves. Most first drafts can be cut by 50 percent—they're swollen with words and phrases that do no new work.

My reason for bracketing the extra words instead of crossing them out was to avoid violating the student's sacred prose. I wanted to leave the sentence intact for the student to analyze. I was saying, "I may be wrong, but I think this can be deleted and the meaning won't be affected at all. But *you* decide: read the sentence without the bracketed material and see if it works." In the early weeks of the term I gave back papers that were festooned with brackets. Entire paragraphs were bracketed. But soon the students learned to put mental brackets around their own clutter, and by the end of the term their papers were almost clean. Today many of those students are professional writers, and they tell me, "I still see your brackets—they're following me through life."

You can develop the same eye. Look for the clutter in your writing and prune it ruthlessly. Be grateful for everything you can throw away. Reexamine each sentence that you put on paper. Is every word doing new work? Can any thought be expressed with more economy? Is anything pompous or pretentious or faddish? Are you hanging on to something useless just because you think it's beautiful?

Simplify, simplify.

4

Style

So much for early warnings about the bloated monsters that lie in ambush for the writer trying to put together a clean English sentence.

"But," you may say, "if I eliminate everything you think is clutter and strip every sentence to its barest bones, will there be anything left of me?" The question is a fair one and the fear entirely natural. Simplicity carried to its extreme might seem to point to a style where the sentences are little more sophisticated than "Dick likes Jane" and "See Spot run."

I'll answer the question first on the level of mere carpentry. Then I'll get to the larger issue of who the writer is and how to preserve his or her identity.

Few people realize how badly they write. Nobody has shown them how much excess or murkiness has crept into their style and how it obstructs what they are trying to say. If you give me an article that runs to eight pages and I tell you to cut it to four, you'll howl and say it can't be done. Then you'll go home and do it, and it will be infinitely better. After that comes the hard part: cutting it to three.

The point is that you have to strip your writing down before you can build it back up. You must know what the essential tools are and what job they were designed to do. If I may labor the metaphor of carpentry, it is first necessary to be able to saw wood neatly and to drive nails. Later you can bevel the edges or add elegant finials, if that's your taste. But you can never forget that you are practicing a craft that is based on certain principles. If the nails are weak, your house will collapse. If your verbs are weak and your syntax is rickety, your sentences will fall apart.

I'll admit that various nonfiction writers, like Tom Wolfe and Norman Mailer, have built some remarkable houses. But these are writers who spent years learning their craft, and when at last they raised their fanciful turrets and hanging gardens, to the surprise of all of us who never dreamed of such ornamentation, they knew what they were doing. Nobody becomes Tom Wolfe overnight, not even Tom Wolfe.

First, then, learn to hammer in the nails, and if what you build is sturdy and serviceable, take satisfaction in its plain strength.

But you will be impatient to find a "style"—to embellish the plain words so that readers will recognize you as someone special. You will reach for gaudy similes and tinseled adjectives, as if "style" were something you could buy in a style store at the mall and drape onto your words in bright decorator colors. (Decorator colors are the colors that decorators come in.) There is no style store. Style is organic to the person doing the writing, as much a part of him as his hair, or, if he is bald, his lack of it. Trying to add style is like adding a toupee. At first glance the formerly bald man looks young and even handsome. But at second glance—and with a toupee there is always a second glance—he doesn't look quite right. The problem is not that he doesn't look well groomed; he does, and we can only admire the wigmaker's almost perfect skill. The point is that he doesn't look like himself.

This is the problem of the writer who sets out deliberately to garnish his prose. You lose whatever it is that makes you unique. The reader will usually notice if you are putting on airs. He wants the person who is talking to him to sound genuine. Therefore a fundamental rule is: Be yourself.

No rule, however, is harder to follow. It requires writers to do two things which by their metabolism are impossible. They must relax and they must have confidence.

Telling a writer to relax is like telling a man to relax while being prodded for a possible hernia, and as for confidence, he is a bundle of anxieties. See how stiffly he sits, glaring at the paper or the screen that awaits his words. See how often he gets up to look for something to eat. A writer will do anything to avoid the act of writing. I can testify from my newspaper days that the number of trips made to the water cooler per reporter-hour far exceeds the body's need for fluids.

What can be done to put the writer out of these miseries? Unfortunately, no cure has yet been found. I can only offer the consoling thought that you are not alone. Some days will go better than others; some will go so badly that you will despair of ever writing again. We have all had many of these days and will have many more.

Still, it would be nice to keep the bad days to a minimum, which brings me back to the matter of trying to relax.

The average writer (as I said earlier) sets out to commit an act of literature. He thinks his article must be of a certain length or it won't seem important. He thinks how august it will look in print. He thinks of all the people who will read it. He thinks it must have the solid weight of authority. He thinks that its style must dazzle. No wonder he tightens: he is so busy thinking of his awesome responsibility to the finished article that he can't even start. Yet he vows to be worthy of the task, and, casting about for heavy phrases that would never occur to him if he weren't trying so hard to make an impression, he plunges in.

Paragraph 1 is a disaster—a tissue of ponderous generalities that seem to have come out of a machine. No *person* could have written them. Paragraph 2 isn't much better. But Paragraph 3 begins to have a somewhat human quality, and by Paragraph 4 the writer begins to sound like himself. He has started to relax. It's amazing how often an editor can simply throw away the first three or four paragraphs of an article and start with the paragraph where the writer begins to sound like himself. Not only are the first few paragraphs hopelessly impersonal and ornate; they also don't really say anything. They are a self-conscious attempt at a fancy introduction, and none is necessary.

A writer is obviously at his most natural and relaxed when he writes in the first person. Writing is a personal transaction between two people, conducted on paper, and the transaction will go well to the extent that it retains its humanity. Therefore I urge people to write in the first person—to use "I" and "me" and "we" and "us." They usually put up a fight.

"Who am I to say what *I* think?" they ask. "Or what *I* feel?"

"Who are you *not* to say what you think?" I reply. "There's only one you. Nobody else thinks or feels in exactly the same way."

"But no one cares about my opinions," they say. "It would make me feel conspicuous."

"They'll care if you tell them something interesting," I say, "and tell them in words that come naturally."

Nevertheless, getting writers to use "I" is seldom easy. They think they must somehow earn the right to reveal their emotions or their deepest thoughts. Or that it's egotistical. Or that it's undignified—a fear that hobbles the academic world. Hence the professorial use of "one" ("One finds oneself not wholly in accord with Dr. Maltby's view of the human condition") and of the impersonal "it is" ("It is to be hoped that Professor Felt's essay will find the wider audience it most assuredly deserves"). I don't want to meet "one"—he's a boring guy. I want a professor with a passion for his subject to tell me why it fascinates *him*.

I realize that there are vast regions of writing where "I" is not allowed. Newspapers don't want "I" in their news stories; many magazines don't want it in their articles; businesses and institutions don't want it in the annual reports and pamphlets that they send so profusely into the American home. Colleges don't want "I" in their term papers or dissertations, and English teachers in elementary and high schools have been taught to discourage any first-person pronoun except the literary "we" ("We see in Melville's symbolic use of the white whale . . ."). Many of these prohibitions are valid. Newspaper articles should consist of news, reported objectively. And I sympathize with teachers who don't want to give students an easy escape into opinion—"I think Hamlet was stupid"—before the students have grappled with the discipline of assessing a work on its merits and on external sources. "I" can be a self-indulgence and a cop-out.

Still, we have become a society fearful of revealing who we are. We have bred a national language of impersonality. The institutions that seek our support by sending us their brochures tend to sound remarkably alike, though surely all of them— hospitals, schools, libraries, museums, zoos—were founded and are still sustained by men and women with different dreams and visions. Where are these people? It's hard to glimpse them among all the passive sentences that say "initiatives were undertaken" and "priorities have been identified."

Even when "I" is not permitted, it's still possible to convey a sense of I-ness. James Reston, for instance, doesn't use "I" in his columns; yet I have a good idea of what kind of person he is, and I could say the same of other essayists and reporters. Good writers are always visible just behind their words. If you aren't allowed to use "I," at least think "I" while you write, or write the first draft in the first person and then take the "I"s out. It will warm up your impersonal style.

Style, of course, is tied to the psyche, and writing has deep psychological roots. The reasons why we express ourselves as we do, or fail to express ourselves because of "writer's block," are buried partly in the subconscious mind. There are as many different kinds of writer's block as there are kinds of writers, and I have no intention of trying to untangle them here. This is a short book, and my name isn't Sigmund Freud.

But I've noticed a new reason for avoiding "I" that runs even deeper than what is not allowed or what is undignified. Americans are suddenly unwilling to go out on a limb. A generation ago our leaders told us where they stood and what they believed. Today they perform the most strenuous verbal feats to escape this fate. Watch them wriggle through TV interviews without committing themselves on a single issue. I remember President Ford trying to assure a group of visiting businessmen that his fiscal policies would work. He said: "We see nothing but increasingly brighter clouds every month." I took this to mean that the clouds were still fairly dark. Ford's sentence, however, was just misty enough to say nothing and still sedate his constituents.

Later administrations brought no relief. Defense Secretary Casper Weinberger, assessing a Polish crisis in 1984, said: "There's continuing ground for serious concern and the situation remains serious. The longer it remains serious, the more ground there is for serious concern." President Bush, taking a stand on assault rifles in 1989, said: "There are various groups that think you can ban certain kinds of guns. I am not in that mode. I am in the mode of being deeply concerned."

But my all-time champ is Elliot Richardson, who held four major cabinet positions in the 1970s—attorney general and secretary of defense, commerce and HEW. It's hard to know even where to begin picking from his vast trove of equivocal statements, but consider this one: "And yet, on balance, affirmative action has, I think, been a qualified success." A thirteen-word sentence with five hedging words. I give it first prize as the most wishy-washy sentence in recent public discourse, though a close rival would be Richardson's analysis of how to ease boredom among assembly-line workers: "And so, at last, I come to the one firm conviction that I mentioned at the beginning: it is that the subject is too new for final judgments."

That's a firm conviction? Leaders who bob and weave like aging boxers don't inspire confidence—or deserve it. The same thing is true of writers. Sell yourself, and your subject will exert its own appeal. Believe in your own identity and your own opinions. Proceed with confidence, generating it by pure will-power. Writing is an act of ego, and you might as well admit it. Use its energy to keep yourself going.

5

The Audience

Soon after you confront this matter of preserving your identity, another question will occur to you: "Who am I writing for?"

It's a fundamental question, and it has a fundamental answer: You are writing for yourself. Don't try to visualize the great mass audience. There is no such audience—every reader is a different person. Don't try to guess what sort of thing editors want to publish or what you think the country is in a mood to read. Editors and readers don't know what they want to read until they read it. Besides, they're always looking for something new.

Don't worry about whether the reader will "get it" if you indulge a sudden impulse for humor or nonsense. If it amuses you in the act of writing, put it in. (It can always be taken out later, but only you can put it in.) You are writing primarily to please yourself, and if you go about it with confidence you will also entertain the readers who are worth writing for. If you lose the dullards back in the dust, that's where they belong. You don't want them anyway.

I realize that I've raised what seems to be a paradox. Earlier I warned that the reader is an impatient bird, perched on the thin edge of distraction or sleep. Now I'm saying that you must write for yourself and not be gnawed by constant worry over whether the reader is tagging along behind.

I'm talking about two different problems. One is craft, the other is attitude. The first is a question of mastering a precise skill; the second is a question of how you use that skill to express your personality.

In terms of craft, there's no excuse for losing the reader through sloppy workmanship. If he drowses off in the middle of your article because you have been careless about a technical detail, the fault is yours. But on the larger issue of whether the reader likes you, or likes what you are saying or how you are saying it, or agrees with it, or feels an affinity for your sense of humor or your vision of life, don't give him a moment's worry. You are who you are, he is who he is, and either you will get along or you won't.

Perhaps this still seems like a paradox—or at least an impossible mental act to perform. How can you think carefully about not losing the reader and still be carefree about his opinion? I can only assure you that they are separate processes.

First, work hard to master the tools. Simplify, prune and strive for order. Think of this as a mechanical act, and soon your sentences will become cleaner. The act will never become as mechanical as, say, shaving or shampooing—you will always have to think about the various ways in which the tools can be used. But at least your sentences will be grounded in solid principles, and your chances of losing the reader will be smaller.

Think of the other process as a creative act—the expressing of who you are. Relax and say what you want to say. And since style is who you are, you only need to be true to yourself to find it gradually emerging from under the accumulated clutter and debris, growing more distinctive every day. Perhaps the style won't solidify for several years as *your* style, *your* voice—and, in fact, it shouldn't. Just as it takes time to find yourself as a person, it takes time to find yourself as a stylist, and even then, inevitably, your style will change as you grow older.

But whatever your age, be yourself when you write. Many old

men still write with the zest they had in their twenties or early thirties; obviously their ideas are still young. Other old writers ramble and repeat themselves; their style is the tip-off that they have turned into garrulous bores. Many college students write as if they were desiccated alumni thirty years out.

Let's look at a few writers to see the sheer pleasure with which they put on paper their passions and their crotchets, not caring whether the reader shares them or not. The first excerpt is from "The Hen (An Appreciation)," written by E. B. White in 1944, at the height of World War II:

Chickens do not always enjoy an honorable position among city-bred people, although the egg, I notice, goes on and on. Right now the hen is in favor. The war has deified her and she is the darling of the home front, feted at conference tables, praised in every smoking car, her girlish ways and curious habits the topic of many an excited husbandryman to whom yesterday she was a stranger without honor or allure.

My own attachment to the hen dates from 1907, and I have been faithful to her in good times and bad. Ours has not always been an easy relationship to maintain. At first, as a boy in a carefully zoned suburb, I had neighbors and police to reckon with; my chickens had to be as closely guarded as an underground newspaper. Later, as a man in the country, I had my old friends in town to reckon with, most of whom regarded the hen as a comic prop straight out of vaudeville. . . . Their scorn only increased my devotion to the hen. I remained loyal, as a man would to a bride whom his family received with open ridicule. Now it is my turn to wear the smile, as I listen to the enthusiastic cackling of urbanites, who have suddenly taken up the hen socially and who fill the air with their newfound ecstasy and knowledge and the relative charms of the New Hampshire Red and the Laced Wyandotte. You would think, from their nervous cries of wonder and praise, that the hen was hatched yesterday in the suburbs of New York, instead of in the remote past in the jungles of India.

To a man who keeps hens, all poultry lore is exciting and endlessly fascinating. Every spring I settle down with my farm journal and read, with the same glazed expression on my face, the age-old story of how to prepare a brooder house. . . .

Now there's a man writing about a subject I have absolutely no interest in. Yet I enjoy this piece thoroughly. I like the simple beauty of its style. I like the rhythms, the unexpected but refreshing words ("deified," "allure," "cackling"), the specific details like the Laced Wyandotte and the brooder house. But mainly what I like is that this is a man telling me unabashedly about a love affair with poultry that goes back to 1907. It's written with humanity and warmth, and after three paragraphs I know quite a lot about what sort of man this hen-lover is.

Or take a writer who is almost White's opposite in terms of style, who relishes the opulent word for its very opulence and does not deify the simple sentence. Yet they are brothers in holding firm opinions and saying what they think. This is H. L. Mencken reporting on the "Monkey Trial"—the trial of John Scopes, a young teacher who taught the theory of evolution in his Tennessee classroom—in the summer of 1925:

It was hot weather when they tried the infidel Scopes at Dayton, Tenn., but I went down there very willingly, for I was eager to see something of evangelical Christianity as a going concern. In the big cities of the Republic, despite the endless efforts of consecrated men, it is laid up with a wasting disease. The very Sunday-school superintendents, taking jazz from the stealthy radio, shake their fire-proof legs; their pupils, moving into adolescence, no longer respond to the proliferating hormones by enlisting for missionary service in Africa, but resort to necking instead. Even in Dayton, I found, though the mob was up to do execution on Scopes, there was a strong smell of antinomianism. The nine churches of the village were all half empty on Sunday, and weeds choked their yards. Only two or three of the resident pastors managed to sustain themselves by their ghostly science; the rest had to take orders for mail-order pantaloons or work in the adjacent strawberry fields; one, I heard, was a barber. . . . Exactly twelve minutes after I reached the village I was taken in tow by a Christian man and introduced to the favorite tipple of the Cumberland Range; half corn liquor and half Coca-Cola. It seemed a dreadful dose to me, but I found that the Dayton illuminati got it down with gusto, rubbing their tummies and rolling their eyes. They were all hot for Genesis, but their faces were too florid to belong to teetotalers, and when a pretty girl came tripping down the main street, they reached for the places where their neckties should have been with all the amorous enterprise of movie stars. . . .

This is pure Mencken, both in its surging momentum and in its irreverence. At almost any page where you open one of his books he is saying something sure to outrage the professed pieties of his countrymen. The sanctity in which Americans bathed their heroes, their churches and their edifying laws—especially Prohibition—was a well of hypocrisy for him that never came close to drying up. Some of his heaviest ammunition he hurled at Presidents and politicians—his portrait of "The Archangel Woodrow" still scorches the pages after half a century—and as for Christian believers and clerical folk in general, they turn up unfailingly as mountebanks and boobs.

It may seem a miracle that Mencken could get away with such heresies in the 1920s, when hero worship was an American religion and the self-righteous wrath of the Bible Belt oozed from coast to coast. In fact, not only did he get away with it; he was the most revered and influential journalist of his generation. The impact he made on subsequent writers of nonfiction is beyond measuring, and even now his topical pieces seem as fresh as if they were written yesterday.

The secret of his popularity—aside from his pyrotechnical use of the American language—was that he was obviously writing for himself and didn't give a damn what the reader might think. It wasn't necessary to share his prejudices to enjoy seeing them expressed with such mirthful abandon. Mencken was never timid or evasive; he didn't kowtow to the reader or curry anyone's favor. It takes courage to be such a writer, but it is out of such courage that revered and influential journalists are born.

Moving forward to our own time, here's an excerpt from *How to Survive in Your Native Land,* a book by James Herndon describing his experiences as a teacher in a California junior high school. Of all the earnest books on this subject that have sprouted in America, Herndon's is—for me—the one that best captures how it really is. His style is not quite like anybody else's, but his voice is absolutely true. Here's how the book starts:

> I might as well begin with Piston. Piston was, as a matter of description, a red-headed medium-sized chubby eighth-grader; his definitive characteristic was, however, stubbornness. Without going into a lot of detail, it became clear right away that what Piston didn't want to do, Piston didn't do; what Piston wanted to do, Piston did.
>
> It really wasn't much of a problem. Piston wanted mainly to paint, draw monsters, scratch designs on mimeograph blanks and print them up, write an occasional horror story— some kids referred to him as The Ghoul—and when he didn't want to do any of those, he wanted to roam the halls and on occasion (we heard) investigate the girls' bathrooms.

We had minor confrontations. Once I wanted everyone to sit down and listen to what I had to say—something about the way they had been acting in the halls. I was letting them come and go freely and it was up to them (I planned to point out) not to raise hell so that I had to hear about it from other teachers. Sitting down was the issue—I was determined everyone was going to do it first, then I'd talk. Piston remained standing. I reordered. He paid no attention. I pointed out that I was talking to him. He indicated he heard me. I inquired then why in hell didn't he sit down. He said he didn't want to. I said I did want him to. He said that didn't matter to him. I said do it anyway. He said why? I said because I said so. He said he wouldn't. I said Look I want you to sit down and listen to what I'm going to say. He said he *was* listening. I'll listen but I won't sit down.

Well, that's the way it goes sometimes in schools. You as teacher become obsessed with an issue—I was the injured party, conferring, as usual, unheard-of freedoms, and here they were as usual taking advantage. It ain't pleasant coming in the teachers' room for coffee and having to hear somebody say that so-and-so and so-and-so from *your* class were out in the halls *without a pass* and *making faces* and *giving the finger* to kids in *my* class during the most *important* part of *my* lesson about *Egypt*—and you ought to be allowed your tendentious speech, and most everyone will allow it, sit down for it, but occasionally someone wises you up by refusing to submit where it isn't necessary. . . . How did any of us get into this? we ought to be asking ourselves.

Any writer who uses "ain't" and "tendentious" in the same sentence, who quotes without using quotation marks, knows what he's doing. This seemingly artless style, so full of art, is ideal for Herndon's purpose. It avoids the pretentiousness that infects so much writing by people who are doing worthy work, and it allows for a rich vein of humor and common sense. Herndon sounds like a good teacher and like a person whose company I would enjoy. But ultimately he is writing for himself: an audience of one.

"Who am I writing for?" The question that begins this chapter has irked some readers; they want me to say "Whom am I writing for?" But I can't bring myself to say it. It's just not me.

6

Words

There's a kind of writing that might be called journalese, and it's the death of freshness in anybody's style. It is the common currency of newspapers and of magazines like *People*—a mixture of cheap words, made-up words and clichés that have become so pervasive that a writer can hardly help using them automatically. You must fight these phrases or you'll sound like every hack who sits down to write. You will never make your mark as a writer unless you develop a respect for words and a curiosity about their shades of meaning that is almost obsessive. The English language is rich in strong and supple words. Take the time to root around and find the ones you want.

What is "journalese"? It's a quilt of instant words patched together out of other parts of speech. Adjectives are used as nouns ("greats," "notables"). Nouns are extended into adjectives ("insightful"). Nouns are used as verbs ("to host"), or they are chopped off to form verbs ("enthuse," "emote"), or they are padded to form verbs ("beef up," "put teeth into"). This is a world where eminent people are "famed" and their associates are "staffers," where the future is always "upcoming" and someone is forever "firing off" a note. Nobody in America has merely sent a note or a memo or a telegram in years. Famed diplomat Henry Kissinger, who hosted foreign notables to beef up the morale of top State Department staffers, sat down and

fired off a lot of notes. Notes that are fired off are always fired
in anger and from a sitting position. What the weapon is I've
never found out.

Here, for example, is an article from a famed newsmagazine
that's hard to match for fatigue:

> Last February, Plainclothes Patrolman Frank Serpico
> knocked at the door of a suspected Brooklyn heroin pusher.
> When the door opened a crack, Serpico shouldered his way
> in only to be met by a .22-cal. pistol slug crashing into his face.
> Somehow he survived, although there are still buzzing frag-
> ments in his head, causing dizziness and permanent deafness
> in his left ear. Almost as painful is the suspicion that he may
> well have been set up for the shooting by other policemen.
> For Serpico, 35, has been waging a lonely, four-year war
> against the routine and endemic corruption that he and oth-
> ers claim is rife in the New York City police department. His
> efforts are now sending shock waves through the ranks of
> New York's finest. . . . Though the impact of the commission's
> upcoming report has yet to be felt, Serpico has little hope
> that . . .

The upcoming report has yet to be felt because it is still
upcoming, and as for the "permanent deafness," it's a little
early to tell. And what makes those buzzing fragments buzz? I
would have thought that by now only Serpico's head would be
buzzing. But apart from these lazinesses of logic, what makes
the story so infinitely tired is the failure of the writer to reach
for anything but the nearest cliché. "Shouldered his way," "only
to be met," "crashing into his face," "waging a lonely war,"
"corruption that is rife," "sending shock waves," "New York's
finest"—these dreary phrases constitute journalese at its worst
and writing at its most banal. We know just what to expect. No
surprise awaits us in the form of a bizarre word, an oblique look.

We are in the hands of a hack and we know it right away. We stop reading.

Don't let yourself get in this position. The only way to fight it is to care deeply about words. If you find yourself writing that someone recently enjoyed a spell of illness or that a business has been enjoying a slump, stop and think how much they enjoyed it. Notice the decisions that other writers make in their choice of words and be finicky about the ones that you select from the vast supply. The race in writing is not to the swift but to the original.

Make a habit of reading what is being written today and what has been written before. Writing is learned by imitation. If anyone asked me how I learned to write, I'd say that I learned by reading the men and women who were doing the kind of writing *I* wanted to do and trying to figure out how they did it. But cultivate the best models. Don't assume that because an article is in a newspaper or a magazine it must be good. Sloppy editing is common in American newspapers, and writers who use clichés by reflex are likely to work for editors who have seen so many clichés that they no longer even recognize them as they go limping by.

Also get in the habit of using dictionaries. My favorite for handy use is *Webster's New World Dictionary,* Second College Edition, though, like all word freaks, I own bigger dictionaries that will reward me in their own fashion when I'm on some more specialized search. (Careful writers, incidentally, cling to their copy of any Webster dictionary based on the superb Second Edition, because the Third Edition is quite permissive.) If you have any doubt of what a word means, look it up. Learn its etymology and notice what curious branches its original root has put forth. See if it has any other meanings that you didn't know it had. Master the small gradations between words that seem to be synonyms. What is the difference between "cajole," "wheedle," "blandish" and "coax"? An excellent guide to these nuances is *Webster's Dictionary of Synonyms.*

And don't scorn that bulging grab bag *Roget's Thesaurus.* It's easy to regard the book as hilarious. Look up "villain," for example, and you'll be awash in such rascality as only a lexicographer could conjure back from centuries of iniquity, obliquity, depravity, knavery, profligacy, frailty, flagrancy, infamy, immorality, corruption, wickedness, wrongdoing, backsliding and sin. You'll find rogues and wretches, ruffians and riffraff, miscreants and malefactors, reprobates and rapscallions, hooligans and hoodlums, scamps and scapegraces, scoundrels and scalawags, jezebels and jades. You'll find adjectives to fit them all (foul and fiendish, devilish and diabolical), and adverbs, and verbs to describe how the wrongdoers do their wrong, and cross-references leading to still other thickets of venality and vice. Still, there is no better friend to have around to nudge the memory than *Roget.* It saves you the time of rummaging in your own memory—that network of overloaded grooves—to find the word that's right on the tip of your tongue, where it doesn't do you any good. The *Thesaurus* is to the writer what a rhyming dictionary is to the songwriter—a reminder of all the choices—and you should use it with gratitude. If, having found the scalawag and the scapegrace, you want to know how they differ, *then* go to the dictionary.

Also bear in mind, when you are choosing words and stringing them together, how they sound. This may seem absurd: readers read with their eyes. But actually they hear what they are reading—in their inner ear—far more than you realize. Therefore such matters as rhythm and alliteration are vital to every sentence. A typical example—maybe not the best, but undeniably the nearest—is the preceding paragraph. Obviously I enjoyed making a certain arrangement of my ruffians and riffraff, my hooligans and hoodlums, and the reader enjoyed it too—far more than if I had provided a mere list. He enjoyed not only the arrangement but the effort to entertain him. He wasn't enjoying it, however, with his eyes. He was enjoying it in his ear.

E. B. White makes the case cogently in *The Elements of Style* (a book that every writer should read at least once a year) when he suggests trying to rearrange any phrase that has survived for a century or two, such as Thomas Paine's "These are the times that try men's souls":

> Times like these try men's souls.
> How trying it is to live in these times!
> These are trying times for men's souls.
> Soulwise, these are trying times.

Paine's phrase is like poetry and the other four are like oatmeal, which, of course, is the divine mystery of the creative process. The good writer of prose must be part poet, always listening to what he writes. E. B. White continues across the years to be my favorite stylist because I'm so conscious of being with a man who cares about the cadences and sonorities of the language. I relish (in my ear) the pattern that his words make as they fall into a sentence. I try to surmise how in rewriting the sentence he reassembled it to end with a phrase that will momentarily linger, or how he chose one word over another because he was after a certain emotional weight. It's the difference between, say, "serene" and "tranquil"—one so soft, the other strangely disturbing because of the unusual "n" and "q."

Such considerations of sound and rhythm should be woven through everything you write. If all your sentences move at the same plodding gait, which even you recognize as deadly but don't know how to cure, read them aloud. (I write entirely by ear and read everything aloud several times before letting it go out into the world.) You will begin to hear where the trouble lies. See if you can gain variety by reversing the order of a sentence, or by substituting a word that has freshness or oddity, or by altering the length of your sentences so that they don't all sound as if they came out of the same mold. An occasional short sentence can carry a tremendous punch. It stays in the reader's ear.

Remember, then, that words are the only tools you will be given. Learn to use them with originality and care. Value them for their strength and their diversity. And also remember: somebody out there is listening.

7

Usage

All this talk about good words and bad words brings us to a gray but important area called "usage." What is good usage? What is good English? What newly minted words is it O.K. to use, and who is to be the judge? Is it O.K. to use "O.K."?

Earlier I mentioned an incident of college students hassling the administration, and in the last chapter I described myself as a word freak. Here are two typical specimens that have crept into the language. "Hassle" is both a verb and a noun, meaning to give somebody a hard time, or the act of being given a hard time, and anyone who has ever been hassled by a petty bureaucrat for not properly filling out Form 35-BT will agree that the word sounds exactly right. "Freak" in this new usage means an enthusiast, and there's no missing the aura of obsession that goes with calling somebody a jazz freak, or a chess freak, or a sun freak, though it would probably be pushing my luck to describe a man who compulsively visits circus sideshows as a freak freak.

Anyway, I accept both of these new arrivals wholeheartedly. I don't consider them slang, or put quotation marks around them to show that I'm mucking about in the argot of the youth culture and really know better. They're good words and we need them to express what they express. But I won't accept "notables" and "greats" and "upcoming" and countless other newcomers. They are cheap words and we *don't* need them.

Why is one word good and another word cheap? I can't give you an answer because usage has no fixed boundaries or rules. Language is a fabric that changes from one week to another, adding new strands and dropping old ones, and even word freaks fight over what is allowable, often reaching their decision on a wholly subjective basis such as taste ("notables" is sleazy). Which still leaves the question of who our tastemakers are.

The question was confronted by the editors of a brand-new dictionary, *The American Heritage Dictionary,* at the outset of their task in the mid-1960s. They assembled a "Usage Panel" to help them appraise the new words and dubious constructions that had come knocking at the door. Which should be ushered in, which thrown out on their ear? The panel consisted of 104 men and women—mostly writers, poets, editors and teachers— who were known for caring about the language and trying to use it well. I was a member of the panel, and over the next few years I kept getting questionnaires. Would I accept "finalize" and "escalate"? How did I feel about "It's me"? Would I allow "like" to be used as a conjunction—like so many people do? How about "mighty," as in "mighty fine"?

We were told that in the dictionary our opinions would be tabulated in a separate "Usage Note" so that readers could tell how we voted. The questionnaire also left room for any comments that we might feel impelled to make—a chance that the panelists seized avidly, as we found when the dictionary was published in 1969 and our comments were released to the press. Passions ran high.

"Good God, no! Never!" cried Barbara W. Tuchman, asked about the verb "to author." Scholarship hath no fury like that of a language purist faced with sludge, and I shared Mrs. Tuchman's vow that "author" should never be authorized, just as I agreed with Lewis Mumford that the adverb "good" should be "left as the exclusive property of Ernest Hemingway" and with

Gerald Carson that "normalcy" should be "permitted only to admirers of the late Warren G. Harding."

But guardians of usage are doing only half their job if they merely keep the language from becoming sloppy. Any boob can rule that the suffix "wise," as in "healthwise," is boobwise, or that being "rather unique" is no more possible than being rather pregnant. The other half of the job is to help the language grow by welcoming any immigrant that will bring strength or color. Therefore I was glad to see that 97 percent of us voted to admit "dropout," which is clean and vivid, but that only 47 percent would accept "senior citizen," which is typical of the pudgy new intruders from the land of sociology, where a janitor is now a maintenance engineer. I'm glad we accepted "escalate," the kind of verbal contraption that I generally dislike but that the Vietnam war endowed with a precise meaning, complete with overtones of blunder.

I'm glad we took into full membership all sorts of robust words that previous dictionaries had derided as "colloquial": adjectives like "rambunctious," verbs like "stall" and "trigger" and "rile," nouns like "shambles" and "tycoon" and "trek," the latter approved by 78 percent to mean any difficult trip, as in "the commuter's daily trek to Manhattan." Originally it was a Cape Dutch word applied to the Boers' arduous journey by ox wagon. But our panel evidently felt that the Manhattan commuter's daily trek is no less arduous.

Still, 22 percent of us were unwilling to let "trek" slip into general usage. This was the virtue of revealing how our panel voted—it put our agreements and our discords on display, and now any writer who is in doubt can conduct himself accordingly. Thus our 95 percent vote against "myself," as in "He invited Mary and myself to dinner," a word condemned as "prissy," "horrible" and "a genteelism," ought to warn off anyone who doesn't want to be prissy, horrible and genteel. As Red

Smith put it, " 'Myself' is the refuge of idiots taught early that 'me' is a dirty word."

On the other hand, only 66 percent of our panel rejected the verb "to contact," and only half opposed the split infinitive and the verbs "to fault" and "to bus." So only 50 percent of your readers will fault you if you decide to voluntarily call your school board and to bus your children to another town. If you contact your school board you risk your reputation by another 16 percent. Our apparent rule of thumb was stated by Theodore M. Bernstein: "We should apply the test of convenience. Does the word fill a real need? If it does, let's give it a franchise." I agree with Bernstein. "Hassle" and "dropout" fill a real need.

All of this merely confirms what lexicographers have always known: that the laws of usage are relative, bending with the taste of the lawmaker. One of our panelists, Katherine Anne Porter, called "O.K." a "detestable vulgarity" and claimed that she had never spoken the word in her life, whereas I freely admit that I have spoken the word "O.K." "Most," as in "most everyone," was scorned as "cute farmer talk" by Isaac Asimov and embraced as a "good English idiom" by Virgil Thomson.

"Regime," meaning any administration, as in "the Truman regime," drew the approval of most everyone on the panel, as did "dynasty." But they drew the wrath of Jacques Barzun, who said, "These are technical terms, you blasted non-historians!" Probably I gave my O.K. to "regime" when I filled out the questionnaire. Now, chided by Barzun for imprecision, I think it looks like journalese. One of the words that *I* railed against was "personality," as in a "TV personality." But now I wonder if it isn't the only word for that vast swarm of people who are famous for being famous—and, possibly, for nothing else. What, for instance, do the Gabor sisters *do*?

In the end it comes down to one question: What is "correct" usage? We have no king to establish the King's English; we only have the President's English—which we don't want. *Webster,* long a defender of the faith, muddied the waters in 1961 with its permissive Third Edition, which argued that almost anything goes as long as somebody uses it, noting that "ain't" is "used orally in most parts of the U.S. by many cultivated speakers."

Just where *Webster* cultivated those speakers I ain't sure. Nevertheless it's true that the spoken language is looser than the written language, and *The American Heritage Dictionary* properly put its question to us in both forms. Often we allowed an oral idiom that we forbade in print as too informal, fully realizing, however, that "the pen must at length comply with the tongue," as Samuel Johnson said, and that today's spoken garbage may be tomorrow's written gold. Certainly the growing acceptance of the split infinitive, or of the preposition at the end of a sentence, proves that formal syntax can't—or shouldn't—hold the fort forever against a speaker's more comfortable way of getting the same thing said. A sentence is a fine thing to put a preposition at the end of. As for "It's me," who would defend to the death "It is I"? Only a purity freak.

Our panel recognized that correctness can even vary within a particular word. We voted heavily against "cohort," for instance, as a synonym for "colleague," except where the tone was jocular. Thus a professor would not be among his cohorts at a faculty meeting, but they would abound at his college reunion, wearing funny hats. We rejected "too" as a synonym for "very," as in "His health is not too good." Whose health is? But we approved it in wry or humorous use, as in "He was not too happy when she ignored him."

These may seem like picayune distinctions. They're not. They are signals to the reader that you are sensitive to the shadings of usage. "Too" when substituted for "very" is clutter—"He didn't feel too much like going shopping"—and should be cut out. But the wry example in the previous paragraph is worthy of Ring Lardner. It adds a tinge of sarcasm that otherwise wouldn't be there.

Did any pattern emerge from the opinions of our panel, or were we just flexing our prejudices and pedantries? Luckily, a pattern did emerge, and it offers a guideline that's still useful. In general we turned out to be liberal in accepting new words and phrases, but conservative in grammar.

It would be foolish, for instance, to reject a word as perfect as "dropout," or to pretend that countless words and phrases are not entering the gates of correct usage every day, borne on the winds of science and technology, fad and fashion, social change and social concern: "meltdown," "skyjacker," "wetlands," "software," "macho," "yuppie," "state-of-the-art," "pro-choice," "gentrify" and hundreds of others. Nor should we forget all the wonderfully short words invented by the counterculture in the 1960s as a way of lashing back at the bloated verbiage of the Establishment: "trip," "rap," "crash," "trash," "funky," "split," "rip-off," "vibes," "downer," "bummer" and many more. If brevity is a prize, these were sure winners. The only trouble with accepting words that entered the language overnight is that they have a tendency to leave as abruptly as they came. The "happenings" of the late 1960s no longer happen, "out of sight" is out of sight, and nobody does his "thing" anymore. Even "awesome" has begun to chill out. Be vigilant, therefore, about instant change. The writer who cares about usage must always know the quick from the dead.

As for the area where our Usage Panel was conservative, we strictly upheld most of the classic distinctions in grammar— "can" and "may," "fewer" and "less," "eldest" and "oldest," etc.—and decried the classic errors, insisting that "flout" still doesn't mean "flaunt," no matter how many writers flaunt their ignorance by flouting the rule, and that "fortuitous" still means "accidental," "disinterested" still means "impartial," and "infer" doesn't mean "imply."

Here we were motivated by our love of the language's beautiful precision. We hate to see our favorite tools mistreated. As Dwight Macdonald put it, "Simple illiteracy is no basis for linguistic evolution." This is where correct usage will win or lose you the readers you would most like to win. Know the difference between a "reference" and an "allusion," between "connive" and "conspire," between "compare with" and "compare to." If you must use "comprise," use it right. It means "include"; the major leagues comprise twenty-six teams.

"I choose always the grammatical form unless it sounds affected," Marianne Moore explained, and that finally is where our panel took its stand. We were not pedants, so hung up on correctness that we didn't want the language to keep refreshing itself with phrases like "hung up." But that didn't mean we had to accept every atrocity that has come stumbling in, like "hopefully."

*

Meanwhile the battle continues. In 1980 the Usage Panel was reconstituted, and we continue to receive ballots soliciting our opinion on new words and locutions: verbs like "definitize" ("Congress definitized a proposal") and "attrit" ("to attrit the population base of the enemy"), nouns like "affordables," colloquialisms like "the bottom line" and "up front," and strays like "into" ("He's into backgammon and she's into jogging").

It no longer takes a panel of experts to notice that jargon is inundating many areas of American life, especially government, business, education and the social sciences. President Carter signed an executive order directing that federal regulations be written "simply and clearly"; corporations and law firms have hired consultants to make their prose less murky and specialized, and even the insurance industry is trying to rewrite its policies to tell us in less disastrous English what redress will be ours when disaster strikes. Whether these efforts will do much good I wouldn't want to bet, nor, probably, would any oddsmaker. Still, there is comfort in the sight of so many people standing Canute-like on the beach, trying to hold back the tide. That's where all careful writers ought to be, looking at every new piece of debris that washes up and asking "Do we need it?"

I remember the first time somebody asked me, "How does that impact you?" I had always thought that "impact" was a noun, except in dentistry, which I try not to think of at all. Then I began to meet "de-impact," usually in connection with programs to de-impact the effects of some adversity. Nouns now turn overnight into verbs. We target goals and we access facts. The train conductor announces that the train won't platform. A sign on an airport door tells me that the door is alarmed.

I see that Detroit is downsizing its cars but still hoping to attract upscale customers. It's part of an ongoing effort to save energy. All efforts in America today are "ongoing." So are all programs and investigations. So, in fact, are all forms of life; when we cease to be ongoing we're dead. "Ongoing" is a jargon word that is unnecessary except to raise morale. We face our daily job with more zest if the boss reminds us that it's an ongoing project; we give more willingly to institutions if they have targeted our funds for ongoing improvements. One hospital recently wrote me about its plan to "modernize, expand and reconfigure" its facilities. When did "reconfigure" poke its haughty nose into our ongoing life? We were all doing fine without it. I would certainly hope that any architect trying to modernize a facility would move things around in response to new needs. "Reconfigure" gives his work the necessary grandeur to raise the necessary cash. Otherwise a donor might fall prey to "disincentivization."

I could go on. I have enough examples to fill a book, but it's not a book I would want anyone to read. We're still left with the question: What is good usage? Perhaps one helpful approach is to try to separate usage from jargon.

I would say, for instance, that "prioritize" is jargon—a pompous new verb that sounds more important than "rank"—and that "bottom line" is usage, a metaphor borrowed from the world of bookkeeping that conveys an image we can picture. As every businessman knows, the bottom line is the one that ultimately matters. It tells how things stand after all the gains and losses have been added up. If someone says, "The bottom line is that we just can't work together," we know what he means. I don't much like the phrase, but the bottom line is that it's here to stay.

New usages also arrive with new political events. Just as Vietnam gave us "escalate," Watergate gave us a whole lexicon of words connoting obstruction and deceit, such as "stonewall," "deep-six" and "launder." It's a fitting irony that under Richard Nixon "launder" became a dirty word. Today when we hear that someone laundered his funds in Mexico to hide the origin of the money and the route it took, the word has a precise meaning. It's short, it's vivid, and we need it. I accept "launder" and "stonewall"; I don't accept "prioritize" and "disincentive."

I would suggest a similar guideline for separating good English from technical English. It's the difference between, say, "printout" and "input." A printout is a specific object that a computer emits. Before the advent of computers it wasn't needed. Now it is. But it has stayed where it belongs—in the world where computers are used. Not so with "input," which was invented to describe the information that's fed to a computer. The word has broken out of the machine and run wild. Our input is sought on every subject, from diets and pets to philosophical discourse ("I'd like your input on whether God really exists").

I don't want to give somebody my input and get his feedback, though I'd be glad to offer my ideas and hear what he thinks of them. To me, good usage consists of using good words if they already exist—as they usually do—to express myself clearly and simply to someone else. You might say it's how I verbalize the interpersonal.

PART II

Forms

8

Nonfiction as Literature

One weekend a few years ago I went to Buffalo to talk at a writers' conference that had been organized by a group of women writers in that city. The women were serious about their craft, and the books and articles they had written were solid and useful. They asked me if I would take part in a radio talk show earlier in the week to publicize the conference—they would be with the host in the studio and I would be on a telephone hookup from my apartment in New York.

The appointed evening arrived, and my phone rang, and the host came on and greeted me with the strenuous joviality of his trade. He said he had three lovely ladies in the studio with him and he was eager to find out what we all thought of the present state of literature and what advice we had for all his listeners who were members of the literati and who had literary ambitions themselves. This hearty introduction dropped like a stone in our midst, and none of the three lovely ladies said anything, which I thought was the proper response. The silence lengthened, and finally I said, "I think we should banish all further mention of the words 'literature' and 'literary' and 'literati.'" I knew that the host had been briefed about what kind of writers we were and what we wanted to discuss. But he had no other frame of reference. "Tell me," he said, "what insights do you all have about the literary experience in America today?" Silence also greeted this question. Finally I said, "We're here to talk about the craft of writing."

He didn't know what to make of that, and he began to invoke the names of authors like Ernest Hemingway and Saul Bellow and William Styron, whom we surely regarded as literary giants. We said that those writers didn't happen to be our models, and we mentioned people like Lewis Thomas and Joan Didion and Stephen Jay Gould and Gary Wills. He had never heard of any of them. One of the women mentioned Tom Wolfe's *The Right Stuff,* and he hadn't heard of that. I mentioned Russell Baker's *Growing Up,* which had just been published to great acclaim. He hadn't heard of that, either. We explained that these were writers we admired for their ability to harness the issues and concerns of the day.

"But don't you want to write anything literary?" our host said. The three women said they felt that they were already doing satisfying work. That brought the program to another halt, and the host began to accept phone calls from his listeners, all of whom were interested in the craft of writing and wanted to know how we went about it. "And yet, in the stillness of the night," the host said to several callers, "don't you ever dream of writing the great American novel?" They didn't. They had no such dreams—in the stillness of the night or at any other time. It was one of the all-time lousy radio talk shows.

The story sums up a situation that any practitioner of nonfiction will recognize. Those of us who are trying to write well about the world we live in, or to teach students to write well about the world *they* live in, are caught in a time warp, where literature by definition consists of forms that were certified as "literary" in the nineteenth century: novels and short stories and poems. But in fact these have become quite rarefied forms in American life. The great preponderance of what writers now write and sell, what book and magazine publishers publish, and what readers demand is nonfiction.

The shift can be documented by all kinds of examples. One is the history of the Book-of-the-Month Club. When the club was founded in 1926 by Harry Scherman, Americans had little access to new literature and were mainly reading junk like *Ben-Hur.* Scherman's idea was that any town that had a post office had the equivalent of a bookstore, and he began sending the best new books to his newly recruited readers all over the country. Much of what he sent was fiction. The list of main selections chosen by the club from 1926 through 1941 is heavily laced with novelists: Ellen Glasgow, Sinclair Lewis, Virginia Woolf, John Galsworthy, Elinor Wylie, Ignazio Silone, Rosamond Lehmann, Edith Wharton, Somerset Maugham, Willa Cather, Booth Tarkington, Isak Dinesen, James Gould Cozzens, Thornton Wilder, Sigrid Undset, Ernest Hemingway, William Saroyan, John P. Marquand, John Steinbeck and many others. That was the high tide of "literature" in America. In fact, members of the Book-of-the-Month Club hardly heard the approach of World War II. Not until 1940 was it brought home to them in a book—*Mrs. Miniver,* a stiff-upper-lip novel about the early days of the Battle of Britain.

All of this changed with Pearl Harbor. World War II sent seven million Americans overseas and opened their eyes to reality: to new places and issues and events. After they came home the trend was reinforced by the advent of television. People who saw reality every evening in their living room suddenly lost patience with the slower rhythms and glancing allusions of the novelist. Overnight, America became a fact-minded nation. Since 1946 the Book-of-the-Month Club's members have predominantly demanded—and therefore received—works of nonfiction.

Magazines were swept along on the same current. The *Saturday Evening Post,* which had long spoon-fed its readers a heavy diet of short stories by writers who all seemed to have three names, like Clarence Budington Kelland and Octavus Roy

Cohen, reversed the ratio in the early 1960s. Ninety percent of the magazine was allotted to nonfiction articles, with just one short story by a three-named author thrown into the mixture to keep the faithful from feeling abandoned. It was the beginning of a golden era of nonfiction—especially in *Life,* which ran finely crafted articles every week; in *The New Yorker,* which elevated the form by originating such landmarks of modern American writing as Rachel Carson's *Silent Spring* and Truman Capote's *In Cold Blood*; and in *Harper's,* which commissioned such remarkable pieces as Norman Mailer's *Armies of the Night.* Nonfiction became the new American literature.

Today there is no area of life that isn't being made accessible to the public by writers writing with high seriousness and grace. I think of Lewis Thomas in biology, Stephen Jay Gould in natural science and evolution, Diane Ackerman in zoology, John McPhee in geology, Freeman Dyson in nuclear disarmament—writers who explain scientific processes with precision and humanity. I think of Wendell Berry and Annie Dillard writing about the fragile balance of nature and ecology, of Robert Coles writing about the gallantry of children under stress. I think of writers who have raised political and social science to literature (Gary Wills, J. Anthony Lukas), and travel writing (Jan Morris, Bruce Chatwin), and sports writing (Roger Angell), and popular culture (Joan Didion), and professional ethics (Janet Malcolm) and memoir (Eileen Simpson, Vivian Gornick).

I think of all the women who are writing strongly and vigilantly about what we are doing to ourselves as a society (Ellen Goodman, Barbara Ehrenreich) and how we are responding to our sick (Susan Sontag). My list is long; these are just a few names. Add to it all the disciplines once regarded as academic, like anthropology and economics, that have become the domain of nonfiction writers and of readers curious to know about the world they live in. Add all the good writing being done in biography (Robert A. Caro, David McCullough, Ronald Steel,

Jean Strouse) and in social history and literature (Phyllis Rose, Judith Thurman, John Updike)—writing that exerts a strong hold over us because it not only summons back the past but makes us think about the present.

My roster of the new literature, in short, would include all the writers who come bearing information, who explain what they know clearly, and who make an arrangement of it that raises their craft to an art. In an age when survival is tenuous and events outrun our ability to make sense of them, these are important writers.

I'm not saying that fiction is dead or that I'm against it. Obviously the novelist can take us into hidden places where no other writer can go: into the deep emotions, into the texture of daily existence, into the interior life. What I am saying is that I have no patience with the snobbery that accompanies "literature"— the snobbery which says that nonfiction is only journalism by another name, and that journalism by any name is a dirty word. While we're redefining literature, let's also redefine journalism. Journalism is writing that first appears in any periodic journal. Lewis Thomas's first two books—*The Lives of a Cell* and *The Medusa and the Snail*—were first written as essays for the *New England Journal of Medicine.* In fact, most of the writers I just mentioned wrote their books first as journalism. Historically, in America, good journalism becomes good literature. H. L. Mencken, Ring Lardner, Joseph Mitchell, Edmund Wilson and dozens of other major American writers were working journalists before they were canonized in the church of literature. They simply did what they did best and never worried about how it was defined.

Ultimately every writer must follow the path that feels most comfortable. For most people who are learning to write, that path is nonfiction. It enables them to write about what they know or can observe or can find out. This is especially true of young people. They will write far more willingly about situations that have reality—experiences that touch their own lives—or subjects that they have an aptitude for. Motivation is at the heart of writing. If nonfiction is where you do your best writing, or your best teaching of writing, don't be buffaloed into the idea that it's an inferior species. Go where your interest lies, or your affection, or your passion. The only important distinction is between good writing and bad writing. Good writing is good writing, whatever form it takes and whatever we call it.

9

Unity

You learn to write by writing. It's a truism, but what makes it a truism is that it's true. The only way to learn to write is to force yourself to produce a certain number of words on a regular basis.

If you went to work for a newspaper that required you to write two or three articles every day, you would be a better writer after six months. You wouldn't necessarily be writing well—your style might still be pedestrian, full of clutter and clichés. But at least you would be exercising your powers of putting the English language on paper, gaining confidence and identifying the most common problems.

All writing is ultimately a question of solving a problem. It may be a problem of where to obtain the facts, or how to organize the material. It may be a problem of approach or attitude, tone or style. Whatever it is, it has to be confronted and solved. Sometimes you will despair of finding the right solution—or any solution. You will think, "If I live to be ninety I'll never get out of this mess I'm in." I've often thought it myself. But when I finally do solve the problem it's because I have written millions of words. Like a surgeon removing his five hundredth appendix, I've been there before and have a surer instinct than the beginner about how to fix what has gone wrong.

So now I'll put you to actual writing. First I wanted to give you a set of principles and to suggest the broad range of opportunities that nonfiction offers. Now the task is to apply these principles to the various forms that nonfiction can take: the interview, travel writing, science writing, business writing, sports, criticism, humor, memoir, and all the hybrid species that can result from mixing them together. Every form has its special pitfalls. But all of them share one horrible problem: how to get started. No element of writing causes so much anguish as "the lead," and with almost no further ado I'll try to wrestle it into partial submission. The only ado that I will first commit is to suggest that before you struggle with the lead you make certain decisions about what tone you want to adopt. Get your unities straight.

Unity is the anchor of good writing. It not only keeps the reader from straggling off in all directions; it satisfies the reader's subconscious need for order and gives reassurance that all is well at the helm. Therefore choose from among the many variables and stick to your choice.

One choice is unity of pronoun. Are you going to write in the first person as a participant, or in the third person as an observer? Or even in the second person, that darling of sportswriters hung up on Hemingway? ("You knew this had to be the most spine-tingling clash of giants you'd ever seen from a pressbox seat, and you weren't just some green kid who was still wet behind the ears.")

Unity of tense is another choice. Most people write mainly in the past tense ("I went up to Boston the other day"), but some people write agreeably in the present ("I'm sitting in the dining car of the Yankee Limited and we're pulling into Boston"). What is not agreeable is to switch back and forth. I'm not saying that you can't use more than one tense. Obviously the whole purpose of tenses is to enable a writer to deal with time in its various gradations from the past to the hypothetical future

("When I telephoned my mother from the Boston station, I realized that if I had written to tell her I would be coming she would have waited for me"). What I am saying is that you must choose the tense in which you are *principally* going to address the reader, no matter how many glances you may take backward or forward along the way.

Another choice is unity of mood. You might want to talk to the reader in the casual and chatty voice that *The New Yorker* has so strenuously refined. Or you might want to approach the reader with a certain formality to describe a serious event or to present a set of important facts. Both tones are acceptable. In fact, *any* tone is acceptable. But don't mix two or three.

Such fatal mixtures are common in the nonfiction of writers who haven't yet learned control. Travel writing is a conspicuous case. "My wife, Ann, and I had always wanted to visit Hong Kong," the writer begins, his blood astir with reminiscence, "and one day last spring we found ourselves looking at an airline poster and I said, 'Let's go!' The kids were grown up or in school," he continues, and he proceeds to describe in genial detail how they stopped off in Hawaii and had such a comical time changing their money at the Hong Kong airport and finding their hotel. Fine. He is a real person taking us along on a real trip, and we can identify with him and Ann.

Suddenly he turns into a travel brochure. "Hong Kong affords many fascinating experiences to the curious sightseer," he writes. "One can ride the picturesque ferry from Kowloon and gawk at the myriad sampans as they scuttle across the teeming harbor, or take a day's trip to browse in the alleys of fabled Macao with its colorful history as a den of smuggling and intrigue. You will want to take the quaint funicular that climbs . . ." Then we get back to him and Ann and their efforts to eat at Chinese restaurants, and again all is well. Everyone is interested in food, and we are being told about a personal quest.

Then suddenly the writer is a guidebook: "To enter Hong

Kong it is necessary to have a valid passport, but no visa is required. You should definitely be immunized against smallpox and you would also be well advised to consult your physician with regard to a possible inoculation for typhoid. The climate in Hong Kong is seasonable except in July and August when . . ." Our writer is gone, and so is Ann, and so—very soon—are we.

It's not that the scuttling sampans and the smallpox shots shouldn't be included. What annoys us is that the writer never decided what kind of article he wanted to write or how he wanted to approach us. He comes at us in many guises, depending on what kind of material he is trying to purvey. Instead of controlling his material, he is allowing his material to control him. This wouldn't happen if he took time to establish certain unities.

Therefore ask yourself some basic questions before you start. For example: "In what capacity am I going to address the reader?" (Reporter? Provider of information? Average man or woman?) "What pronoun and tense am I going to use?" "What style?" (Impersonal reportorial? Personal but formal? Personal and casual?) "What attitude am I going to take toward the material?" (Involved? Detached? Judgmental? Ironic? Amused?) "How much do I want to cover?" "What one point do I want to make?"

The last two questions are more important than they might seem. Most nonfiction writers have a definitiveness complex. They feel that they are under some obligation—to the subject, to their honor, to the gods of writing—to make their article the last word. It's a commendable impulse, but there is no last word. What you think is definitive today will turn undefinitive by tomorrow, and writers who doggedly pursue every last fact will find themselves pursuing the rainbow and never settling down to write. Nobody can write a book or an article "about" something. Even Tolstoy couldn't write a book about war and peace, or Melville a book about whaling. They made certain reductive decisions about time and place and about individual characters in that time and place. Every writing project must be reduced before you start to write it.

Therefore think small. Decide what corner of your subject you're going to bite off, and be content to cover it well and stop. Often you'll find that along the way you've managed to say almost everything you wanted to say about the entire subject. This is also a matter of energy and morale. An unwieldy writing project is a drain on your enthusiasm. Enthusiasm is the force that keeps you going; it also conveys itself to the reader. When your zest begins to ebb, the reader is the first person to know it.

As for what point you want to make, every successful piece of nonfiction should leave the reader with one provocative thought that he or she didn't have before. Not two thoughts, or five—just one. So try to decide what single point you most want to leave in the reader's mind. It will not only give you a better idea of what route you ought to follow and what destination you hope to reach; it will affect your decision about tone and attitude. Some points are best made by dry understatement, some by heavy irony.

Once you have all these unities decided, there is no material you can't work into your frame. If the man writing about Hong Kong had chosen to write solely in the conversational vein about what he and Ann did, he would have found a natural way to weave into his narrative whatever he wanted to tell us about the Kowloon ferry and the local weather. His personality and purpose would have been intact, and his article would have held together.

Now it's possible that you'll make these prior decisions and then discover they were not the right ones. The material seems to be leading you in an unexpected direction, where you are more comfortable writing in a different tone. That's not abnormal—the very act of writing often generates some cluster of thoughts or memories that you didn't anticipate. Don't fight such a current if it feels right. Trust your material if it's taking you into terrain that you didn't intend to enter but where the vibrations are good. Adjust your style and your mood accordingly and proceed to whatever destination you reach. Don't ever become the prisoner of a preconceived plan. Writing is no respecter of blueprints—it's too subjective a process, too full of surprises.

Of course if this happens, the second part of your article will be badly out of joint with the first. But at least you know which part is truest to your instincts. Then it's just a matter of making repairs. Go back to the beginning and rewrite it so that the mood and style are consistent from start to finish.

There's nothing in such a method to be ashamed of. Scissors and paste—or their equivalents on a word processor—are honorable writers' tools. Just remember that all the unities must be fitted into the edifice that you finally put together, however backwardly they may fall into place, or it will soon come tumbling down.

10

The Lead

The most important sentence in any article is the first one. If it doesn't induce the reader to proceed to the second sentence, your article is dead. And if the second sentence doesn't induce him to continue to the third sentence, it's equally dead. Of such a progression of sentences, each tugging the reader forward until he is safely hooked, a writer constructs that fateful unit, the "lead."

How long should the lead be? One or two paragraphs? Four or five? There is no pat answer. Some leads hook the reader with just a few well-baited sentences; others amble on for several pages, exerting a slow but steady pull. Every article poses a different problem, and the only valid test is: Does it work? Your lead may not be the best of all possible leads, but if it does the job it's supposed to do, be thankful and proceed.

Sometimes the length may depend on the audience that you are writing for. Readers of a literary review, for instance, expect the writer to start somewhat discursively, and they will stick with him for the pleasure of wondering where he will emerge as he moves in leisurely circles toward his eventual point. But I urge you not to count on the reader to stick around. He is a fidgety fellow who wants to know—very soon—what's in it for him.

Therefore your lead must capture the reader immediately

and force him to keep reading. It must cajole him with freshness or novelty or paradox, or with humor, or with surprise, or with an unusual idea, or with an interesting fact or a question. Anything will do, as long as it nudges his curiosity and tugs at his sleeve.

Next the lead must do some real work. It must provide a few hard details that tell the reader why the piece was written and why he ought to read it. But don't dwell on the reason. Coax the reader a little more; keep him inquisitive.

Continue to build. Every paragraph should amplify the one that preceded it. Give more thought to adding solid detail and less to entertaining the reader. But take special care with the last sentence of each paragraph—it's the crucial springboard to the next paragraph. Try to give that sentence an extra twist of humor or surprise, like the periodic "snapper" in the routine of a stand-up comic. Make the reader smile and you've got him for at least one more paragraph.

Let's look at a few leads that vary in pace but are alike in maintaining pressure. I'll start with two columns of my own that first appeared in *Life* and *Look*—magazines which, judging by the comments of readers, found their consumers mainly in barbershops, hairdressing salons and airplanes ("I was getting a haircut the other day and I saw your article"). I mention this as a reminder that far more periodical reading is done under the dryer than under the reading lamp, so there isn't much time for the writer to fool around.

The first is the lead of a piece called "Block That Chicken-furter":

> I've often wondered what goes into a hot dog. Now I know and I wish I didn't.

Two very short sentences. But it would be hard not to continue to the second paragraph:

My trouble began when the Department of Agriculture published the hot dog's ingredients—everything that may legally qualify—because it was asked by the poultry industry to relax the conditions under which the ingredients might also include chicken. In other words, can a chickenfurter find happiness in the land of the frank?

One sentence that explains the incident that the column is based on. Then a snapper to restore the easygoing tone.

Judging by the 1,066 mainly hostile answers that the Department got when it sent out a questionnaire on this point, the very thought is unthinkable. The public mood was most felicitously caught by the woman who replied: "I don't eat feather meat of no kind."

Another fact and another smile. Whenever you're lucky enough to get a quotation as funny as that one, find a way to use it—preferably at the end of a paragraph.

The article then specifies what the Department of Agriculture says may go into a hot dog—a list that includes "the edible part of the muscle of cattle, sheep, swine or goats, in the diaphragm, in the heart or in the esophagus . . . [but not including] the muscle found in the lips, snout or ears."

From there it progresses—not without an involuntary reflex around the esophagus—into an account of the controversy between the poultry interests and the frankfurter interests, which in turn leads to the point that Americans will eat anything that even remotely resembles a hot dog. Implicit at the end is the larger point that Americans don't know, or care, what goes into the food they eat. The style of the article has remained casual and touched with humor throughout. But its content turns out to be more serious than the reader expected when he was drawn into it by a whimsical lead.

A slower lead, luring the reader more with curiosity than with humor, introduced a piece called "Thank God for Nuts":

> By any reasonable standard, nobody would want to look twice—or even once—at the piece of slippery elm bark from Clear Lake, Wisc., birthplace of pitcher Burleigh Grimes, that is on display at the National Baseball Museum and Hall of Fame in Cooperstown, N.Y. As the label explains, it is the kind of bark that Grimes chewed during games "to increase saliva for throwing the spitball. When wet, the ball sailed to the plate in deceptive fashion." This would seem to be one of the least interesting facts available in America today.
>
> But baseball fans can't be judged by any reasonable standard. We are obsessed by the minutiae of the game and nagged for the rest of our lives by the memory of players we once saw play. No item is therefore too trivial that puts us back in touch with them. I am just old enough to remember Burleigh Grimes and his well-moistened pitches sailing deceptively to the plate, and when I found his bark I studied it as intently as if I had come upon the Rosetta Stone. "So *that's* how he did it," I thought, peering at the odd botanical relic. "Slippery elm! I'll be damned."
>
> This was only one of several hundred encounters that I had with my own boyhood as I prowled through the Museum, a handsome brick building on Main Street, only a peanut bag's throw from the pasture where Abner Doubleday allegedly invented the game in 1839. Probably no other museum is so personal a pilgrimage to our past. . . .

The reader is now safely hooked, and the hardest part of the writer's job is over.

One reason for citing this lead is to point out that salvation often lies not in the writer's style but in some odd fact he was able to discover. I remember that I went up to Cooperstown and spent a whole afternoon in the museum, taking voluminous notes. Jostled everywhere by nostalgia, I gazed with reverence at Lou Gehrig's locker and Bobby Thomson's game-winning bat. I sat in a grandstand seat brought from the Polo Grounds, dug my unspiked soles into the home plate from Ebbets Field, and dutifully copied all the labels and captions that might be useful.

"These are the shoes that touched home plate as Ted finished his journey around the bases," said the label identifying the shoes worn by Ted Williams when he hit a home run on his last time at bat. The shoes were in much better shape than the pair—rotted open at the sides—that belonged to Walter Johnson. But again the caption provided exactly the kind of justifying fact that a baseball nut would want. "My feet must be comfortable when I'm out there a-pitching," the great Walter said.

The museum closed at five and I returned to my motel secure in my memories and my research. But instinct told me to go back the next morning for one more tour, and it was only then that I noticed Burleigh Grimes's slippery elm bark, which struck me as an ideal lead. It still does.

One moral of this story is that you should always collect more material than you will use. Every article is strong in proportion to the surplus of details from which you can choose the few that will serve you best—if you don't go on gathering facts forever. At some point you must stop researching and start writing.

Another moral is to look for your material everywhere, not just by reading the obvious sources and interviewing the obvious people. Look at signs and at billboards and at all the junk written along the American roadside. Read the labels on our packages and the instructions on our toys, the claims on our medicines and the graffiti on our walls. Read the fillers, so rich in self-esteem, that come spilling out of your monthly statement from the electric company and the telephone company and the bank. Read menus and catalogues and second-class mail. Nose about in obscure crannies of the newspaper, like the Sunday real estate section—you can tell the temper of a society by what patio accessories it wants. Our daily landscape is thick with absurd messages and portents. Notice them. They not only have a certain social significance; they are often just quirky enough to make a lead that's different from everybody else's.

And speaking of everybody else's lead, there are several categories I'd be glad never to see again. One is the future archaeologist: "When some future archaeologist stumbles upon the remains of our civilization, what will he make of the jukebox?" I'm tired of him already and he's not even here. I'm also tired of the visitor from Mars: "If a creature from Mars landed on our planet tomorrow he would be amazed to see hordes of scantily clad earthlings lying on the sand and barbecuing their skins." And I'm tired of the cute event that just happened to happen "one day not long ago" or on a conveniently recent Saturday afternoon. "One day not long ago a small button-nosed boy was walking with his dog, Terry, in a field outside Paramus, N.J., when he saw something that looked strangely like a balloon rising out of the ground." Let's retire the future archaeologist and the man from Mars and the button-nosed boy. Try to give your lead a freshness of perception or detail.

Consider this lead, by Joan Didion, on a piece called "7000 Romaine, Los Angeles 38":

> Seven Thousand Romaine Street is in that part of Los Angeles familiar to admirers of Raymond Chandler and Dashiell Hammett: the underside of Hollywood, south of Sunset Boulevard, a middle-class slum of "model studios" and warehouses and two-family bungalows. Because Paramount and Columbia and Desilu and the Samuel Goldwyn studios are nearby, many of the people who live around here have some tenuous connection with the motion-picture industry. They

once processed fan photographs, say, or knew Jean Harlow's manicurist. 7000 Romaine looks itself like a faded movie exterior, a pastel building with chipped *art moderne* detailing, the windows now either boarded or paned with chicken-wire glass and, at the entrance, among the dusty oleander, a rubber mat that reads WELCOME.

Actually no one is welcome, for 7000 Romaine belongs to Howard Hughes, and the door is locked. That the Hughes "communications center" should lie here in the dull sunlight of Hammett-Chandler country is one of those circumstances that satisfy one's suspicion that life is indeed a scenario, for the Hughes empire has been in our time the only industrial complex in the world—involving, over the years, machinery manufacture, foreign oil-tool subsidiaries, a brewery, two airlines, immense real-estate holdings, a major motion-picture studio, and an electronics and missile operation—run by a man whose *modus operandi* most closely resembles that of a character in *The Big Sleep.*

As it happens, I live not far from 7000 Romaine, and I make a point of driving past it every now and then, I suppose in the same spirit that Arthurian scholars visit the Cornish coast. I am interested in the folklore of Howard Hughes. . . .

What is pulling us into this article—toward, we hope, some glimpse of how Hughes operates, some hint of the riddle of the Sphinx—is the steady accretion of facts that have pathos and faded glamour. Knowing Jean Harlow's manicurist is such a minimal link to glory, the unwelcoming welcome mat such a queer relic of a golden age when Hollywood's windows weren't paned with chicken-wire glass and the roost was ruled by giants like Mayer and De Mille and Zanuck, who could actually be seen exercising their mighty power. We want to know more; we read on.

Another approach is to just tell a story. It's such a simple solution, so obvious and unsophisticated, that we often forget about it. But narrative is the oldest and most compelling method of holding someone's attention; everybody wants to be told a story. Keep looking for ways to couch your information in narrative form.

What follows is the lead of Edmund Wilson's account of the discovery of the Dead Sea Scrolls, one of the most astonishing relics of antiquity to turn up in modern times. Wilson doesn't waste any time setting the stage or warming up his audience. He starts right in—whap!—and we are caught:

At some point rather early in the spring of 1947, a Bedouin boy called Muhammed the Wolf was minding some goats near a cliff on the western shore of the Dead Sea. Climbing up after one that had strayed, he noticed a cave that he had not seen before, and he idly threw a stone into it. There was an unfamiliar sound of breakage. The boy was frightened and ran away. But he later came back with another boy, and together they explored the cave. Inside were several tall clay jars, among fragments of other jars. When they took off the bowl-like lids, a very bad smell arose, which came from dark oblong lumps that were found inside all the jars. When they got these lumps out of the cave, they saw that they were wrapped up in lengths of linen and coated with a black layer of what seemed to be pitch or wax. They unrolled them and found long manuscripts, inscribed in parallel columns on thin sheets that had been sewn together. Though these manuscripts had faded and crumbled in places, they were in general remarkably clear. The character, they saw, was not Arabic. They wondered at the scrolls and kept them, carrying them along when they moved.

These Bedouin boys belonged to a party of contrabanders, who had been smuggling their goats and other goods out of Transjordan into Palestine. They had detoured so far to the south in order to circumvent the Jordan bridge, which the customs officers guarded with guns, and had floated their commodities across the stream. They were now on their way to Bethlehem to sell their stuff in the black market, and they had come to the Dead Sea in order to stock up with water at the spring of Ain Feshkha, the only water to be found for miles in that dry, hot and desolate region. They were quite safe from discovery there: it was a locality that had no attractions, to which nobody ever came. In Bethlehem they sold their contraband and showed their scrolls to the merchant who was buying it. He did not know what they were and refused to pay the twenty pounds they asked for them; so they took them to another merchant, from whom they always bought their supplies. Being a Syrian, he thought that the language might be ancient Syriac and he sent word by another merchant to the Syrian Metropolitan at the Monastery of St. Mark in Old Jerusalem.

The Metropolitan, Mar Athanasius Yeshue Samuel, expressed a decided interest. He knew that nobody since the first Christian centuries had lived anywhere near Ain Feshkha, and he had been struck by the visitors' telling him that the scrolls were "wrapped up like mummies". . . .

And yet there can be no fixed rules for how to write a lead. Within the broad principle of not letting the reader get away, all writers must approach their subject in a manner that most naturally suits what they are writing about and who they are. In proof of which, I'll close with the lead of an article on rugby written by the actor Richard Burton. Its second sentence is one of the longest I've ever seen, but it's under control all the way. Besides, it sounds very Welsh, and if that's how Welshmen talk it's how they ought to write:

It's difficult for me to know where to start with rugby. I come from a fanatically rugby-conscious Welsh miner's family, know so much about it, have read so much about it, have heard with delight so many massive lies and stupendous exaggerations about it and have contributed my own fair share, and five of my six brothers played it, one with some distinction, and I mean I even knew a Welsh woman from Taibach who before a home match at Aberavon would drop goals from around 40 yards with either foot to entertain the crowd, and her name, I remember, was Annie Mort and she wore sturdy shoes, the kind one reads about in books as "sensible," though the recipient of a kick from one of Annie's shoes would have been not so much sensible as insensible, and I even knew a chap called Five-Cush Cannon who won the sixth replay of a cup final (the previous five encounters having ended with the scores 0–0, 0–0, 0–0, 0–0, 0–0, including extra time) by throwing the ball over the bar from a scrum 10 yards out in a deep fog and claiming a dropped goal. And getting it.

11

The Ending

After so many words suggesting how to get started I should add a few on how to stop. Knowing when to end an article is far more important than most writers realize. In fact, you should give as much thought to choosing your last sentence as you did to your first. Well, almost as much.

This may seem absurd. If the reader has stuck with you from the beginning, trailing you around blind corners and over bumpy terrain, surely he won't leave when the end is in sight. But he will—because the end that's in sight often turns out to be a mirage. Like the minister's sermon that builds to a series of perfect conclusions that never conclude, an article that doesn't stop at its proper stopping place is suddenly a drag and therefore, finally, a failure.

We are most of us still prisoners of the lesson pounded into us by the composition teachers of our youth: that every story must have a beginning, a middle and an end. We can still visualize the outline, with its Roman numerals (I, II and III), which staked out the road we would faithfully trudge, and its subnumerals (IIa and IIb) denoting lesser paths down which we would briefly poke. But we always promised to get back to III and summarize our journey.

That's all right for elementary and high school students uncertain of their ground. It forces them to see that every piece of writing should have a logical design which introduces and develops a theme. It's a lesson worth knowing at any age—even professional writers are adrift more often than they would like to admit. But if you are going to write good nonfiction you must wriggle out of III's dread grip.

You'll know you have arrived at III when you see emerging on your screen a sentence that begins, "In sum, therefore, it can be noted that . . ." Or a question that asks "What insights, then, have we been able to glean from . . . ?" These are signals to the reader that you are about to repeat in compressed form what you have already said in detail. The reader's interest begins to falter; the tension you have built begins to sag.

Yet you will be true to Miss Potter, your teacher, who made you swear fealty to the holy outline. You remind the reader of what can, in sum, therefore, be noted. You go gleaning one more time in insights that you have already adduced.

But your readers hear the laborious sound of cranking. They see what you are doing and how bored you are by it. They feel the stirrings of resentment. Why didn't you give more thought to how you were going to wind this thing up? Or are you summarizing because you think they're too dumb to get the point? Still, you keep cranking. But the reader has another option. He quits.

This is the negative reason for realizing the importance of the last sentence. Failure to know where that sentence should occur—and what it should consist of—can wreck an article that until its final stage has been tightly constructed.

The positive reason for ending well is not just to avoid ending badly but because a good last sentence—or paragraph—is a joy in itself. It has its own virtues, which give the reader a lift and which linger when the article is over.

The perfect ending should take the reader slightly by surprise and yet seem exactly right to him. He didn't expect the article to end so soon, or so abruptly, or to say what it said. But he knows it when he sees it. Like a good lead, it works. It's like the curtain line in a theatrical comedy. We are in the middle of a scene (we think) when suddenly one of the actors says something funny, or outrageous, or epigrammatic, and the lights go out. We are momentarily startled to find the scene over, and then delighted by the aptness of how it ended. What delights us, subconsciously, is the playwright's perfect control.

For the nonfiction writer, the simplest way of putting this into a rule is: When you're ready to stop, stop. If you have presented all the facts and made the point you want to make, look for the nearest exit.

Often it takes just a few sentences to wrap things up. Ideally they should encapsulate the idea of the piece and conclude with a sentence that stuns with its fitness or unexpectedness. The following passage is from a chapter in Gary Wills's *Nixon Agonistes* which analyzes how the Republicans chose the egregious Spiro Agnew as their nominee for vice-president at the 1968 convention in Miami. Earlier Wills has described Agnew as "a guided missile, swung into place, aimed, activated, launched with the minute calculation that marks Nixon. Once the missile was fired, the less attention it drew to itself the better—like a torpedo churning quiet toward its goal." This is how Wills ends:

There is a difference between ambition and opportunism. Leisurely "Ted" [Agnew] is not driven by Nixon's demons. He does not knock himself out; he does not even do his homework. But he is opportunistic—not cynically so; when lucky breaks come, one takes them, grateful. Man's function is to reap the fruits of our beneficent system. How foolish of "the kids" not to understand this. As he told them in the campaign: "You may give us your symptoms; we will make the diagnosis and we, the Establishment, will implement the cure." It is a message that he did not try to take to Miami's blacks.

The blunt irony of that final sentence brings echoes of Mencken rumbling down the decades again, as so often happens for me when one of America's bleakest truths is seen through a glass plainly. Here is how Mencken ends his appraisal of President Calvin Coolidge, whose appeal to the "customers" was that his "government governed hardly at all; thus the ideal of Jefferson was realized at last, and the Jeffersonians were delighted":

> We suffer most, not when the White House is a peaceful dormitory, but when it [has] a tin-pot Paul bawling from the roof. Counting out Harding as a cipher only, Dr. Coolidge was preceded by one World Saver and followed by two more. What enlightened American, having to choose between any of them and another Coolidge, would hesitate for an instant? There were no thrills while he reigned, but neither were there any headaches. He had no ideas, and he was not a nuisance.

Both the Agnew sentence and the Coolidge sentence send the reader on his way quickly and with an arresting thought to take along. The notion of Coolidge having no ideas and not being a nuisance is bound to leave a residue of enjoyment. It works.

Here's another ending that works. It's from *Iron and Silk*, a memoir by Mark Salzman of the two years he spent teaching English at a medical college in China after graduating from Yale in 1982. The incident involves a clerical worker who took her own life. She had complained that her superior had long mistreated her, but nobody wanted to take responsibility for the investigation. The important question, one student asked, is "what will happen to her family now?"

> He explained to me that, according to Chinese law, most suicides are considered criminal offenses against Socialism

and the Communist Party. When someone takes his own life, members of his family are often punished, on the principle that they must have either condoned or been influenced by the "incorrect thought" that led to the suicide. My student predicted that the woman's children would lose their chances of work assignments in our unit when they came of age. . . .

Four days passed, during which the woman's family was not allowed to hold any kind of memorial service, and, I was told, few dared visit the family to offer condolences. No one talked about her in my classes, though it was clear she was on everyone's mind.

On the fifth day a poster went up at the gate of our college. The Leaders had announced their decision: "Although Comrade M's suicide was the wrong course of action to take, it was not a crime against Socialism or the Chinese Communist Party because she left no note blaming the Party or any of its representatives for her despair, indicating that her problems were personal and not political. A thorough investigation of the case has proven that her superior, Manager L, is competent and totally without blame. Comrade M's gesture of hanging herself in the office of Manager L was the result of misunderstanding on her part."

A memorial service was held right away, and the woman's house was crowded with friends and neighbors who came to help with the cooking and cleaning. For several days afterward my students talked fondly about her in class, for she had been very popular during her lifetime, and everyone agreed how tragic it was that she had had this misunderstanding.

Something that I often do in my own work is to bring my story full circle—to strike at the end an echo of a note that was sounded at the beginning. It gratifies my sense of symmetry, and I like to think that it also pleases the reader, completing with its resonance the journey we set out on together. But what usually works best is a quotation. Go back through your notes to try to find some remark that has a sense of finality, or that's funny, or that adds an unexpected closing detail. Sometimes it will jump out at you during the interview—I've often thought, "That's my ending!"—or during the process of writing. Put it aside and save it.

In the mid-1960s, when Woody Allen was just becoming established as America's resident neurotic, still mainly doing nightclub monologues, I wrote the first long magazine piece that took note of his arrival. It ended like this:

> "If people come away relating to me as a person," Allen says, "rather than just enjoying my jokes; if they come away wanting to hear me again, no matter what I might talk about, then I'm succeeding." Judging by the returns, he is. Woody Allen is Mr. Related-To, Mr. Pop Therapy, and he seems a good bet to hold the franchise for many years.
>
> Yet he does have a problem all his own, unshared by, unrelated to, the rest of America. "I'm obsessed," he says, "by the fact that my mother genuinely resembles Groucho Marx."

There's a remark from so far out in left field that nobody could see it coming. The surprise that it carries is tremendous. How could it not be a perfect ending?

Surprise is one of the most refreshing commodities in writing. If something surprises you it will almost surely surprise—and delight—the people you are writing for.

12

The Interview

Get people talking. Learn to ask questions that will elicit answers about what is most interesting or vivid in their lives. Nothing so animates writing as someone telling what he thinks or what he does—in his own words.

His own words will always be better than your words, even if you are the most elegant stylist in the land. They carry the inflection of his speaking voice and the idiosyncrasies of how he puts a sentence together. They contain the regionalisms of his conversation and the lingo of his trade. They convey his enthusiasms. This is a person talking to the reader directly, not through the filter of a writer. As soon as a writer steps in, everybody else's experience becomes secondhand.

Therefore learn how to conduct an interview. Whatever form of nonfiction you write, it will come alive in proportion to the number of "quotes" you can weave into it naturally as you go along. Often, in fact, you will find yourself embarking on an article so apparently lifeless—the history of an institution, perhaps, or some local issue such as storm sewers—that you will quail at the prospect of keeping your readers, or even yourself, awake.

Take heart. You will find the solution if you look for the human element. Somewhere in every drab institution are men and women who have a fierce attachment to what they are doing and are rich repositories of lore. Somewhere behind every storm sewer is a politician whose future hangs on getting it installed and a widow who has always lived on the block and is outraged that some damn-fool legislator thinks it will wash away. Find these people to tell your story and it won't be drab.

I have proved this to myself many times—first when I was invited to write a small book for the New York Public Library to celebrate the fiftieth anniversary of its main building on Fifth Avenue. On the surface it seemed to be just the story of a marble building and millions of musty volumes. But behind the facade I found that the library had nineteen research divisions, each with a curator supervising a hoard of treasures and oddities, from Washington's handwritten Farewell Address to 750,000 movie stills. I decided to interview all these curators to learn what was in their collections, what they were adding to keep up with new areas of knowledge, and how their rooms were being used.

I found, for instance, that the Science and Technology division had a collection of patents second only to that of the United States Patent Office and was therefore almost a second home to the city's patent lawyers. But it also had a daily stream of men and women who obviously thought they were on the verge of discovering perpetual motion. "Everybody's got something to invent," the curator explained, "but they won't tell us what they're looking for—maybe because they think we'll patent it ourselves." The whole building turned out to be just such a mixture of scholars and searchers and crackpots, and my story, though ostensibly the chronicle of an institution, was really a story about people.

I used the same approach in a long article about Sotheby's, the thriving London auction firm. Sotheby's was also divided into various domains, such as silver and porcelain and art, each with an expert in charge, and, like the Library, it subsisted on the whims of a capricious public. The experts were like depart-

ment heads in a small college, and all of them had anecdotes
that were unique both in substance and in the manner of telling:

> "We just sit here like Micawber waiting for things to come
> in," said R. S. Timewell, head of the furniture department.
> "Recently an old lady near Cambridge wrote that she wanted
> to raise two thousand pounds and asked if I would go through
> her house and see if her furniture would fetch that much. I
> did, and there was absolutely nothing of value. As I was about
> to leave I said, 'Have I seen *every*thing?' She said I had,
> except for a maid's room that she hadn't bothered to show
> me. The room had a very fine 18th-century chest that the old
> lady was using to store blankets in. 'Your worries are over,' I
> told her, 'if you sell that chest.' She said, 'But that's quite
> impossible—where will I store my blankets?' "

My worries were over, too. By listening to the quizzical scholars who ran the business and to the men and women who
flocked there every morning bearing unloved objects found in
British attics ("I'm afraid it *isn't* Queen Anne, madam—much
nearer Queen Victoria, unfortunately"), I got as much human
detail as a writer could want.

Finally, when I was asked in 1966 to write a history of the
Book-of-the-Month Club to mark its fortieth birthday, I thought
I might encounter nothing but inert matter. But again I found
a peppery human element on both sides of the fence, for the
books had always been selected by a panel of strong-minded
judges and sent to equally stubborn subscribers, who never
hesitated to wrap up a book they didn't like and send it right
back.

I was given more than a thousand pages of transcribed interviews with the five original judges (Heywood Broun, Henry
Seidel Canby, Dorothy Canfield, Christopher Morley and Wil-

liam Allen White), to which I added my own interviews with the club's founder, Harry Scherman, and with the judges who were then active. The result was four decades' worth of personal memories on how America's reading tastes had changed, and why, and even the books took on a life of their own and became characters in my story:

> "Probably it's difficult for anyone who remembers the prodigious success of *Gone With the Wind,*" Dorothy Can-field said, "to think how it would have seemed to people who encountered it simply as a very, very long and detailed book about the Civil War and its aftermath. We had never heard of the author and didn't have anybody else's opinion on it. It was chosen with a little difficulty, because some of the charac-terization was not very authentic or convincing. But as a narrative it had the quality which the French call *attention:* it made you want to turn over the page to see what happens next. I remember that someone commented, 'Well, people may not like it very much, but nobody can deny that it gives a lot of reading for your money.' Its tremendous success was, I must say, about as surprising to us as to anybody else."

These three examples are typical of the kind of information that is locked inside people's heads, which a good nonfiction writer must unlock. The best way to practice is to go out and interview people. The interview itself is one of the most com-mon and popular nonfiction forms, so you might as well master it early.

How should you start? First, decide what person you want to interview. If you are a college student, don't interview your roommate. With all due respect for what a fine fellow he is, he probably doesn't have much to say that the rest of us want to hear. To learn the craft of nonfiction you must push yourself out into the real world—your town or your city or your county—

and pretend that you're writing for a real publication. If it helps, decide which publication you are hypothetically writing for. In any case, choose as your subject someone whose job is so important, or so interesting, or so unusual that the average reader would want to read about him.

This doesn't mean that he or she has to be president of the bank. It can be the owner of the local pizza parlor or supermarket or hairdressing academy. It can be the fisherman who puts out to sea every morning, or the Little League manager, or the nurse. It can be the butcher, the baker or—better yet, if you can find him—the candlestick maker. Look for the women in your community who are unraveling the old myths about what the two sexes were foreordained to do. Choose, in short, someone who touches some corner of the reader's life.

Interviewing is one of those skills that you can only get better at. You will never again feel so ill at ease as when you try it for the first time, and probably you'll never feel entirely comfortable prodding another person for answers that he or she may be too shy or too inarticulate to reveal. But at least half of the skill is mechanical. The rest is instinct—knowing how to make the other person relax, when to push, when to listen, when to stop. This can all be learned with experience.

The basic tools for an interview are paper and two or three well-sharpened pencils. Is that the most insultingly obvious advice? You'd be surprised how many writers venture forth to stalk their quarry with no pencil, or with one that breaks, or with a pen that doesn't work, and with nothing to write on. "Be prepared" is as apt a motto for the nonfiction writer on his rounds as it is for the Boy Scout.

But keep your notebook or paper out of sight until you need it. There's nothing less likely to relax a person than the arrival of a stranger with a stenographer's pad. Both of you need time to get to know each other. Take a while just to chat, gauging what sort of person you're dealing with, getting him or her to trust you.

Never go into an interview without doing whatever homework you can. If you are interviewing a town official, know his or her voting record. If it's an actress, know what plays or movies she has been in. You will be resented if you inquire about facts you could have learned in advance.

Make a list of likely questions—it will save you the vast embarrassment of going dry in mid-interview. Perhaps you won't need it; better questions will occur to you, or the person being interviewed will veer off at an angle you couldn't have foreseen. Here you can only go by intuition. If he strays hopelessly off the subject, drag him back. If you like the new direction, follow him and forget the questions you intended to ask.

Many beginning interviewers are crippled by the fear that they are imposing on the other person and have no right to invade his privacy. This fear is almost wholly unfounded. Unless the other person is a Howard Hughes, he is delighted that somebody wants to interview him. Most men and women lead lives, if not of quiet desperation, at least of desperate quietness, and they jump at a chance to talk about their work to an outsider who seems eager to listen.

This doesn't necessarily mean it will go well. In general you will be talking to people who have never been interviewed before, and they will warm to the process awkwardly, self-consciously, perhaps not giving you anything you can use. Come back another day; it will go better. You will both even begin to enjoy it—proof that you aren't forcing your victims to do something they don't really want to do.

Speaking of tools, is it all right (you ask) to use a tape recorder? Why not just take one along, start it going, and forget all that business of pencil and paper?

Obviously the tape recorder is a superb instrument for capturing what people have to say—especially people who, for reasons of their culture or education or temperament, would never get around to writing it down. In this realm of social anthropology the machine is invaluable. I admire the books of Studs Terkel, such as *Hard Times: An Oral History of the Great Depression,* which he "wrote" by recording long interviews with ordinary people and stitching the results into coherent shape. I also like the question-and-answer interviews, obtained by tape recorder, that have long been published in certain magazines. They have the sound of spontaneity and the refreshing absence of a writer hovering over the product and burnishing it to a high gloss.

But strictly, this isn't writing. It's a process of asking questions and then pruning and splicing and repairing the answers, and it takes endless time and care and labor. People who seem to be talking into the tape recorder with linear precision turn out, when the interview is transcribed, to have been stumbling so aimlessly over the sands of language that they haven't completed a single decent sentence. The ear makes allowances for absent syntax that the eye won't tolerate in print. Hence my admiration for Terkel and other stewards of the spoken word. The seemingly simple use of a tape recorder isn't simple.

My main reasons for warning you off it, however, are practical ones. One hazard is that you don't usually have a tape recorder with you—you are more apt to have a pencil. Another is that tape recorders malfunction. Few moments in journalism are as glum as the return of a reporter with "a really great story," followed by his pushing of the PLAY button and total silence. But above all, a writer should be able to see his materials. If your interview is on tape you become a listener, forever fussing with the machine, running it backward to find a brilliant remark that you can never quite find, running it forward, stopping, starting, driving yourself crazy. Be a writer. Write things down.

Still, taking notes has one big problem. The person you're interviewing often starts talking faster than you can write. You are still scribbling Sentence A when he zooms into Sentence B. You drop Sentence A and pursue him into Sentence B, meanwhile trying to hold the rest of Sentence A in your inner ear and hoping that Sentence C will be a dud that you can skip altogether, using the time to catch up. Unfortunately, you now have your subject going at high speed. He is at last saying all the things you have been trying to cajole out of him for an hour, and saying them with what seems to be Churchillian eloquence. Your inner ear is clogging up with sentences you want to grab before they slip away.

Tell him to stop. Just say, "Hold it a minute, please," and write until you catch up. What you are trying to do with your feverish scribbling, after all, is to quote him correctly, and nobody wants to be misquoted.

With practice you will write faster and develop some form of shorthand. You'll find yourself devising abbreviations for often-used words and also omitting the small connective syntax. As soon as the interview is over, fill in all the missing words that you can remember. Complete the uncompleted sentences. Most of them will still be lingering just within the bounds of recall.

When you get home, type out your notes—probably an almost illegible scrawl—so that you can read them easily. This not only makes the interview accessible, along with any clippings or other materials you may have assembled. It enables you to review in tranquillity a torrent of words that you wrote in haste, and thereby discover what the person really said.

You will find that he said much that is redundant or dull. Single out the quotations that are most important or colorful. You will be tempted to use all the words that are in your notes because you performed the laborious chore of getting all the words down. But that's a self-indulgence—no excuse for putting the reader to the same effort. Your job is to distill the essence.

What about your obligation to the person you interviewed?

To what extent can you cut or juggle his words? This question vexes every writer returning from a first interview—and it should. But the answer is not hard if you keep in mind two standards: brevity and fair play.

Your ethical duty to the person being interviewed is to present his position accurately. If he carefully weighed two sides of an issue and you only quote his views of one side, making him seem to favor that position, you will misrepresent what he told you. Or you might misrepresent him by quoting him out of context, or by choosing only some flashy remark without adding the serious afterthought. You are dealing with a person's honor and reputation—and also with your own.

But after that your duty is to the reader. He or she deserves the smallest package. Most people meander in their conversation, filling it with irrelevant tales and trivia. Much of it is delightful, but it's still trivia. Your interview will be strong to the extent that you get the main points made without waste.

Therefore if you find on page 5 of your notes a comment that perfectly amplifies a point on page 2—a point made earlier in the interview—you will do everyone a favor if you link the two thoughts, letting the second sentence follow and illustrate the first. This may violate the truth of how the interview progressed, but you will be true to the intent of what was said. Play with the quotes by all means—selecting, rejecting, thinning, transposing their order, saving a good one for the end. Just make sure the play is fair. Don't change any words or let the cutting of a sentence distort the proper context of what remains.

Do I literally mean "don't change any words"? Yes and no. If a speaker chooses his words carefully, you should make it a point of professional pride to quote him verbatim. Most interviewers are sloppy about this; they think that if they achieve a rough approximation it's good enough. It's not good enough: nobody wants to see himself in print using words or phrases he

wouldn't ever use. But if the speaker's conversation is ragged—
if his sentences trail off, if his thoughts are disjointed, if his
syntax is so tangled that it would embarrass him—the writer has
no choice but to clean up the English and provide the missing
links.

Sometimes, in fact, you can fall into a trap in your effort to be
true to the speaker. As you write your article, you type his
words exactly as you took them down. You even allow yourself
a moment of satisfaction at being such a faithful scribe. Later,
editing what you've written, you realize that several of the
quotes don't quite make sense. When you first heard them, they
sounded so felicitous that you didn't give them a second
thought. Now, on second thought, there's a hole somewhere in
the language or the logic. To leave the hole is no favor to the
reader or the speaker—and no credit to the writer. You have
to patch the damage. Often you only need to add one or two
clarifying words. Or you might find another quote in your notes
that makes the same point. But don't forget that you can always
call the person you interviewed. Tell him you want to check a
few of the things he said. Get him to rephrase his points until
they're clear. Don't ever become the prisoner of your quotes—
so lulled by how wonderful they sound that you never stop to
analyze them.

As for how to organize the interview, the lead, like all leads,
should obviously tell the reader why the person is worth reading about. What is his claim to our time and attention? Thereafter, try to achieve a balance between what the subject is
saying in *his* words and what you are writing in *your* words to
explain and to connect. If you quote a person for three or four
consecutive paragraphs it becomes monotonous. Quotes are
livelier when you break them up, making periodic appearances
in your role as guide. You are still the writer—don't relinquish
control. But make your appearances useful; don't just insert one
of those dreary sentences that shout to the reader that your sole

purpose is to break up a string of quotations ("He tapped his pipe on a nearby ashtray and I noticed that his fingers were quite long." "She toyed idly with her arugula salad").

When you use a quotation, start the sentence with it. Don't lead up to it with a vapid phrase saying what the man said.

> BAD: Mr. Smith said that he liked to "go downtown once a week and have lunch with some of my old friends."
> GOOD: "I usually like to go downtown once a week," Mr. Smith said, "and have lunch with some of my old friends."

The second sentence has vitality, the first one is dead. In fact, nothing is deader than to start a sentence with a "Mr. Smith said" construction—it's where countless readers stop reading. If the man said it, let him say it and get the sentence off to a warm, human start.

But be careful where you break the quotation. Do it as soon as you naturally can, so that the reader knows who is talking, but not where it will destroy the rhythm or the sense. Notice how the following three variants all inflict some kind of damage:

> "I usually like," Mr. Smith said, "to go downtown once a week and have lunch with some of my old friends."
> "I usually like to go downtown," Mr. Smith said, "once a week and have lunch with some of my old friends."
> "I usually like to go downtown once a week and have lunch," Mr. Smith said, "with some of my old friends."

Finally, don't strain to find synonyms for "he said." Don't make your man assert, aver and expostulate just to avoid repeating "he said," and please—please!—don't write "he smiled" or "he grinned." I have never heard anybody smile. The reader's eye skips over "he said" anyway, so it's not worth a lot of fuss. If you crave variety, choose synonyms that catch the shifting nature of the conversation. "He pointed out," "he explained," "he replied," "he added"—these all carry a particular meaning. But don't use "he added" if the man is merely averring and not putting a postscript on what he just said.

I'll close with a passage from *The Bottom of the Harbor,* by Joseph Mitchell, the writer of long nonfiction articles I most admired when I was trying to learn the craft myself. (Among writers writing today I would choose Calvin Trillin and Ian Frazier as models.) The book consists of various articles that Mitchell wrote for *The New Yorker* about people who live and work around the waterfront. He is a master of the uncommonly difficult art of writing about the so-called common man without patronizing him. In this interview with the captain of a fishing boat called a "dragger," note the deceptively simple style, the exactness of detail, and especially the deft interweaving of Mitchell's words with those of the captain, Ellery Thompson:

> Ellery is a self-taught B-flat trumpet player. While living on the *Eleanor,* he spent many evenings in the cabin by himself practicing hymns and patriotic music. Sometimes, out on the grounds, if he had a few minutes to kill, he would go below and practice. One afternoon, blundering around the Hell Hole in a thick summer fog, he grew tired of cranking the foghorn and got out his trumpet and stood on deck and played "The Star-Spangled Banner" over and over, alarming the crews of other draggers fogbound in the area, who thought an excursion boat was bearing down on them. After he went back to sleeping at home, he continued to practice in the evenings, but he had to give it up before long because of its effect on his mother's health. . . .
>
> Ellery walks with a pronounced stoop, favoring his left shoulder, where the rheumatism has settled, and he takes his time. "If I start to hustle and bustle," he says, "everything I eat repeats and repeats." He abhors hurry; he thinks that

humanity in general has got ahead of itself. He once threatened to fire a man in his crew because he worked too hard. . . .

Ellery is about as self-sufficient as a man can be. He has no wife, no politics and no religion. "I put off getting married until I got me a good big boat," he says. "When I got the boat and got it paid for, the Depression struck. There's mighty few women that'll eat fish three times a day, and that's about all I had to offer. I kept putting it off until times got better. When times got better, I got the rheumatism. And a man in his middle forties with the chronic rheumatism, there's not much of the old Romeo left in him."

Ellery is a member of only one organization. "I'm a Mason," he says. "Aside from that, the only thing I belong to is the human race." His father was a Republican and his mother is a Democrat; he says he has never put any dependence in either party and has never once voted for anybody. His family belongs to the Baptist Church; he says he has somehow managed to get along without it. "I enjoy hymns," he says. "I enjoy the old ones, the gloomy ones. I used to go to church just to hear the good old hymns, but the sermons finally drove me away."

13

Writing About a Place

Next to knowing how to write about people, you should know how to write about a place. People and places are the twin pillars on which most nonfiction is built. Every human event happens somewhere, and the reader wants to know what that somewhere was like.

In a few cases you'll need only a paragraph or two to sketch the setting of an event. But more often you'll need to evoke the mood of a whole neighborhood or town to give texture to the story you're telling. And in certain cases, such as the travel piece itself—that perennial form in which you recount how you lived on a houseboat in Kashmir or went camping in the Rockies—descriptive detail will be the main substance.

Whatever the proportion, it would seem to be relatively easy. The dismal truth is that it's very hard. It must be hard, because it's in this area that most writers—professional and amateur—produce not only their worst work but work that is just plain terrible. The terrible work has nothing to do with some terrible flaw of character. On the contrary, it results from the virtue of enthusiasm. Nobody turns so quickly into a bore as a traveler home from his travels. He enjoyed his trip so much that he wants to tell us all about it—and "all" is what we don't want to hear. We only want to hear some. What made his trip different from everybody else's? What can he tell us that we don't already know? We don't want him to describe every ride at Disneyland, or tell us that the Grand Canyon is awesome, or that Venice has canals. If one of the rides at Disneyland got stuck, if somebody fell into the awesome Grand Canyon, *that* would be worth hearing about.

It's natural for all of us when we have gone to a certain place to feel that somehow we are the first people who ever went there or thought such sensitive thoughts about it. Fair enough: it's what keeps us going and validates our experience. Who can visit the Tower of London without musing on the wives of Henry VIII, or visit Egypt and not be moved by the size and antiquity of the pyramids? But this is ground already covered by many people. As a writer you must keep a tight rein on your subjective self—the traveler touched by new sights and sounds and smells—and keep an objective eye on the reader. The article that records what you did every day on your trip will fascinate you because it was your trip. Will it fascinate the reader? Nine times out of ten it won't. The mere agglomeration of detail is no free pass to the reader's interest. The detail must in some way be significant.

The other big trap is style. Nowhere else in nonfiction do writers use such syrupy words and groaning platitudes. Adjectives that you would squirm to use in conversation—"roseate," "wondrous," "fabled," "scudding"—are common currency. Half the sights seen in a day's sightseeing are "quaint," especially windmills and covered bridges. They are certified for quaintness.

It's a style of soft words that under hard examination mean nothing, or that mean different things to different people: "attractive," "charming," "romantic." To write that "the city has its own attractiveness" is no help. And who will define "charm," except possibly the owner of a charm school? Or "romantic"? These are subjective concepts in the eye of the beholder. One man's romantic sunrise is another man's hangover.

Travelese is a land "where old meets new." I'm amazed at the number of places where old meets new. Old never meets old. The meeting occurs in the "twisting alleys" and "bustling thoroughfares" of storied Tangier or picturesque Zanzibar. This is terrain dotted with "byways," usually half forgotten or at least hidden. It's a world where inanimate objects spring to life: storefronts smile, buildings boast, ruins beckon, and the very chimney tops sing their immemorial song of welcome. The clichés bloom with very fertility.

How can you overcome such fearful odds and write well about a place? My advice can be reduced to two principles—one of style, the other of substance.

First, choose your words with unusual care. If a phrase comes to you easily, look at it with deep suspicion—it's probably one of the innumerable clichés that have woven their way so tightly into the fabric of travel writing that it takes a special effort *not* to use them. Also resist straining for the luminous lyrical phrase to describe the wondrous waterfall. At best it will make you sound artificial—unlike yourself—and at worst pompous. Strive for fresh words and images. Leave "myriad" and their ilk to the poets. Leave "ilk" to anyone who will take it away.

As for substance, be intensely selective. If you are describing a beach, don't write that "the shore was scattered with rocks" or that "occasionally a seagull flew over." Shores have a tendency to be scattered with rocks and to be flown over by seagulls. Eliminate every such fact that is a known attribute: don't tell us that the sea had waves and the sand was white. Find details that are significant. They may be important to your narrative; they may be unusual, or colorful, or comic, or entertaining. But make sure they are details that do useful work.

I'll give you some examples from various writers, widely different in temperament but alike in the power of the details they choose. The first is from an article by Joan Didion called "Some Dreamers of the Golden Dream." It's about a lurid crime that occurred in the San Bernardino Valley of California, and in this early passage the writer is taking us, as if in her own car, away from urban civilization to the lonely stretch of road where Lucille Miller's Volkswagen so unaccountably caught fire:

This is the California where it is easy to Dial-A-Devotion, but hard to buy a book. This is the country of the teased hair and the Capris and the girls for whom all life's promise comes down to a waltz-length white wedding dress and the birth of a Kimberly or a Sherry or a Debbi and a Tijuana divorce and a return to hairdresser's school. "We were just crazy kids," they say without regret, and look to the future. The future always looks good in the golden land, because no one remembers the past. Here is where the hot wind blows and the old ways do not seem relevant, where the divorce rate is double the national average and where one person in every 38 lives in a trailer. Here is the last stop for all those who come from somewhere else, for all those who drifted away from the cold and the past and the old ways. Here is where they are trying to find a new life style, trying to find it in the only places they know to look: the movies and the newspapers. The case of Lucille Marie Maxwell Miller is a tabloid monument to the new style.

Imagine Banyan Street first, because Banyan is where it happened. The way to Banyan is to drive west from San Bernardino out Foothill Boulevard, Route 66: past the Santa Fe switching yards, the Forty Winks Motel. Past the motel that is 19 stucco tepees: "SLEEP IN A WIGWAM—GET MORE FOR YOUR WAMPUM." Past Fontana Drag City and Fontana Church of the Nazarene and the Pit Stop A Go-Go; past Kaiser Steel, through Cucamonga, out to the Kapu Kai Restaurant-Bar and Coffee Shop, at the corner of Route 66 and Carnelian Avenue. Up Carnelian Avenue from the Kapu Kai, which means "Forbidden Seas," the subdivision flags whip in

the harsh wind. "HALF-ACRE RANCHES! SNACK BARS! TRAV-
ERTINE ENTRIES! $95 DOWN." It is the trail of an intention
gone haywire, the flotsam of the New California. But after a
while the signs thin out on Carnelian Avenue, and the houses
are no longer the bright pastels of the Springtime Home
owners but the faded bungalows of the people who grow a
few grapes and keep a few chickens out here, and then the
hill gets steeper and the road climbs and even the bungalows
are few, and here—desolate, roughly surfaced, lined with
eucalyptus and lemon groves—is Banyan Street.

In only two paragraphs we have a feeling not only for the
tackiness of the New California landscape, with its stucco tepees
and instant housing and borrowed Hawaiian romance, but for
the pathetic impermanence of the lives and pretensions of the
people who have alighted there. All the details—statistics and
names and signs—are doing useful work.

Concrete detail is also the anchor of John McPhee's prose.
Coming into the Country, his book about Alaska—to choose one
example from his many craftsmanlike books—has a section devoted to the quest for a possible new state capital. It takes
McPhee only a few sentences to give us a sense of what's wrong
with the present capital, both as a place to live and as a place
for lawmakers to make good laws:

A pedestrian today in Juneau, head down and charging, can
be stopped for no gain by the wind. There are railings along
the streets by which senators and representatives can haul
themselves to work. Over the past couple of years, a succession of wind gauges were placed on a ridge above the town.
They could measure velocities up to 200 miles per hour. They
did not survive. The taku winds tore them apart after driving
their indicators to the end of the scale. The weather is not
always so bad; but under its influence the town took shape,

and so Juneau is a tight community of adjacent buildings and
narrow European streets, adhering to its mountainsides and
fronting the salt water. . . .

The urge to move the capital came over Harris during
those two years [in the Alaska State Senate]. Sessions began
in January and ran on at least three months, and Harris developed what he called "a complete sense of isolation—stuck
there. People couldn't get at you. You were in a cage. You
talked to the hard lobbyists every day. Every day the same
people. What was going on needed more airing."

The oddity of the city, so remote from the ordinary American
experience, is instantly clear. One possibility for the legislators
was to move the capital to Anchorage. There at least people
wouldn't feel that they were in an alien town. McPhee distills
its essence in a paragraph that is brilliant both in detail and in
metaphor:

> Almost all Americans would recognize Anchorage, because
> Anchorage is that part of any city where the city has burst its
> seams and extruded Colonel Sanders. Anchorage is some-
> times excused in the name of pioneering. Build now, civilize
> later. But Anchorage is not a frontier town. It is virtually
> unrelated to its environment. It has come in on the wind, an
> American spore. A large cookie cutter brought down on El
> Paso could lift something like Anchorage into the air. Anchor-
> age is the northern rim of Trenton, the center of Oxnard, the
> ocean-blind precincts of Daytona Beach. It is condensed, in-
> stant Albuquerque.

What could be luckier for a nonfiction writer than to live in
America? The country is unendingly various and surprising.
Whether the locale you write about is urban or rural, east or
west, every place has a look, a cast of characters and a set of

cultural assumptions that make it unlike any other place. Find those distinctive traits. The following three passages describe parts of America that could hardly be more different. Yet in each case the writer has given us so many precise images that we feel we are there. The first excerpt is from Vivian Gornick's *Fierce Attachments,* a memoir that vividly describes the Bronx tenement where she grew up:

> There were no trees or bushes or grasses of any kind in the alley [behind the apartment]—only concrete, wire fencing, and wooden poles. Yet I remember the alley as a place of clear light and sweet air, suffused, somehow, with a perpetual smell of summery green.
>
> The alley caught the morning sun (our kitchen was radiant before noon), and it was a shared ritual among the women that laundry was done early on a washboard in the sink and hung out to dry in the sun. Crisscrossing the alley, from first floor to fifth, were perhaps fifty clotheslines strung out on tall wooden poles planted in the concrete ground. Each apartment had its own line stretching out among ten others on the pole. The wash from the line often interfered with the free flap of the wash on the line above or below, and the sight of a woman yanking hard at a clothesline, trying to shake her wash free from an indiscriminate tangle of sheets and trousers, was common. While she was pulling at the line she might also be calling "Berth-a-a. Berth-a-a. Ya home, Berth-a-a?" Friends were scattered throughout the buildings on the alley, and called to one another all during the day to make various arrangements. . . . [My mother's] running commentary on the life outside the window was my first taste of the fruits of intelligence: she would convert gossip into knowledge. She would hear a voice go up one octave and observe: "She had a fight with her husband this morning." Or it would go down an octave and, "Her kid's sick."

Go from there to a small town in East Texas, just across the border from Arkansas. This piece by Prudence Mackintosh ran in *Texas Monthly,* a magazine I've been enjoying for years for the aliveness with which she and her fellow Texas writers take me—a resident of mid-Manhattan—to every corner of their state. It's regional writing of a high order.

I gradually realized that much of what I had grown up believing was Texan was really Southern. The cherished myths of Texas had little to do with my part of the state. I knew dogwood, chinaberry, crape myrtle, and mimosa, but no bluebonnets or Indian paintbrush. Although the Four States Fair and Rodeo was held in my town, I never really learned to ride a horse. I never knew anyone who wore cowboy hats or boots as anything other than a costume. I knew farmers whose fences were bois d'arc and "bob wire" and whose property was known as Old Man So-and-so's place, not ranches with their cattle brands arched over entrance gates. I knew ponds, not tanks. Streets in my town were called Wood, Pine, Olive, and Boulevard, not Guadalupe and Lavaca.

Go still farther west—to Muroc Field, in California's Mojave Desert, the one place in America that was hard and desolate enough, as Tom Wolfe explains in the brilliant early chapters of *The Right Stuff,* for the Army Air Force to use when it set out a generation ago to break the sound barrier.

It looked like some fossil landscape that had long since been left behind by the rest of territorial evolution. It was full of huge dry lake beds, the biggest being Rogers Lake. Other than sagebrush the only vegetation was Joshua trees, twisted freaks of the plant world that looked like a cross between cactus and Japanese bonsai. They had a dark petrified green

color and horribly crippled branches. At dusk the Joshua trees
stood out in silhouette on the fossil wasteland like some ar-
thritic nightmare. In the summer the temperature went up
to 110 degrees as a matter of course, and the dry lake beds
were covered in sand, and there would be windstorms and
sandstorms right out of a Foreign Legion movie. At night it
would drop to near freezing, and in December it would start
raining, and the dry lakes would fill up with a few inches of
water, and some sort of putrid prehistoric shrimps would
work their way up from out of the ooze, and sea gulls would
come flying in a hundred miles or more from the ocean, over
the mountains, to gobble up these squirming little throw-
backs. A person had to see it to believe it. . . .

When the wind blew the few inches of water back and
forth across the lake beds, they became absolutely smooth
and level. And when the water evaporated in the spring, and
the sun baked the ground hard, the lake beds became the
greatest natural landing fields ever discovered, and also the
biggest, with miles of room for error. That was highly desir-
able, given the nature of the enterprise at Muroc.

Besides the wind, sand, tumbleweed, and Joshua trees,
there was nothing at Muroc except for two quonset-style han-
gars, side by side, a couple of gasoline pumps, a single concrete runway, a few tarpaper shacks, and some tents. The
officers stayed in the shacks marked "barracks," and lesser
souls stayed in the tents and froze all night and fried all day.
Every road into the property had a guardhouse on it manned
by soldiers. The enterprise the Army had undertaken in this
godforsaken place was the development of supersonic jet and
rocket planes.

Practice writing this kind of travel piece, and just because I
call it a travel piece I don't mean that you have to go to the
Mojave Desert or Mombasa. Go to your local mall, or bowling

alley, or park. Or write about your vacation. But whatever place
you write about, go there often enough to isolate the qualities
that make it special. Usually this will be some combination of
the place and the people who inhabit it. If it's your local bowling
alley it will be a mixture of the ambience inside and the regular
patrons. If it's a foreign city it will be some mixture of the
ancient culture and its present populace. Try to find it.

A master of this feat of detection is the English author V. S.
Pritchett, one of the best and most versatile of nonfiction writers. Consider what he squeezes out of a visit to Istanbul:

> Istanbul has meant so much to the imagination that the
> reality shocks most travelers. We cannot get the sultans out
> of our minds. We half expect to find them still cross-legged
> and jewelled on their divans. We remember tales of the
> harem. The truth is that Istanbul has no glory except its situa-
> tion. It is a city of steep, cobbled, noisy hills. . . .
>
> Mostly the shops sell cloth, clothes, stockings, shoes, the
> Greek traders rushing out, with cloth unrolled, at any poten-
> tial customer, the Turks passively waiting. Porters shout; ev-
> eryone shouts; you are butted by horses, knocked sideways by
> loads of bedding, and, through all this, you see one of the
> miraculous sights of Turkey—a demure youth carrying a
> brass tray suspended on three chains, and in the exact center
> of the tray a small glass of red tea. He never spills it; he
> maneuvers it through chaos to his boss, who is sitting on the
> doorstep of his shop.
>
> One realizes there are two breeds in Turkey: those who
> carry and those who sit. No one sits quite so relaxedly, ex-
> pertly, beatifically as a Turk; he sits with every inch of his
> body; his very face sits. He sits as if he inherited the art from
> generations of sultans in the palace above Seraglio Point.
> Nothing he likes better than to invite you to sit with him in
> his shop or in his office with half a dozen other sitters: a few

polite inquiries about your age, your marriage, the sex of your children, the number of your relations, and where and how you live, and then, like the other sitters, you clear your throat with a hawk that surpasses anything heard in Lisbon, New York or Sheffield, and join the general silence.

I like the phrase "his very face sits"—just four short words, but they convey an idea so fanciful that they take us by surprise. They also tell us a great deal about Turks. I'll never be able to visit Turkey again without noticing its sitters. With one quick insight Pritchett has caught a whole national trait. This is the essence of good writing about other countries. Distill the important from the immaterial.

I'm reminded by Pritchett's own nationality that the English have long excelled at a distinctive form of travel writing—the article that is less notable for what the writer extracts from a place than for what the place extracts from him. New sights touch off thoughts that otherwise would never have entered his mind. If travel is broadening, it should broaden more than just our knowledge of how a Gothic cathedral looks or how the French make wine. It should generate a whole constellation of ideas about how men and women work and play, raise their children, worship their gods, live and die. Certainly the books written by Britain's "desert eccentrics"—scholar-adventurers like Charles Doughty, T. E. Lawrence and Wilfred Thesiger who chose to live among the Arabs—derive much of their strange power from the reflections born of surviving in so harsh and minimal an environment.

So when you write about a place, try to draw the best out of it. But if the process should work in reverse, let it draw the best out of you. Probably the finest travel book written by an American is *Walden*, though Thoreau only went a few miles out of town, and today a growing number of nonfiction writers are finding their voice by hitting the road, going back to the land or pondering the mysteries of nature.

One last form of travel writing is the literature of adventure and exploration, especially when it involves the history of a remote region and the reconstruction of old events. For me, the best hand at this intricate work is Alan Moorehead. I've followed him across much of Africa and Asia and Australia and the Pacific, always struck with admiration bordering on disbelief that he could collate such a wealth of present and past experience and write about it with seemingly effortless warmth.

Nowhere were Moorehead and his subject more perfectly paired than in *The White Nile.* The story has everything, starting with the enigma of Africa itself. The continent had so thoroughly repulsed the efforts of outsiders to reach its interior that by 1856, when Moorehead's story begins, "that impenetrable blank space had become filled in imagination with a thousand monstrosities, dwarf men and cannibals with tails, animals as strange as the fabulous griffin and the salamander, huge inland seas, and mountains so high they defied all nature by bearing on their crests, in this equatorial heat, a mantle of perpetual snow."

Of all the riddles locked in that blank space, none was more tantalizing than the secret of where the Nile originated. Herodotus, who turned back at the first cataract in 460 B.C., wrote that "it enters Egypt from parts beyond," and those parts were still unfound in 1856 when Richard Burton and John Speke set out from Zanzibar to look for them. They were the first in a succession of driven explorers, missionaries and journalists—including Samuel Baker, David Livingstone and Henry M. Stanley—whose expeditions to the elusive lakes and rivers of central Africa, so full of hardships and wrong guesses, Moorehead brings back to life, meanwhile weaving through them a thread that forms the dark center of his book: the almost unbearable story of the African slave trade.

To say that Moorehead is one of the great travel writers is to not quite catch his accomplishment. Great travel writers write about themselves in the present—as modern pilgrims to some older site. Moorehead's domain is the past, and he inhabits *The White Nile* only as a writer who has followed the trail of the explorers who went before him. He has obviously read and digested everything written by them and about them: diaries, letters, contemporary newspapers, annals of scientific societies, Foreign Office files, military archives. Here is how he describes General Gordon's final journal entry, scribbled as the siege of Khartoum was about to end with the fall of the city to the Mahdi and his own martyrdom in the hearts of Victorian England:

> Khartoum in its death throes is almost as real to us as a catastrophe that has taken place in our own lives. The journal is an astonishing document. No other English soldier has revealed his heart so emphatically, so simply or so movingly as Gordon does in these wild jottings, sometimes written on telegraph forms and flimsy scraps of paper, sometimes heavily underscored or crossed out, sometimes decorated with oddly exact little maps and ribald caricatures, sometimes pathetic, ironical or recklessly unfair, but always absolutely honest.

But Moorehead is no mere researcher; he also needs to see the places he is writing about. Describing the isolated village of Tabora, where Livingstone spent five months waiting for the supplies sent by Stanley from Zanzibar to reach him, holding small Bible classes under the mango trees, Moorehead writes: "Even now there is a feeling of solitude and claustrophobia about the place." Tabora wasn't on Moorehead's way to anywhere; he didn't have to visit it. The point is that he did. Wherever Moorehead takes me, I know he has been there himself; I can feel it in his writing. This compulsion to be a witness to his material is what I finally most admire about Alan Moorehead's books. It's a matter of character.

What I finally most enjoy are the paragraphs that turn up periodically—small jewels of insight and compression—in which he steps aside from his narrative and puts into context a chain of events or a man's life. I'll leave you with this one from *The White Nile:*

> Burton belongs decidedly to that small perennial group of English men and women who are born with something lacking in their lives: a hunger, a nostalgia, that can be set at rest only in the deserts of the East. Whatever the reason may have been—whether it was a natural revulsion from the narrow horizons and the wet and cloudy climate of England, or from the constricting Victorian code of manners there—it was the tinkling of the camel bell that beckoned him until the day he died.

14

Bits & Pieces

This is a chapter of scraps and morsels—small admonitions on many points that I have collected under one, as they say, umbrella.

*

VERBS. Use active verbs unless there is no comfortable way to get around using a passive verb. The difference between an active-verb style and a passive-verb style—in clarity and vigor—is the difference between life and death for a writer.

"Joe hit him" is strong. "He was hit by Joe" is weak. The first is short and vivid and direct; it leaves no doubt about who did what. The second is necessarily longer and it has an insipid quality; something was done by somebody to someone else. A style that consists mainly of passive constructions, especially if the sentences are long, saps the reader's energy. Nobody quite knows what is being perpetrated by whom and on whom.

I use "perpetrated" because it's the kind of word that passive-voice writers are fond of. They prefer long words of Latin origin to short Anglo-Saxon words—which compounds their trouble and makes their sentences still more glutinous. Short is generally better than long. (Of the 701 words in Lincoln's Second Inaugural Address, a marvel of economy in itself, 505 are words of one syllable and 122 are words of two syllables.)

Verbs are the most important of all your tools. They push the sentence forward and give it momentum. Active verbs push hard; passive verbs tug fitfully. Active verbs also enable us to visualize an activity because they require a pronoun or a noun to put them in motion. Many verbs also carry in their imagery or in their sound a suggestion of what they mean: flail, poke, dazzle, squash, beguile, pamper, swagger, wheedle, vex. Probably no other language has such a vast supply of verbs so bright with color. Don't choose one that is dull or merely serviceable. Make active verbs activate your sentences, and try to avoid the kind that need an appended preposition to complete their work. Don't set up a business that you can start or launch. Don't say that the president of the company stepped down. Did he resign? Did he retire? Did he get fired? Be precise. Use precise verbs.

If you want to see how active verbs give vitality and flair to the written word, don't just go back to Hemingway or Thurber or Thoreau. I commend the King James Bible and William Shakespeare.

*

ADVERBS. Most adverbs are unnecessary. You will clutter your sentence and annoy the reader if you choose a verb that has a precise meaning and then add an adverb that carries the same meaning. Don't tell us that the radio blared loudly— "blare" connotes loudness. Don't write that someone clenched his teeth tightly—there's no other way to clench teeth. Again and again in careless writing, strong verbs are weakened by redundant adverbs.

So are countless adjectives and other parts of speech: "effortlessly easy," "slightly spartan," "totally flabbergasted." The beauty of "flabbergasted" is that it implies an astonishment that is total; I can't picture someone being partly flabbergasted. If an action is so easy as to be effortless, use "effortless." And what is "slightly spartan"? Perhaps a monk's cell with wall-to-wall carpeting. Don't use adverbs unless they do necessary work. Spare us the news that the losing athlete moped dejectedly and the winner grinned widely.

*

ADJECTIVES.   Most adjectives are also unnecessary. Like adverbs, they are sprinkled into sentences by writers who don't stop to think that the concept is already in the noun. This kind of prose is littered with precipitous cliffs and lacy spiderwebs and friendly smiles. It's also littered with adjectives denoting the color of an object whose color is well known: yellow daffodils and brownish dirt. If you want to make a value judgment about daffodils, choose an adjective like "garish." If you're in a section of the country where the dirt is red, feel free to mention the red dirt. These adjectives would do a job that the noun alone wouldn't be doing.

Redundant adjectives are only part of the problem. Most writers sow adjectives almost unconsciously into the soil of their prose to make it more lush and pretty. The sentences become longer and longer as they fill up with stately elms and frisky kittens and hard-bitten detectives and sleepy lagoons. This is adjective-by-habit, and it's a habit you should get rid of. Not every oak has to be gnarled. The adjective that exists solely as decoration is a self-indulgence for the writer and an obstacle for the reader.

Again, the rule is simple: Make your adjectives do work that needs to be done. "He looked at the gray sky and the black clouds and decided to sail back to the harbor." The darkness of the sky is the reason for the decision. If it's important to tell the reader that a house was drab or a girl was beautiful, by all means use "drab" and "beautiful." They will have their proper power because you have learned to use adjectives sparsely.

*

LITTLE QUALIFIERS.　Prune out the small words that qualify how you feel and how you think and what you saw: "a bit," "a little," "sort of," "kind of," "rather," "quite," "very," "too," "pretty much," "in a sense," and dozens more. They dilute both your style and your persuasiveness.

Don't say you were a bit confused and sort of tired and a little depressed and somewhat annoyed. Be confused. Be tired. Be depressed. Be annoyed. Don't hedge your prose with little timidities. Good writing is lean and confident.

Don't say you weren't too happy because the hotel looked pretty expensive. Say you weren't happy because the hotel looked expensive. Don't tell us that you were quite fortunate. How fortunate is that?

Don't describe an event as rather spectacular or very awesome. Words like "spectacular" and "awesome" don't submit to measurement. "Very" is a useful word to achieve emphasis, but far more often it is clutter. There's no need to call someone very methodical. Either he is methodical or he isn't.

The larger point here is one of authority. Every little qualifier whittles away some fraction of trust on the part of the reader. Readers want a writer who believes in himself and in what he is saying. Don't diminish this belief. Don't be kind of bold. Be bold.

*

PUNCTUATION.　These are brief thoughts on punctuation, in no way intended as a primer. If you don't know how to punctuate—and many college students still don't—get a grammar book.

The Period. There's not much to be said about the period except that most writers don't reach it soon enough. If you find yourself hopelessly mired in a long sentence, it's probably because you're trying to make the sentence do more than it can reasonably do—perhaps express two dissimilar thoughts. The quickest way out is to break the long sentence into two short sentences, or even three. There is no minimum length for a sentence that's acceptable in the eyes of God. Among good writers it is the short sentence that predominates, and don't tell me about Norman Mailer—he's a genius. If you want to write long sentences, be a genius. Or at least make sure that the sentence is under control from beginning to end, in syntax and punctuation, so that the reader knows where he is at every step of the winding trail.

The Exclamation Point. Don't use it unless you must to achieve a certain effect. It has a gushy aura—the breathless excitement of a debutante commenting on an event that was exciting only to her: "Daddy says I must have had too much champagne!" "But honestly, I just could have danced all night!" We have all suffered more than our share of these sentences in which an exclamation point knocks us over the head with how cute or wonderful something was. Instead construct your sentence so that the order of the words will put the emphasis where you want it. Also resist using the exclamation point to notify the reader that you are making a joke or being ironic. "It never occurred to me that the water pistol might be loaded!" Readers are annoyed by your reminder that this was a comical moment. They are also robbed of the pleasure of making the discovery themselves. Humor is best achieved by understatement, and there's nothing subtle about an exclamation point.

The Semicolon. There is a nineteenth-century mustiness that hangs over the semicolon. We associate it with the carefully balanced sentences, the judicious weighing of "on the one hand" and "on the other hand," of Conrad and Thackeray and Hardy. Therefore it should be used sparingly by writers of non-fiction today. Yet I notice that it turns up quite often in the excerpts I've quoted in this book, and I've used it fairly often myself—usually to append a related thought to the first half of a sentence. Still, the semicolon brings the reader, if not to a halt, at least to a considerable pause. So use it with discretion, remembering that it will slow to a Victorian pace the late-twentieth-century momentum you are striving for, and rely instead on the period and the dash.

The Dash. Somehow this invaluable tool is widely regarded as not quite proper—a bumpkin at the genteel dinner table of good English. But it has full membership and will get you out of many tight corners. The dash is used in two different ways. One is to amplify or justify in the second part of the sentence a thought you have stated in the first part. "We decided to keep going—it was only 100 miles more and we could get there in time for dinner." By its very shape the dash pushes the sentence ahead and explains why they decided to keep going. The other use involves two dashes, which set apart a parenthetical thought within a longer sentence. "She told me to get in the car—she had been after me all summer to have a haircut—and we drove silently into town." An explanatory detail that might otherwise have required a separate sentence is dispatched along the way.

The Colon. The colon has begun to look even more antique than the semicolon, and many of its functions have been taken over by the dash. But it still serves well its pure role of bringing your sentence to a brief halt before you plunge into, say, an itemized list. "The brochure said that the ship would stop at the following ports: Oran, Algiers, Naples, Brindisi, Piraeus, Istanbul and Beirut." You can't beat the colon for work like that.

*

MOOD CHANGERS. Learn to alert the reader as early as possible in a sentence to any change in mood from the previous sentence. At least a dozen words will do this job for you: "but," "yet," "however," "nevertheless," "still," "instead," "thus," "therefore," "meanwhile," "now," "later," "today," "subsequently," and several more. I can't overstate how much easier it is for readers to process a sentence if you start with "but" when you're shifting direction, or, conversely, how much harder it is if they must wait until the end to realize that you're now in a different gear.

Many of us were taught that no sentence should begin with "but." If that's what you learned, unlearn it—there's no stronger word at the start. It announces total contrast with what has gone before, and the reader is primed for the change. If you need relief from too many sentences beginning with "but," switch to "however." It is, however, a weaker word and therefore needs careful placement. Don't start a sentence with "however"—it hangs there like a wet dishrag. And don't end with "however"—by that time it has lost its howeverness. Put it as early as you reasonably can—as I did three sentences ago. Its abruptness then becomes a virtue.

"Yet" does almost the same job as "but," though its meaning is closer to "nevertheless." Either of these words at the beginning of a sentence—"Yet he decided to go" or "Nevertheless he decided to go"—can replace a whole long phrase that summarizes what the reader has just been told: *Despite the fact that all these dangers had been pointed out to him,* he decided to go." Look for all the places where one of these short words will quickly convey the same mood and meaning as a long and dismal clause. "Instead I took the train." "Still I had to admire him." "Thus I learned how to smoke." "It was therefore easy to meet him." "Meanwhile I had talked to John." What a vast amount of huffing and puffing these pivotal words save! (The exclamation point is to show that I really mean it.)

As for "meanwhile," "now," "today" and "later," what they also save is confusion, for writers often change their time frame without remembering to tip the reader off. "Now I know better." "Today you can't find such an item." "Later I found out why." Always make sure that the reader is oriented. Always ask yourself where you left him in the previous sentence.

*

CONTRACTIONS. Your style will obviously be warmer and truer to your personality if you use contractions like "I'll" and "won't" when they fit comfortably into what you're writing. "I'll be glad to see them if they don't get mad" is less stiff than "I will be glad to see them if they do not get mad." There's no rule against such informality—trust your ear and your instincts. I only suggest avoiding one form—"I'd," "he'd," "we'd," etc.— because "I'd" can mean both "I had" and "I would," and readers often get well into a sentence before learning which meaning it is. Frequently it turns out to be not the one they thought it was. Also, don't invent contractions, like "could've." Stick with the ones you can find in the dictionary.

*

OVERSTATEMENT. "The living room looked as if an atomic bomb had gone off there," writes the inexperienced writer, describing what he saw on Sunday morning after a Saturday night party that got out of hand. Well, we all know that he's exaggerating to make a droll point, but we also know that an atomic bomb *didn't* go off there, or any other bomb except maybe a water bomb. "I felt as if ten 747 jets were flying through my brain," he writes, "and I seriously considered jumping out the window and killing myself." These verbal high jinks can get just so high—and I'm already well over the limit— before the reader feels an overpowering drowsiness. It's like being trapped with a man who can't stop reciting limericks. Don't overstate. You didn't really consider jumping out the window. Life has more than enough truly horrible funny situations. Let the humor sneak up so that we hardly hear it coming.

*

CREDIBILITY.   Credibility is just as fragile for a writer as for a President. Don't inflate an incident to make it more flamboyant or bizarre than it actually was. If the reader catches you in just one bogus statement that you are trying to pass off as true, everything you write thereafter will be suspect. It's too great a risk, and not worth taking.

*

CONCEPT NOUNS.   Nouns that express a concept are commonly used in bad writing instead of verbs that tell what somebody did. Here are three typical dead sentences:

"The common reaction is incredulous laughter."

"Bemused cynicism isn't the only response to the old system."

"The current campus hostility is a symptom of the change."

What is so eerie about these sentences is that they have no people in them. They also have no working verbs—only "is" or "isn't." The reader can't visualize anybody performing some activity; all the meaning lies in impersonal nouns that embody a vague concept: "reaction," "cynicism," "response," "hostility." Turn these cold sentences around. Get people doing things:

"Most people just laugh with disbelief."

"Some people respond to the old system by turning cynical; others say . . ."

"It's easy to notice the change—you can see how angry all the students are."

My revised sentences aren't jumping with vigor, partly because the material I'm trying to knead into shape is shapeless dough. But at least they have real people and real verbs. Don't get caught holding a bag that doesn't have anything in it but abstract nouns. You'll sink to the bottom of the lake and never be seen again.

*

CREEPING NOUNISM. This is a new American disease that strings two or three nouns together where one noun—or, better yet, one verb—will do. Nobody goes broke now; we have money problem areas. It no longer rains; we have precipitation activity or a thunderstorm probability situation. Please, let it rain.

*

SEXISM. Probably the most vexing new question for writers is what to do about sexist language, especially the "he-she" pronoun. The feminist movement has revealed how much sexism lurks in our language, not only in the bothersome "he" but in the hundreds of words that carry an invidious meaning or some overtone of judgment. They are words that patronize ("gal"), or that imply second-class status ("poetess") or a second-class role ("housewife") or a certain kind of empty-headedness ("the girls"), or that demean the ability of a woman to do a man's job ("lady lawyer"), or that are deliberately prurient ("divorcée," "coed," "blonde") and are seldom applied to men. Men get mugged; a woman who gets mugged is a shapely stewardess or a pert brunette.

Just as damaging—and more subtle—are the countless usages that treat women as possessions of the family male, not as people with their own identity who played an equal part in the family saga: "Early settlers pushed west with their wives and children." Turn those settlers into pioneer families, or pioneer couples who went west with their sons and daughters, or men and women who settled the West. Today there are very few roles or jobs that aren't open to both sexes. Don't ever use constructions which suggest that only men can be settlers or farmers or cops or firefighters. Good writers and editors are now pushing these stereotypes out of the language.

A thornier problem is raised by the feminists' annoyance with words that contain "man," such as "chairman" and "spokesman." Their point is that women can chair a committee as well as a man and are equally good at spoking. Hence the flurry of new words like "chairperson" and "spokeswoman." These makeshift words from the 1960s have greatly helped to raise our consciousness about sex discrimination both in words and in attitudes. But in the end they are makeshift words, perhaps hurting the cause more than helping it. One solution is to find or invent another word—"chair" for "chairman," "company representative" for "spokesman." You can also convert the noun into a verb: "Speaking for the company, Ms. Jones said. . . ." In cases where a certain occupation has both a masculine and a feminine form, look for a generic substitute. Actors and actresses, for instance, can become performers.

This still leaves the offensive pronoun. Obviously "he" and "him" and "his" are words that rankle. "Every employee should decide what he thinks is best for him and his dependents." What are we to do about these countless sentences? One solution is to turn them into the plural: "All employees should decide what they think is best for them and their dependents." But this is good only in small doses. A style that converts every "he" into a "they" will quickly turn to mush.

Another solution is to use "or": "Every employee should decide what he or she thinks is best for him or her." But again, it can only be used sparingly. Often a writer will find several situations in an article where he or she can use "he or she," or "him or her," if it seems natural. By "natural" I mean that the writer is serving notice that he (or she) has the problem in mind and is trying his (or her) best within reasonable limits. But let's face it: the English language is stuck with the generic masculine ("Man shall not live by bread alone"). To turn every "he" into a "he or she," and every "his" into a "his or her," would clog the language.

In the three earlier editions of *On Writing Well*, for instance, I used "he" and "him" throughout to refer to "the reader," "the writer," "the critic," "the humorist," etc. I felt that the book would be much harder to read if I used "he or she" with every such mention. (I reject "he/she" altogether; the slant has no place in good English.) Lately, however, various women have written to nudge me about this. They say that as writers and readers themselves they resent always having to visualize a man doing the reading and the writing, and they're right; I stand nudged. In this Fourth Edition I've tried to repair the damage.

Most of the nudgers urged me to adopt the plural: to use "readers" and "writers," followed thereafter by "they." I don't like plurals; they weaken writing because they are less specific than the singular, less easy to visualize. I'd like every writer to visualize *one* reader struggling to read what he or she has written. Nevertheless I found more than a hundred places where I was able to eliminate "he," "him," "his," "himself" or "man," mainly by switching to the plural, with no real harm done; the sky didn't fall in. In the places where the male pronoun remains, I felt that it was the only clean solution.

Another suggestion from the nudgers was to alternate "he" and "she": to use "he" as the generic pronoun in one paragraph, or in one chapter, and to use "she" in the next. That struck me as too confusing and also too tricky. My cardinal goal in writing—even beyond the respect of my women readers—is clarity. Anything that gets in the way of clarity is bad, and a reader suddenly confronted with alternating pronouns would end up constantly wondering, "Who's *she?*" and "Where did *he* come from?" The device is also too self-dramatizing; it calls attention to itself as a political statement and pulls the reader's attention away from where it belongs: on the writing.

The best solutions simply eliminate "he" and its connotations of male ownership by using other pronouns or by alternating some other component of the sentence. "We" is a handy replacement for "he"; "our" and "the" can often replace "his." (A) "First *he* notices what's happening to *his* kids and he blames it on *his* neighborhood." (B) "First *we* notice what's happening to *our* kids and we blame it on *the* neighborhood." General nouns can replace specific nouns. (A) "Doctors often neglect their wives and children." (B) "Doctors often neglect their families." Countless sins can be erased by such small changes.

One other pronoun that helped me in my surgery was "you." Instead of talking about what "the writer" does and the trouble *he* gets into, I found more places where I could address the writer directly ("You'll often find . . ."). It's not a remedy that works for every kind of writing, but it's a godsend to anyone writing a textbook or an instructional book or a self-help book. The voice of a Dr. Spock talking to the father or mother of a child with a fever, or the voice of a Julia Child talking to the cook stalled in mid-recipe, is one of the most reassuring sounds a reader can hear. Always look for ways to make yourself available to the people you're trying to reach.

The pedants, of course, have other solutions. They have proposed various unisex pronouns, deriving from Nordic or Anglo-Saxon roots that only they have dug up, which they claim would fall easily into our speech if we just started teaching them in our schools and writing them in our writings. One of their typical candidates is "thon," a third-person pronoun that applies to either gender and has a handy possessive ("thons") and reflexive ("thonself"). Maybe I don't speak for the average American, but I doubt that thon wants that word in thons language or that thon would use it thonself. This is not how language changes.

*

PARAGRAPHS. Keep your paragraphs short, especially if you're writing for a newspaper or a magazine that sets its type in a narrow width. This is purely visual and psychological advice.

Short paragraphs put air around what you write and make it look inviting, whereas one long chunk of type can discourage the reader from even starting to read. A newspaper paragraph generally shouldn't have more than two or three sentences. You may worry that such frequent paragraphing will damage the logical development of your idea. (Obviously *The New Yorker* is obsessed by this fear—a reader can go for several columns without relief.) Don't worry; the gains far outweigh the hazards.

*

DICTATION. Much of the "writing" done in America is done by dictation. Administrators, executives, managers, bureaucrats, educators and other officials think in terms of using their time efficiently. To them, the quickest way of getting something "written" is to dictate it to a secretary and never look at it. This is false economy—they save a few hours and blow their whole personality. Dictated sentences tend to be pompous, sloppy and redundant. Executives who are so busy that they can't avoid dictating should at least find time to edit what they have dictated, crossing words out and putting words in, making sure that what they finally write is a true reflection of who they are, especially if it's a document that will go to a large number of readers who will judge their personality and their character on the basis of their style.

*

WRITING IS NOT A CONTEST. Every writer is starting from a different point and is bound for a different destination. Yet many writers are paralyzed by the thought that they are competing with everybody else who is trying to write and is presumably doing it better. This can often happen in a writing class. Inexperienced students are chilled to find themselves in the same class with students whose byline has appeared in the college newspaper. But writing for the college paper is no great credential; in fact, I've often found that the hares who write for the paper are overtaken by the tortoises who move studiously toward the goal of mastering the craft. The same fear cripples free-lance writers, who see the work of other writers appearing in magazines while their own keeps returning in the mail. Forget the competition and go at your own pace. Ultimately your only contest is with yourself.

*

THE SUBCONSCIOUS MIND.   Your subconscious mind does more writing than you think. Often you'll spend a whole day trying to fight your way out of some verbal thicket in which you seem to be tangled beyond salvation. Frequently a solution will occur to you the next morning when you plunge back in. While you slept, your writer's mind didn't. To some extent a writer is always working. Stay alert to the currents around you. Much of what you see and hear will come back, having percolated for days or even months through your subconscious mind, just when your conscious mind, laboring to write, needs it.

*

THE QUICKEST FIX.   Surprisingly often a difficult problem in a sentence can be solved by simply getting rid of it. Unfortunately, this solution is usually the last one that occurs to writers in a jam. First they will put the troublesome phrase through all kinds of exertions—moving it to some other part of the sentence, trying to rephrase it, adding new words to clarify the thought or to oil whatever is stuck. These efforts only make the situation worse, and the writer is left to conclude that there *is* no solution to the problem—not a comforting thought. When you find yourself at such an impasse, look at the troublesome element and ask, "Do I need it at all?" Probably you don't. It was trying to do an unnecessary job all along—that's why it was giving you so much grief. Remove it and watch the afflicted sentence spring to life and breathe normally. It's the quickest possible cure and very often the best.

*

BREEZINESS. There is a kind of writing that's so seemingly relaxed that you think you hear the author talking to you. E. B. White was probably its best practitioner, though many other masters of the form—James Thurber, Lewis Thomas, Virgil Thomson—come to mind. I'm partial to it because it's a style that I've always tried to write myself. The common assumption is that it's effortless. Just the opposite is true: the effortless style is achieved by strenuous effort and rewriting. The nails of grammar and syntax are all in place; the English is as good as the writer can make it, and the total piece has a design that pulls the reader along from start to finish.

Here, for instance, is how a typical piece by E. B. White begins:

> I spent several days and nights in mid-September with an ailing pig and I feel driven to account for this stretch of time, more particularly since the pig died at last, and I lived, and things might easily have gone the other way round and none left to do the accounting.

At first glance the sentence is so folksy that we imagine ourselves sitting in the parlor of White's house in rural Maine. A wood fire is burning and White is in a rocking chair, puffing on a pipe. He wants to tell us a yarn, and the words just tumble out. But look at the sentence again. It's a thing of beauty; nothing about it is accidental. Its use of the English language is disciplined, the punctuation is formal, the words are plain and precise, and the rhythm is that of a poet, a man who writes by ear.

This is the effortless style at its best: a methodical act of writing that disarms us with its generated warmth. The writer knows exactly what he's doing; he's writing with confidence, and—most important—he's writing to please himself. He's not trying to ingratiate himself with the reader. He knows that if he pleases himself a certain number of readers will also enjoy what he has to say.

Inexperienced writers miss this point. They think that all they have to do to achieve a casual effect is to be "just folks"—good old Bob or Betty chatting over the back fence. They're so eager not to appear highbrow that they don't even try to write good English. They want to be a pal to the reader and to make his reading simple. What they write is the breezy style.

How would a breezy writer handle E. B. White's vigil with the pig? It might come out like this:

> Ever stay up late baby-sitting for a sick porker? Believe me, you can lose a heckuva lot of shut-eye. I did this bit for three nights back in September and my better half thought I'd lost my marbles. (Just kidding, Pam!) Frankly, the whole deal kind of bummed me out. Because, you see, the pig up and died on me. To tell you the truth, I wasn't feeling in the pink myself, so I suppose it could have been yours truly and not old Porky who kicked the bucket. And you can bet your bottom dollar Mr. Pig wasn't going to write any book about it.

I won't labor all the obvious reasons why this stuff is so terrible. It's crude. It's corny. It's verbose. It's disdainful of the English language. It's condescending. (I stop reading writers who say "You see.") But the most pathetic thing about the breezy style is that it's harder to read than good English. In the writer's desperate attempt to simplify the reader's journey he has strewn the path with obstacles: cheap slang, shoddy sentences, windy musings. E. B. White's style is infinitely easier to read. He knows that the tools of grammar haven't survived for so many centuries by chance—they are roadmarks that the reader not only needs but subconsciously wants. Nobody ever stopped reading E. B. White or V. S. Pritchett because the writing was too good. But a reader will stop if he thinks the writer is talking down to him. Nobody wants to be patronized.

Write with respect for the English language at its best and for readers at their best.

*

TASTE. What finally separates the good writer from the breezy writer is a quality so intangible that nobody even knows what it is: taste. It can't be defined, but we know it when we see it. A woman with taste in clothes delights us with her ability to turn herself out every day in a combination that's not only stylish and surprising; it's also exactly right. Taste is the instinct to know what works and to avoid what doesn't.

In the arts, knowing what *not* to do is a major component of taste. Two jazz pianists may be equally proficient at the keyboard. The one with taste will put every note to useful work in telling his story; the one without taste will drench us in ripples and other unnecessary ornaments. A painter with taste will trust his eye to tell him what needs to be on his canvas and what doesn't; the one without taste will give us a landscape that's too pretty, or too cluttered, or too gaudy in its colors—anyway, too something.

I realize that I'm trying to pin down a matter that's highly subjective and has no firm rules. One person's beautiful painting is another person's kitsch. It's also true that taste changes with the decades—yesterday's charm is rejected today as junk, but tomorrow it will be back in vogue, certified again as charming. So why do I even bring up the problem? Mainly to remind you that it exists. Taste is an invisible current that runs through all writing, and you should be aware of it.

Sometimes, in fact, it's not invisible. Every art form has a hard core of verities that survive the fickleness of time. There must be something innately pleasing in the proportions of the Parthenon; Western man continues to let the Greeks of two thousand years ago design his major public buildings. In music, the fugues of Bach have a timeless elegance that's rooted in the timeless laws of mathematics.

Does writing have any such guideposts for us? Not many—writing is the expression of every person's individuality, and in general we can only say that we know what we like when it comes along. Still, as in the other arts, taste is partly a question of knowing what to omit. Clichés, for example. If a writer litters his prose with platitudes—if every idea that doesn't hit the nail on the head has to go back to the drawing board—we can safely infer that the writer lacks an instinct for what gives language its freshness. Faced with a choice between the novel and the banal, he goes unerringly for the banal.

Extend the point beyond clichés to include a writer's larger use of words. Again, freshness is a critical factor. Taste chooses words that have originality, strength and precision; non-taste veers into the breezy vernacular of the alumni magazine's class notes—a world where people in authority are the top brass or the powers that be. What exactly is wrong with "the top brass"? Nothing—and everything. Taste is knowing that it's better to call people in authority what they are: officials, or executives, or the president of the company. Non-taste reaches for the corny synonym.

But finally taste is a mixture of qualities that are beyond defining: an ear, for instance, that can hear the difference between a sentence that limps and a sentence that lilts, or an intuition that knows when a casual phrase dropped into a formal sentence will not only feel right but will seem to be the inevitable choice. Does this mean that taste can't be learned? Yes and no. Perfect taste, like perfect pitch, is a gift from God. But a certain amount can be acquired. The trick is to study writers who have it.

*

IMITATION. Don't ever hesitate to imitate another writer—every artist learning a craft needs models. Eventually you'll find your own voice and will shed the skin of the writer you imitated. But pick only the best models. If you want to write about medicine, read Lewis Thomas; if you want to write travel or memoir, read Alan Moorehead or Eudora Welty.

The best way to learn to write is to study the work of the men and women who are doing the kind of writing you want to do. I often read E. B. White to get myself warmed up. I want to get his cadences into my ear—and also his taste, by which I mean his attitude toward language. I still read some S. J. Perelman before starting a piece of humor. I want to get into my head his relish of nonsense and his pleasure in pushing the language to its outer limits. Find the models that are right for you and make them your mentors.

*

ELOQUENCE AND THE USES OF THE PAST.   By reading other writers you plug yourself into a longer tradition that enriches you. Sometimes you will tap a vein of eloquence or racial memory that gives your writing a depth it could never attain on its own. Let me illustrate what I mean by a roundabout route.

Normally I don't read the proclamations issued by state officials to designate important days of the year as important days of the year. But in 1976, when I was teaching at Yale, the governor of Connecticut, Ella Grasso, had the pleasant idea of reissuing the Thanksgiving Proclamation written forty years earlier by Governor Wilbur Cross, which she called "a masterpiece of eloquence." I've often wondered whether eloquence has vanished from American life and speech, or whether we even still consider it a goal worth striving for. So I studied Governor Cross's words to see how they had weathered the passage of time, that cruel judge of the rhetoric of earlier generations. I was delighted to find that I agreed with Governor Grasso. It was a piece written by a master:

Time out of mind at this turn of the seasons when the hardy oak leaves rustle in the wind and the frost gives a tang to the air and the dusk falls early and the friendly evenings lengthen under the heel of Orion, it has seemed good to our people to join together in praising the Creator and Preserver, who has brought us by a way that we did not know to the end of another year. In observance of this custom, I appoint Thursday, the 26th of November, as a day of Public Thanksgiving for the blessings that have been our common lot and have placed our beloved state with the favored regions of earth—for all the creature comforts: the yield of the soil that has fed us and the richer yield from labor of every kind that has sustained our lives—and for all those things, as dear as breath to the body, that quicken man's faith in his manhood, that nourish and strengthen his word and act; for honor held above price; for steadfast courage and zeal in the long, long search after truth; for liberty and for justice freely granted by each to his fellow and so as freely enjoyed; and for the crowning glory and mercy of peace upon our land;—that we may humbly take heart of these blessings as we gather once again with solemn and festive rites to our Harvest Home.

Governor Grasso added a postscript urging the citizens of Connecticut "to renew their dedication to the spirit of sacrifice and commitment which the Pilgrims invoked during their first harsh winter in the New World," and I made a mental note to look at Orion that night. I was glad to be reminded that I was living in one of the favored regions of earth. I was also glad to be reminded that peace is not the only crowning glory to be thankful for; so is the English language when it is gracefully used for the public good. The cadences of Jefferson, Lincoln, Churchill, Roosevelt and Adlai Stevenson came rolling down to me. (The cadences of Eisenhower, Nixon and Reagan did not.)

I posted the Thanksgiving proclamation on a bulletin board

for my students to enjoy. From their comments I realized that several of them thought I was being facetious. Knowing my obsession with simplicity, they assumed that I regarded Governor Cross's message as florid excess.

The incident left me with several questions. Had I sprung Wilbur Cross's prose on a generation that had never been exposed to nobility of language as a means of addressing the populace? I couldn't recall a single attempt since John F. Kennedy's inaugural speech in 1961. (More recently, Mario Cuomo and Jesse Jackson have partly restored my faith.) This was a generation reared on television, where the picture is valued more highly than the word—where the word, in fact, is devalued, used as mere punctuation or chatter, and often misused and mispronounced. It was also a generation reared on music—songs and rhythms meant primarily to be heard and felt. With so much noise in the air from TV and stereo, was any American child being trained to listen? Was anyone calling attention to the majesty of a well-constructed sentence?

My other question raised a more subtle mystery: What is the line that separates eloquence from bombast? Why are we exalted by the words of Wilbur Cross and anesthetized by the speeches of most politicians and public officials who ply us with oratorical ruffles and flourishes?

Part of the answer takes us back to taste. A writer with an ear for language will reach for fresh imagery and avoid phrases that are trite. The hack will reach for the very clichés that the good writer spurns, thinking he will enrich his thoughts with currency that is, as he would put it, tried and true. Another part of the answer lies in simplicity. Writing that will endure tends to consist of words that are short and strong; words that anesthetize are words of three, four and five syllables, mostly of Latin origin, many of them ending in "ion" and embodying a vague concept. In Wilbur Cross's Thanksgiving Proclamation there are no four-syllable words and only ten three-syllable words, three of which are proper nouns that he was stuck with. Notice how many of the governor's words are anything but vague: leaves, wind, frost, air, evening, earth, comforts, soil, labor, breath, body, justice, courage, peace, land, rites, home. They are homely words in the best sense; they catch the rhythm of the seasons and the dailiness of life. Also notice that all of them are nouns. After verbs, plain nouns are your strongest tools; they resonate with emotion.

But ultimately eloquence runs on a deeper current. It moves us with what it leaves unsaid, touching off echoes in what we already know from our reading, our religion and our heritage. Eloquence invites us to bring some part of ourselves to the transaction. It was no accident that Lincoln's speeches resounded with echoes of the King James Bible; he knew it almost by heart from his boyhood, and he had so soaked himself in its sonorities that his formal English was more Elizabethan than American. The Second Inaugural Address reverberates with Biblical phrases and paraphrases: "It may seem strange that any men should dare to ask a just God's assistance in wringing their bread from the sweat of other men's faces, but let us judge not, that we be not judged." The first half of the sentence borrows a metaphor from Genesis, the second half reshapes a famous command in Matthew, and "a just God" is from Isaiah.

If this speech affects me more than any other American document, it's not only because I know that Lincoln was killed five weeks later, or because I'm moved by all the pain that culminated in this plea for a reconciliation that would have malice toward none and charity for all. It's also because Lincoln tapped some of Western man's oldest teachings about slavery, clemency and judgment. His words carried stern overtones for the men and women who heard him in 1865, reared, as he was, on the Bible. But even in the 1990s it's hard not to feel a wrath almost too ancient to grasp in Lincoln's notion that God might will the Civil War to continue "until all the wealth piled by the bondsman's two hundred and fifty years of unrequited toil shall be sunk, and until every drop of blood drawn with the lash shall be paid by another drawn with the sword, as was said three thousand years ago."

Wilbur Cross's Thanksgiving Proclamation also echoes with truths that we know in our bones. To such mysteries as the changing of the seasons and the bounty of the earth we bring strong emotions of our own. Who hasn't looked with awe at Orion? To such democratic processes as "the long search after truth" and "liberty and justice freely granted" we bring fragments of our own searches after truth, our own grantings and receivings, in a nation where so many human rights have been won and so many still elude us. Governor Cross doesn't take our time to explain these processes, and I'm grateful to him for that. I hate to think how many clichés a hack orator would marshal to tell us far more—and nourish us far less.

Therefore remember the uses of the past when you tell your story. What moves us in writing that has regional or ethnic roots—black writing, Southern writing, Jewish-American writing—is the sound of voices far older than the narrator's, talking in cadences that are more than ordinarily rich. Toni Morrison, one of the most eloquent of black writers, once said: "I remember the language of the people I grew up with. Language was so important to them. All that power was in it. And grace and metaphor. Some of it was very formal and Biblical, because the habit is that when you have something important to say you go into parable, if you're from Africa, or you go into another level of language. I wanted to use language that way. Because my feeling was that a black novel was not black because I wrote it, or because there were black people in it, or because it was about black things. It was the style. It had a certain style. It was inevitable. I couldn't describe it, but I could produce it."

Go with what seems inevitable in your own heritage. Embrace it and it may lead you to eloquence.

15

Science, Technology and Nature

Take a class of writing students in a liberal arts college, tell them that their next assignment is to write about some aspect of science, and a pitiful moan will go around the room. "No! Not science!" the moan says. "Don't make us dive into those terrifying waters!"

I used to be such a student myself, as fearful of science as James Thurber's grandmother, who, as he recalled her in *My Life and Hard Times,* thought that "electricity was dripping invisibly all over the house" from wall sockets. But as a writer I've learned that scientific and technical subjects can be made as accessible to the layman as any other subject. It's just a matter of putting one sentence after another. The "after," however, is crucial. Nowhere else must you work so hard to write sentences that form a linear sequence. This is no place for fanciful leaps or implied truths. Fact and deduction are the ruling family.

The science assignment that I give to students is a simple one. I just ask them to describe how something works. I don't care about style or any other graces. I only want them to tell me, say, how a sewing machine does what it does, or how a pump operates, or why an apple falls down, or how the eye tells the brain what it sees. Any process will do, and "science" can be defined loosely to include technology, medicine and nature.

A basic tenet of journalism is that "the reader knows nothing." As tenets go, it's not too flattering, but a writer of science or technology can never forget it. You just can't assume that your readers know what you assume any boob knows, or that they still remember what was once explained to them. Speaking as one boob, I doubt if I could get into one of those life jackets that hundreds of airline flight attendants have shown me how to get into: something about "simply" putting my arms through the straps, "simply" pulling two toggle knobs sharply downward (or is it sideways?) and "simply" blowing it up—but not too soon. The only step I'm confident I could perform is to blow it up too soon.

Describing how a process works is valuable for two reasons. First, it forces you to make sure *you* know how it works. Then it forces you to take the reader through the same sequence of ideas and deductions that made the process clear to you. I've found it to be a breakthrough assignment for many students who couldn't disentangle themselves from disorderly thinking. One of them, a bright Yale sophomore still spraying the page with fuzzy generalities at midterm, came to class in a high mood and asked if he could read aloud his paper on how a fire extinguisher works. I was dubious; I was sure we were in for chaos. But his piece moved with simplicity and logic. It clearly explained how three different kinds of fires were attacked by three different kinds of fire extinguishers. I was elated by his overnight change into a writer who had learned to write sequentially, and so was he. By the end of his junior year he had written a how-to book that sold better than any book *I* had written.

Many other fuzzy students put themselves through the same cure and have written with clarity ever since. For the principle of science writing applies to all nonfiction writing. It's the principle of leading readers who know nothing, step by step, to a grasp of subjects they didn't think they had an aptitude for or were afraid they were too dumb to understand.

Let me tilt the linear example by ninety degrees and ask you to imagine science writing as an upside-down pyramid. Start at the bottom with the one fact that a reader must know before he can learn any more. The second sentence broadens what was stated first, making the pyramid wider, and the third sentence broadens the second, so that gradually you can move beyond mere fact into significance and speculation—how a new discovery alters what was known, what new avenues of research it might open, where the research might be applied. There's no limit to how wide the inverted pyramid can become, but the reader will understand the broad implications only if he starts with a narrow fact.

A good example is an article by Harold M. Schmeck, Jr., which ran on page 1 of the *New York Times*.

> WASHINGTON—There was a chimpanzee in California with a talent for playing ticktacktoe. Its trainers were delighted with this evidence of learning, but they were even more impressed by something else. They found they could tell from the animal's brain whether any particular move would be right or wrong. It depended on the chimpanzee's state of attention. When the trained animal was properly attentive, he made the right move.

Well, that's a reasonably interesting fact. But why is it worth page 1 of the *Times*? Paragraph 2 tells me:

> The significant fact was that scientists were able to recognize that state. By elaborate computer analysis of brain wave signals they were learning to distinguish what might be called "states of mind."

But hadn't this been possible before?

This was far more ambitious than simply detecting gross states of arousal, drowsiness or sleep. It was a new step toward understanding how the brain works.

How is it a new step?

The chimpanzee and the research team at the University of California at Los Angeles have graduated from the tick-tacktoe stage, but the work with brain waves is continuing. It has already revealed some surprising insights to the brain's behavior during space flight. It shows promise of application to social and domestic problems on earth and even to improvements in human learning.

Good. I could hardly ask for a broader application of the research: space, human problems and the cognitive process. But is it an isolated effort? No indeed.

It is part of the large ferment of modern brain research in progress in laboratories throughout the United States and abroad. Involved are all manner of creatures from men and monkeys to rats and mice, goldfish, flatworms and Japanese quail.

I begin to see the total context. But what is the purpose?

The ultimate goal is to understand the human brain—that incredible three-pound package of tissue that can imagine the farthest reaches of the universe and the ultimate core of the atom but cannot fathom its own functioning. Each research project bites off a little piece of an immense puzzle.

So now I know where the chimp at U.C.L.A. fits into the spectrum of international science. Knowing this, I'm ready to learn more about his particular contribution.

In the case of the chimpanzee being taught to play tick-tacktoe, even the trained eye could see nothing beyond the ordinary in the wavy lines being traced on paper to represent electrical waves from an animal's brain. But through analysis by computer it was possible to tell which traces showed that the animal was about to make the right move and which preceded a mistake.

An important key was the system of computer analysis developed largely by Dr. John Hanley. The state of mind that always foreshadowed a correct answer was one that might be described as trained attentiveness. Without the computer's ability to analyze the huge complexities of the recorded brain waves, the "signatures" of such states could not have been detected.

The article goes on for four columns to describe potential uses of the research—measuring causes of domestic tension, for instance, or reducing the rush-hour stress of drivers—and eventually it touches on work being done in many corners of the world and in various pockets of medicine and psychology. But it started with one chimpanzee playing ticktacktoe.

You can take much of the mystery out of science writing by helping the reader to identify with the scientific work being done. This means, once again, looking for the human element—and if you have to settle for a chimpanzee, at least that's the next-highest rung on the Darwinian ladder.

One obvious human element is yourself. Use your own experience to connect the reader to some mechanism that also touches his life. In the following article on memory and how it operates, note how the writer, Will Bradbury, gives us at the start a personal handle with which to grab a complex subject:

Even now I see the dark cloud of sand before it hits my eyes, hear my father's calm voice urging me to cry the sting away, and feel anger and humiliation burn in my chest. More than 30 years have passed since that moment when a play-mate, fighting for my toy ambulance, tossed a handful of sand in my face. Yet the look of the sand and ambulance, the sound of my father's voice and the throb of my bruised feelings all remain sharp and clear today. They are the very first things I can remember, the first bits of visual, verbal and emotional glass imbedded in the mosaic I have come to know as *me* by what is certainly the brain's most essential function—memory.

Without this miracle function that enables us to store and recall information, the brain's crucial systems for waking and sleeping, for expressing how we feel about things and for performing complicated acts could do little more than fumble with sensory inputs of the moment. Nor would man have a real feeling of self, for he would have no gallery of the past to examine, learn from, enjoy and, when necessary, hide away in. Yet after thousands of years of theorizing, of reading and misreading his own behavioral quirks, man is just begin-ning to have some understanding of the mysterious process that permits him to break and store bits of passing time.

One problem has been to decide what memory is and what things have it. Linseed oil, for example, has a kind of memory. Once exposed to light, even if only briefly, it will change consistency and speed the *second* time it is exposed. It will "remember" its first encounter with the light. Electronic and fluidic circuits also have memory, of a more sophisticated kind. Built into computers, they are able to store and retrieve extraordinary amounts of information. And the human body has at least four kinds of memory. . . .

That's a fine lead. Who doesn't possess some cluster of vivid images that he can recall from an inconceivably early age? The reader is eager to learn how such a feat of storage and retrieval is accomplished. The example of the linseed oil is just piquant enough to make us wonder what "memory" really is, and then the writer reverts to the human frame of reference, for it is man who has built the computer circuits and who has four kinds of memory himself.

Another method is to weave a scientific story around some-one else. This is the continuing appeal of the articles called "Annals of Medicine" that Berton Roueché has long been writing in *The New Yorker*. They are detective stories, almost always involving a victim—some ordinary person struck by a mystifying ailment—and a gumshoe obsessed with finding the villain. Here's how one of them begins:

> At about 8 o'clock on Monday morning, Sept. 25, 1944, a ragged, aimless old man of 82 collapsed on the sidewalk on Dey Street, near the Hudson Terminal. Innumerable people must have noticed him, but he lay there alone for several minutes, dazed, doubled up with abdominal cramps, and in an agony of retching. Then a policeman came along. Until the policeman bent over the old man he may have supposed that he had just a sick drunk on his hands; wanderers dropped by drink are common in that part of town in the early morning. It was not an opinion that he could have held for long. The old man's nose, lips, ears and fingers were sky-blue.

By noon, eleven blue men have been admitted to nearby hospitals. But never fear—Dr. Ottavio Pellitteri, field epidemiologist, is quickly on the scene and telephoning Dr. Morris Greenberg at the Bureau of Preventable Diseases. Slowly the two men piece together fragments of evidence that seem to defy medical history until the case is at last nailed down and the villain identified as a type of poisoning so rare that many standard texts on toxicology don't even mention it.

Roueché's secret is as old as the art of storytelling. We are in on a chase and a mystery. But he doesn't start with the medical history of poisoning, or talk about standard texts on toxicology. He gives us a man—and not only a man but a blue one.

Another way of helping the reader to understand unfamiliar facts is to relate them to sights he *is* familiar with. Reduce the abstract principle to an image he can visualize. Moshe Safdie, the architect who conceived Habitat, the innovative housing complex at Montreal's Expo 67, explains in his book *Beyond Habitat* that man would build better than he does if he took the time to see how nature does the job, since "nature makes form, and form is a by-product of evolution":

> One can study plant and animal life, rock and crystal formations, and discover the reasons for their particular form. The nautilus has evolved so that when its shell grows, its head will not get stuck in the opening. This is known as gnomonic growth; it results in the spiral formation. It is, mathematically, the only way it can grow.
>
> The same is true of achieving strength with a particular material. Look at the wings of a vulture, at its bone formation. A most intricate three-dimensional geometric pattern has evolved, a kind of space frame, with very thin bones that get thicker at the ends. The main survival problem for the vulture is to develop strength in the wing (which is under tremendous bending movement when the bird is flying) without building up weight, as that would limit its mobility. Through evolution the vulture has the most efficient structure one can imagine—a space frame in bone.

"For each aspect of life there are responses of form," Safdie writes, noting that the maple and the elm have wide leaves to absorb the maximum amount of sun for survival in a temperate climate, whereas the olive tree has a leaf that rotates because it must preserve moisture and can't absorb heat, and the cactus turns itself perpendicular to light. We may not know anything about botany, but we can all picture a maple leaf and a cactus plant. With every hard principle Safdie gives us a simple illustration:

> Economy and survival are the two key words in nature. Examined out of context, the neck of the giraffe seems uneconomically long, but it is economical in view of the fact that most of the giraffe's food is high on the tree. Beauty as we understand it, and as we admire it in nature, is never arbitrary.

Or take this article about bats, by Diane Ackerman. Most of us know only three facts about bats: they're mammals, we don't like them, and they've got some kind of radar that enables them to fly at night without bumping into other things. Obviously anyone writing about bats must soon get around to explaining how that mechanism of "echo-location" works. In the following passage Ackerman gives us details so precise—and so easy to relate to what we know—that the process becomes a pleasure to read about:

> It's not hard to understand echo-location if you picture bats as calling or whistling to their prey with high-frequency sounds. Most of us can't hear these. At our youngest and keenest of ear, we might detect sounds of twenty thousand vibrations a second, but bats can vocalize at up to two hundred thousand. They do it not in a steady stream but at intervals—twenty or thirty times a second. A bat listens for the sounds to return to it, and when the echoes start coming faster and louder it knows that the insect it's stalking has flown nearer. By judging the time between echoes, a bat can tell how fast the prey is moving and in which direction. Some bats are sensitive enough to register a beetle walking on sand,

and some can detect the movement of a moth flexing its wings as it sits on a leaf.

That's my idea of sensitive; I couldn't ask a writer to give me two more wonderful examples. But there's more to my admiration than gratitude. I also wonder: How many other examples of bat sensitivity did she collect—dozens? hundreds?—to be able to choose those two? Always start with too much material. Then give your reader just enough.

As the bat closes in, it may shout faster, to pinpoint its prey. And there's a qualitative difference between a steady, solid echo bouncing off a brick wall and the light, fluid echo from a swaying flower. By shouting at the world and listening to the echoes, bats can compose a picture of their landscape and the objects in it which includes texture, density, motion, distance, size and probably other features, too. Most bats really belt it out; we just don't hear them. This is an eerie thought when one stands in a silent grove filled with bats. They spend their whole lives yelling. They yell at their loved ones, they yell at their enemies, they yell at their dinner, they yell at the big, bustling world. Some yell faster, some slower, some louder, some softer. Long-eared bats don't need to yell; they can hear their echoes perfectly well if they whisper.

Another way of making science accessible is to write like a person and not like a scientist. It's the same old question of warmth, of being yourself. Just because you're dealing with a scholarly discipline that's usually reported in a style of dry pedantry is no reason why you shouldn't write in good fresh English. Loren Eiseley is an example of a naturalist who refused to be cowed by nature as he passed on to us—in *The Immense Journey*—not only his knowledge but his enthusiasms:

I have long been an admirer of the octopus. The cephalopods are very old, and they have slipped, protean, through many shapes. They are the wisest of the mollusks, and I have always felt it to be just as well for us that they never came ashore, but—there are other things that have.

There is no need to be frightened. It is true that some of the creatures are odd, but I find the situation rather heartening than otherwise. It gives one a feeling of confidence to see nature still busy with experiments, still dynamic, and not through or satisfied because a Devonian fish managed to end as a two-legged character with a straw hat. There are other things brewing and growing in the oceanic vat. It pays to know this. It pays to know there is just as much future as past. The only thing that doesn't pay is to be sure of man's own part in it.

Eiseley's gift to us is that he enables us to feel what it's like to be a scientist. The central transaction in his writing is the naturalist's love affair with nature, just as in Lewis Thomas's writing it's the cell biologist's love of the cell. "Watching television," Dr. Thomas writes in *The Lives of a Cell*, "you'd think we lived at bay, in total jeopardy, surrounded on all sides by human-seeking germs, shielded against infection and death only by a chemical technology that enables us to keep killing them off. We explode clouds of aerosol, mixed for good luck with deodorants, into our noses, mouths, underarms, privileged crannies—even into the intimate insides of our telephones." But even at our most paranoid, Dr. Thomas says, "we have always been a relatively minor interest of the vast microbial world":

I can think of a few microorganisms, possibly the tubercle bacillus, the syphilis spirochete, the malarial parasite and a few others, that have a selective advantage in their ability to infect human beings, but there is nothing to be gained, in an evolutionary sense, by the capacity to cause illness or death. Pathogenicity may be something of a disadvantage for most microbes, carrying lethal risks more frightening to them than to us. The man who catches a meningococcus is in considerably less danger for his life, even without chemotherapy, than meningococci with the bad luck to catch a man.

At the opposite pole of magnitude from bacteria and bats are disciplines so big, like astronomy, or so old, like geology, that they frighten writers away. Yet they are part of the world we live in, and a good science writer can find a way to scale them down to human size. One such writer, Dava Sobel, explaining the various geological situations that produce waterfalls, reminds us along the way that "waterfalls are often named for their shapes and colors (Horseshoe, Rainbow, Silver Apron, plus many Ribbons and Bridal Veils)" and that their names also "commemorate everyone from Winston Churchill to Sitting Bull." But her purpose is to instruct, not, like most waterfall watchers, to rhapsodize:

> Technically, a waterfall is a stream descending precipitously over an exaggerated steepening of its bed. . . . Some waterfalls—like those in Hawaii, Iceland and East Africa—are the result of volcano-associated faulting. Other kinds of waterfalls flow over rapidly receding sea cliffs, down fault scarps and even into the box canyons of the badlands during torrential rains.
>
> The down-sloping boundary between the Piedmont Upland and the Atlantic Coastal Plain of the eastern United States turns every crossing river into a waterfall. This Fall Line is a vein of power that runs through Trenton, Philadelphia, Wilmington, Baltimore, Washington, Richmond, Petersburg and Columbia. "For cities built along the Fall Line,"

writes Edward S. Deevey, Jr., of the University of Florida, "geology has been destiny." At a waterfall, ships going upriver had to stop; inns, portages, depots and warehouses sprang up. At a waterfall, mills for grist and textiles tapped the cheap muscle of the river.

I've quoted from so many writers, writing about so many facets of the physical world, to show that they all come across first as people—men and women finding a common thread of humanity between themselves and their specialty and their readers. They aren't afraid of their task; on the contrary, they seem to be relaxed and having a good time. They all write clearly and without pretense, using the vocabulary of everyday life and seldom taking refuge in the jargon of their field. If Lewis Thomas uses "pathogenicity" it's because the word fits what he wants to say as tightly as a glove, and he trusts us to be intellectually curious enough to look it up (as I just did) and to find that it means "the production or development of a disease." He's not putting on airs or being deliberately obscure.

You can achieve the same rapport with your subject. Though I've used science as a demonstration model in this chapter, the principle applies to every field where the reader must be led across new and bewildering terrain. In the life sciences alone, think of all the issues—drugs, AIDS, abortion, health delivery, care of the old, toxic waste, pollution, global warming, gene splicing, surrogate motherhood—where biology and chemistry are entangled with ethics, religion, politics and economics. Only through clear writing can the rest of us make educated choices in these urgent areas where we have little or no education.

Finally, somewhere between the hard and soft sciences is the one that most Americans find scariest of all—mathematics—and I'll close with that, partly because it's a subject that might seem too abstract to lend itself to warm writing. But mainly I like this passage by S. M. Ulam, from his likable *Adventures of a Mathematician,* because he doesn't just tell me *what* he thinks about his subject. He tells me *how* he thinks about it.

> The world of mathematics is a creation of the brain and can be visualized without external help. Mathematicians are able to work on their subject without any of the equipment or props needed by other scientists. . . . This may explain why so many mathematicians appear turned inward or preoccupied while performing other activities.
>
> Ever since I started learning mathematics I would say that I have spent—regardless of any other activity—on the average of two to three hours a day thinking and two to three hours reading or conversing about mathematics. Sometimes when I was twenty-three I would think about the same problem with incredible intensity for several hours without using paper or pencil. By the way, this is infinitely more strenuous than making calculations with symbols to look at and manipulate. . . .
>
> I always preferred to try to imagine new possibilities rather than merely to follow specific lines of reasoning or make concrete calculations. Some mathematicians have this trait to a greater extent than others. . . . Paul Erdöes concentrates all the time, but usually on lines which are already begun or which are connected to what he was thinking about earlier. He doesn't wipe his memory clean like a tape recorder to start something new.
>
> Banach used to say, "Hope is the mother of fools," a Polish proverb. Nevertheless, it is good to be hopeful and to believe that with luck one will succeed. If one insists only on complete solutions to problems, this is less rewarding than repeated tries which result in partial answers or at least in some experience. It is analogous to exploring an unknown country where one does not immediately have to reach the end of the

trail or all the summits to discover new realms.

It is most important in creative science not to give up. If you are an optimist you will be willing to "try" more than if you are a pessimist. It is the same in games like chess. A really good chess player tends to believe (sometimes mistakenly) that he holds a better position than his opponent. This, of course, helps to keep the game moving and does not increase the fatigue that self-doubt engenders. Physical and mental stamina are of crucial importance in chess and also in creative scientific work.

16

Business Writing

Although this is a book about writing, it's not meant just for "writers." Its points are valid for all the people who have to do some writing just to get along in their job. The interoffice memo, the business letter and the marketing analysis are forms of writing, and many a career rises or falls on the ability or inability of an employee to state an idea or a set of facts clearly and concisely.

Most people work for institutions—businesses and banks, insurance firms and law firms, government agencies, school systems, nonprofit organizations and various other entities. Many of them are executives whose writing goes out to the public: the corporation president addressing the stockholders, the bank manager explaining a change in procedure, the school principal writing a newsletter to parents. Whoever they are, they are so fearful and so uncomfortable with words that their sentences lack all humanity—and so do their institutions. It's hard to imagine that these are real places where real men and women come to work every morning.

But just because people work for an institution they don't have to write like one. Institutions can be warmed up. Administrators and managers can be turned into human beings. Information can be imparted clearly and without pomposity. It's a question of remembering that readers identify with people, not with abstractions like "profitability," or with Latinate nouns like "utilization" and "implementation," or with inert constructions in which nobody can be visualized doing something ("prefeasibility studies are in the paperwork stage").

Nowhere has the point been made better than in George Orwell's translation into modern bureaucratic fuzz of this famous verse from Ecclesiastes:

> I returned and saw under the sun, that the race is not to the swift, nor the battle to the strong, neither yet bread to the wise, nor yet riches to men of understanding, nor yet favor to men of skill; but time and chance happeneth to them all.

Orwell's version goes:

> Objective consideration of contemporary phenomena compels the conclusion that success or failure in competitive activities exhibits no tendency to be commensurate with innate capacity, but that a considerable element of the unpredictable must invariably be taken into account.

First notice how the two passages look. The one at the top invites us to read it. The words are short and have air around them; they convey the rhythms of human speech. The second one is clotted with long words. It tells us instantly—at a glance—that a ponderous mind is at work. We don't want to go anywhere with a mind that expresses itself in such suffocating language. We don't even start reading.

Also notice the content of the two passages. Gone from the second one are the short words and vivid images from everyday life—the race and the battle, the bread and the riches—and in their place have waddled the long and flabby nouns of generalized meaning. Gone is any sense of what one person did ("I returned") or what he realized ("saw") about one of life's central mysteries: the capriciousness of fate.

Let me illustrate how this disease infects our everyday life. I'll use school principals as my first example, not because they are the worst offenders (they aren't) but because I happen to have such an example. My points are intended, however, for all the men and women who work in all the organizations where language has lost its humanity and nobody knows what the people in charge are trying to say.

My encounter with the principals began when I got a call from Ernest B. Fleishman, superintendent of schools in Greenwich, Connecticut. "We'd like you to come and 'dejargonize' us," he said. "We don't think we can teach students to write unless all of us at the top of the school system clean up our own writing." He said he would send me some typical materials that had originated within the system. His idea was for me to analyze the writing and then conduct a workshop.

What appealed to me was the willingness of Dr. Fleishman and his colleagues to make themselves vulnerable. Vulnerability, I think, has a strength of its own. We decided on a date, and soon a fat envelope arrived. It contained various internal memos and mimeographed newsletters that had been mailed to parents from the sixteen elementary, junior and senior high schools.

The newsletters had a cheery and informal look. Obviously the system was making an effort to communicate warmly with its families. But even at first glance certain chilly phrases caught my eye—"prioritized evaluative procedures," "modified departmentalized schedule"—and one principal promised that his school would provide "enhanced positive learning environments." Just as obviously the system wasn't communicating as warmly as it thought it was.

I studied the principals' material and divided it into good and bad examples. On the appointed morning in Greenwich I found forty principals and curriculum coordinators assembled and eager to learn. I told them that I could only applaud them for submitting to a process that so threatened their identity. In the national clamor over why Johnny can't write, Dr. Fleishman was the first adult in my experience who admitted that youth has no monopoly on verbal sludge and that the problem must also be attacked at the top.

I told the principals that we want to think of the men and women who run our children's schools as people not unlike ourselves. We are suspicious of pretentiousness, of all the fad words that the social scientists have coined to avoid the horrid necessity of making themselves clear to ordinary mortals. I urged them to be natural. How we write and how we talk is how we define ourselves.

I asked them to listen to how they were defining themselves to the community. I had made copies of certain bad examples, changing the names of the schools and the principals. I explained that I would read some of the examples aloud. Later we would see if they could turn what they had written into plain English. This was my first example:

Dear Parent:

We have established a special phone communication system to provide additional opportunities for parent input. During this year we will give added emphasis to the goal of communication and utilize a variety of means to accomplish this goal. Your inputs, from the unique position as a parent, will help us to plan and implement an educational plan that meets the needs of your child. An open dialogue, feedback and sharing of information between parents and teachers will enable us to work with your child in the most effective manner.

DR. GEORGE B. JONES
Principal

That's the kind of communication I don't want to receive, unique though my parent inputs might be. I'd like to be told that the school is going to make it easier for me to telephone the teachers and that they hope I'll call often to discuss how my children are getting along. Instead the parent gets junk: "special phone communication system," "added emphasis to the goal of communication," "plan and implement an educational plan." As for "open dialogue, feedback and sharing of information," they are three ways of saying the same thing.

Dr. Jones is clearly a man who means well, and his plan is one that we all want: a chance to pick up the phone and tell the principal what a great kid Johnny is despite that unfortunate incident in the playground last Tuesday. But Dr. Jones doesn't sound like a person I want to call. In fact, he doesn't sound like a person. His message could have been tapped out by a computer. He is squandering a rich resource: himself.

Another example that I chose was a "Principal's Greeting" sent to parents at the start of the year. It consisted of two paragraphs that were very different:

> Fundamentally, Foster is a good school. Pupils who require help in certain subjects or study skills areas are receiving special attention. In the school year ahead we seek to provide enhanced positive learning environments. Children, and staff, must work in an atmosphere that is conducive to learning. Wide varieties of instructional materials are needed. Careful attention to individual abilities and learning styles is required. Cooperation between school and home is extremely important to the learning process. All of us should be aware of desired educational objectives for every child.
>
> Keep informed about what is planned for our children this year and let us know about your own questions and about any special needs your child may have. I have met many of you in the first few weeks. Please continue to stop in to introduce

yourself or to talk about Foster. I look forward to a very productive year for all of us.

DR. RAY B. DAWSON
Principal

In the second paragraph I'm being greeted by a person; in the first I'm hearing from an educator. I like the real Dr. Dawson of Paragraph 2. He talks in warm and comfortable phrases: "Keep informed," "let us know," "I have met," "Please continue," "I look forward."

By contrast, Educator Dawson of Paragraph 1 never uses "I" or even suggests a sense of "I." He falls back on the jargon of his profession, where he feels safe, not stopping to notice that he really isn't telling the parent anything. What are "study skills areas" and how do they differ from "subjects"? What are "enhanced positive learning environments" and how do they differ from "an atmosphere that is conducive to learning"? What are "wide varieties of instructional materials": pencils, textbooks, filmstrips? What exactly are "learning styles"? What "educational objectives" are "desired," and who desires them?

The second paragraph, in short, is warm and personal; the other is pedantic and vague. This was a pattern I found repeatedly. Whenever the principals wrote to notify the parents of some human detail they wrote with humanity:

It seems that traffic is beginning to pile up again in front of the school. If you can possibly do so, please come to the rear of the school for your child at the end of the day.

I would appreciate it if you would speak with your children about their behavior in the cafeteria. Many of you would be totally dismayed if you could observe the manners of your children while they are eating. Check occasionally to see if they owe money for lunch. Sometimes children are very slow in repaying.

But when the educators wrote to explain how they proposed to do their educating, they vanished without a trace:

> In this document you will find the program goals and objectives that have been identified and prioritized. Evaluative procedures for the objectives were also established based on acceptable criteria.

> Prior to the implementation of the above practice, students were given very little exposure to multiple choice questions. It is felt that the use of practice questions correlated to the unit that a student is presently studying has had an extremely positive effect as the test scores confirm.

After I had read various good and bad examples, the principals began to hear the difference between their true selves and their educator selves. The problem was how to close the gap. I recited my articles of faith: clarity, simplicity, economy, humanity. I explained about using active verbs and avoiding windy "concept nouns." I told them not to use the private vocabulary of education as a crutch; almost any subject can be made accessible in good English.

These were all basic tenets, but the principals wrote them down as if they had never heard them before—and maybe they hadn't, or at least not for many years. Perhaps this is why bureaucratic prose becomes so turgid, whatever the bureaucracy. Once an administrator rises to a certain level, nobody ever points out to him again the beauty of a simple declarative sentence, or shows him how his writing has become swollen with ornate generalizations.

Finally our workshop got down to work. I distributed my

copies and asked the principals to rewrite the more knotty sentences. It was a grim moment. They had met the enemy for the first time. They scribbled on their pads and scratched out what they had scribbled. Some didn't write anything. Some crumpled their paper. They began, in fact, to look like writers. An awful silence hung over the room, broken only by the crossing out of sentences and the crumpling of paper. They began to sound like writers.

As the day went on, they slowly relaxed. They began to write in the first person and to use active verbs. For a while they still couldn't loose their grip on long words and vague nouns ("parent communication response"). But gradually their sentences became human. When I asked them to tackle "Evaluative procedures for the objectives were also established based on acceptable criteria," one of them wrote: "At the end of the year we will evaluate our progress." Another wrote: "We will see how well we have succeeded."

That's the kind of plain talk that a parent wants. It's also what stockholders want from their corporation, what customers want from their bank, what the widow wants from the government office that is handling her social security. There is a deep yearning for human contact and a resentment of bombast. Any institution that won't take the trouble in its writing to be both clear and personal will lose friends, customers and money. Let me put it another way for business executives: a shortfall will be experienced in anticipated profitability.

Here's an example of how organizations throw away their humanity with pompous language. It's a "customer bulletin" distributed by a major industrial corporation. The sole purpose of a customer bulletin is to give helpful information to a customer. This one begins: "Companies are increasingly turning to capacity planning techniques to determine when future processing loads will exceed processing capabilities." That sentence is no favor to the customer; it's congealed with Orwellian nouns like "capacity" and "capabilities" that have no specific procedures that the customer can picture. What *are* capacity planning techniques? Whose capacity is being planned? By whom? The second sentence says: "Capacity planning adds objectivity to the decision-making process." More pompous nouns. The third sentence says: "Management is given enhanced decision participation in key areas of information system resources."

The customer has to stop after every sentence and translate it. The bulletin might as well be in French. He starts with the first sentence—the one about capacity planning techniques. Translated, that means "It helps to know when you're giving your computer more than it can handle." The second sentence—"Capacity planning adds objectivity to the decision-making process"—means that you should know the facts before you decide. The third sentence—the one about enhanced decision participation—means "The more you know about your system, the better it will work." It could also mean several other things.

But the customer isn't going to keep translating much longer. Soon he's going to start looking for another company. He thinks, "If these guys are so smart, why can't they tell me what they do? Maybe they're *not* so smart." The bulletin goes on to say that "for future cost avoidance, productivity has been enhanced." That seems to mean that the product will be free: all costs have been avoided. Next the bulletin assures the customer that "the system is delivered with functionality." That means it works. I should hope so.

Finally, at the end, we get a glimmer of humanity. The writer of the bulletin asks a satisfied customer why he chose this system. The man says he chose it because of the company's reputation for service. He says: "A computer is like a sophisticated pencil. You don't care how it works, but if it breaks you want someone there to fix it." Notice how refreshing that sentence is after all the garbage that preceded it: in its language (comfortable words), in its details that we can visualize (the pencil), and above all in its humanity. The writer has taken the coldness out of a technical process by relating it to an experience we're all familiar with—waiting for the repairman to come when something breaks.

Still, plain talk will not be easily achieved in corporate America. Too much vanity is on the line. Executives and managers at every level are prisoners of the notion that a simple style reflects a simple mind. Actually a simple style is the result of hard work and hard thinking; a muddled style reflects a muddled thinker or a person too dumb or too lazy to organize his thoughts. Remember that what you write is often the only chance you'll get to present yourself to someone whose business you want. If what you write is ornate or pompous or fuzzy, that's how you'll be perceived. The reader has no other choice.

I learned about corporate America by venturing out into it, after Greenwich, to conduct workshops for some of the country's biggest corporations, which also asked to be dejargonized. "We don't even understand our own memos anymore," they told me. I worked with the men and women who write the vast amounts of material that these companies generate for internal and external consumption. The internal material consists of house organs and newsletters whose purpose is to tell employees what's happening at their "facility" and to give them a sense of belonging. The external material includes the glossy magazines and annual reports that go to stockholders, the speeches that are delivered by high executives, the releases that are sent to the press, and the consumer manuals that explain how the product works. I found almost all of it lacking in human juices and much of it impenetrable.

Typical of the sentences in the newsletters was this one:

> Announced concurrently with the above enhancements were changes to the System Support Program, a program

product which operates in conjunction with the NCP. Among the additional functional enhancements are dynamic reconfiguration and inter-systems communications.

There's no joy for the writer in such work, and certainly none for the reader. It's language out of *Star Trek,* and if I were an employee I would not be cheered—or informed—by these efforts to raise my morale. In fact, I would soon stop reading them. I told the corporate writers that they had to find the people behind the fine achievements that were being described. "Go to the engineer who conceived the new system," I said, "or to the designer who designed it, or to the technician who assembled it, and get them to tell you in their own words how the idea came to them, or how they put it together, or how it will be used by real people out in the real world." The way to warm up any institution is to locate the missing "I" in it. "I" is the most interesting element of any story.

The writers explained that they often did interview the engineer but couldn't get him to talk English. They showed me some typical quotes in their newsletters that proved the point all too well. The engineers spoke in an arcane language studded with acronyms ("Sub-system support is available only with VSAG or TNA"). I said that the writers had to keep going back to the engineer until he finally made himself intelligible. They said that the engineer didn't *want* to be made intelligible: if he spoke too simply he would look like a jerk to his peers. I said that their responsibility was to the facts and to the reader, not to the vanity of the engineer. I urged them to believe in themselves as writers and not to relinquish control. They replied that this was easier said than done in hierarchical corporations, where approval of written reports is required at various higher levels. I sensed an undercurrent of fear: do things the company way and don't risk your job trying to make the company human.

High executives were equally victimized by the syndrome of wanting to sound important. One corporation had a monthly newsletter to enable "management" to share its concerns with middle managers and lower employees. Prominent in every issue was a message of exhortation from the division vice-president, whom I'll call Vernon Smith. Judging by his monthly message, he was a pompous ass, saying nothing and saying it in inflated verbiage.

When I mentioned this, the writers said that Vernon Smith was actually a diffident man and a good executive with a good mind. They pointed out that he doesn't write the message himself; it's written for him. I said that Vernon Smith was being done a disservice—that the writers should go to him every month (with a tape recorder, if necessary) and stay there until he talked about his concerns in the same language that he would use when he got home and talked to Mrs. Smith.

What I realized was that most executives in America don't write what appears over their signature or what they say in their speeches. They have surrendered the qualities that make them unique. If they and their institutions seem cold and pretentious it's because they acquiesce in the process of being pumped up and dried out. Preoccupied with their high technology, they forget that some of the most powerful tools they possess—for good and for bad—are words.

If you work for an institution, whatever your job, whatever your level, be yourself when you write. You will stand out as a real person among the robots, and your example might even persuade Vernon Smith to write his own stuff.

17

Sports

I learned about the circuit clout before I learned about the electrical circuit. I also learned early—as a child addict of the sports pages—that a hurler (or twirler) who faces left when he toes the slab is a southpaw or a portsider. Southpaws were always lanky, portsiders always chunky, though I've never heard "chunky" applied to anything else except peanut butter (to distinguish it from "creamy") and I have no idea what a chunky person would look like. When hurlers fired the old horsehide, a batsman would try to solve their slants. If he succeeded he might rap a sharp bingle to the outfield, garnering a win for the home contingent, or at least knotting the count. If not, he might bounce into a twin killing, snuffing out a rally and dimming his team's hopes in the flag scramble.

I could go on, mining every sport for its lingo and extracting from the mother lode a variety of words found nowhere else in the mother tongue. Do we ever garner anything except a win? I could write of hoopsters and pucksters, grapplers and matmen, strapping oarsmen and gridiron standouts. I could rhapsodize about the old pigskin—far more passionately than any pig farmer—and describe the frenzied bleacherites caught up in the excitement of the autumn classic. I could, in short, write in sports English instead of good English, as if they were two different languages. Of course they're not. As in the case of writing about science or any other special subject, there's no substitute for the best.

What, you might ask, is wrong with "southpaw"? Shouldn't we be grateful for the addition to our language of a word so picturesque? Why isn't it a relief to have twirlers and circuit clouts instead of the same old pitchers and home runs? The answer is that these words have become even cheaper currency than the coins they were meant to replace. They come flooding automatically out of the typewriter of every scribe (sportswriter) in every press box.

The man who first thought of "southpaw" had a right to be pleased. I like to think he allowed himself the small smile that is the due of anyone who invents a good novelty. But how long ago was that? The color that "southpaw" added to the language has paled with decades of repetition, along with the hundreds of other idioms that now form the fabric of daily sportswriting. There is a weariness about them that leaves us numb. We read the articles to find out who won, and how, but we don't read them with any enjoyment.

The best sportswriters know this. They avoid the exhausted synonyms and strive for freshness elsewhere in constructing a sentence. You can search the columns of Red Smith and never find a batsman bouncing into a twin killing; Smith was never afraid to let a batter hit into a double play. But you will find hundreds of unusual words—good English words—chosen with precision and fitted into situations where no other sportswriter would put them. They gratify us because the writer obviously cared about using fresh imagery in a field where his competitors settled for the same old stuff. That's why Red Smith was still king of his field after more than half a century of writing, and why his competitors had long since been sent—as they would be the first to say—to the showers.

I remember countless phrases in Red Smith's columns that took me by surprise with their humor and originality. It was a pleasure to read about a quarterback who was "scraped off the turf like apple butter." I remember many times when Smith, a devout angler, baited his hook and came up with that slippery fish, a sports commissioner, gasping for air.

"In most professional sports the bottom has just about dropped out of the czar business," he wrote in 1971, noting once again that the cupidity of team owners has a tendency to outrun the courage of a sport's monitors. "The first and toughest of the overlords was Kenesaw Mountain Landis, who came to power in 1920 and ruled with a heavy hand until his death in 1944. But if baseball started with Little Caesar, it wound up with Ethelred the Unready." Red Smith was the daily guardian of our perspective, a writer who kept us honest. But that was largely because he was writing good English. His style was not only graceful; it was strong enough to carry strong convictions.

What keeps the average sportswriter from writing good English is the misapprehension that he shouldn't be trying to. He has been reared on so much jargon, so many clichés, that he thinks they are the required tools of the trade. He is also obsessed by synonyms. He has a dread of repeating the word that's easiest for the reader to visualize—batter, runner, golfer, boxer—if a synonym can be found. And usually, with exertion, it can. This excerpt from a college newspaper is typical:

Bob Hornsby extended his skein yesterday by toppling Dartmouth's Jerry Smithers, 6–4, 6–2, to lead the netmen to victory over a surprisingly strong foe. The gangling junior put his big serve to good use in keeping the Green captain off balance. The Memphis native was in top form as he racked up the first four games, breaking the Indian's service twice in the first four games. The Exeter graduate faltered and the Hanover mainstay rallied to cop three games. But the racquet ace was not to be denied, and the Yankee's attempt to knot the first stanza at 4–4 failed when he was passed by a cross-court volley on the sixth deuce point. The redhead was simply too determined, and . . .

What ever became of Bob Hornsby? Or, for that matter, Jerry Smithers? Well might you ask. Hornsby has been metamorphosed within one paragraph into the gangling junior, the Memphis native, the Exeter graduate, the racquet ace and the redhead, and Smithers turns up as the Green captain, the Indian, the Hanover mainstay and the Yankee. The reader doesn't know them in these various disguises—or care. He only wants the clearest picture of what happened. Never be afraid to repeat the player's name and to keep the details of the game simple. A set or an inning doesn't have to be recycled into a stanza or a frame just to avoid redundancy. The cure is worse than the ailment.

Another obsession is with numbers. True, every sports addict lives with a head full of statistics, cross-filed for ready access, and many a baseball fan who once flunked simple arithmetic can perform prodigies of instant calculation in the ballpark on a summer afternoon. Still, some statistics are more important than others. If a pitcher wins his twentieth game, if a golfer shoots a 61, if a runner runs the mile in 3:48, please mention it. But don't get carried away:

AUBURN, Ala., Nov. 1 (UPI)—Pat Sullivan, Auburn's sophomore quarterback, scored two touchdowns and passed for two today to hand Florida a 38–12 defeat, the first of the season for the ninth-ranked Gators.

John Reaves of Florida broke two Southeastern Conference records and tied another. The tall sophomore from Tampa, Fla., gained 369 yards passing, pushing his six-game season total to 2,115. That broke the S.E.C. season record of 2,012 set by the 1966 Heisman trophy winner, in 10 games.

Reaves attempted 66 passes—an S.E.C. record—and tied

the record of 33 completions set this fall by Mississippi's Archie Manning.

Fortunately for Auburn, nine of Reaves's passes were intercepted—breaking the S.E.C. record of eight interceptions suffered by Georgia's Zeke Bratkowski against Georgia Tech in 1951.

Reaves's performance left him only a few yards short of the S.E.C. season total offense record of 2,187 set by Georgia's Frank Sinkwich in 11 games in 1942. And his two touchdown passes against Auburn left him only one touchdown pass short of the S.E.C. season record of 23 set in 1950 by Kentucky's Babe Parilli. . . .

Those are the first five paragraphs of a six-paragraph story that was prominently displayed in my New York newspaper, a long way from Auburn. It has a certain mounting hilarity—a figure freak amok at his typewriter. But can anybody read it? And does anybody care? Only Zeke Bratkowski—finally off the hook.

Sports is one of the richest fields now open to the nonfiction writer. Many authors better known for "serious" books have done some of their most solid work as observers of athletic combat. John McPhee's *Levels of the Game,* George Plimpton's *Paper Lion* and George F. Will's *Men at Work*—books about tennis, pro football and baseball—take us deeply into the lives of the players. In mere detail they have enough information to keep any fan happy. But what makes them special is their humanity. Who is this strange bird, the winning athlete, and what engines keep him going?

One of the classics in the literature of baseball is John Updike's account of Ted Williams's final game, on September 28, 1960. The article builds to the almost mythical moment in the eighth inning when the forty-two-year-old "Kid," coming up for his last time at bat in Fenway Park, hits one over the wall. But before that Updike has compressed much of the career of "this brittle and temperamental player" in one paragraph that is as graceful as Williams's own swing:

> I remember watching one of his home runs from the bleachers of Shibe Park; it went over the first baseman's head and rose meticulously along a straight line and was still rising when it cleared the fence. The trajectory seemed qualitatively different from anything anyone else might hit. For me, Williams is the classic ballplayer of the game on a hot August weekday, before a small crowd, when the only thing at stake is the tissue-thin difference between a thing done well and a thing done ill. Baseball is a game of the long season, of relentless and gradual averaging-out. Irrelevance—since the reference point of most individual games is remote and statistical—always threatens its interest, which can be maintained not by the occasional heroics that sportswriters feed upon but by players who always care; who care, that is to say, about themselves and their art. Insofar as the clutch hitter is not a sportswriter's myth, he is a vulgarity, like a writer who writes only for money. It may be that, compared to managers' dreams, such as Joe DiMaggio and the always helpful Stan Musial, Williams is an icy star. But of all team sports, baseball, with its graceful intermittences of action, its immense and tranquil field sparsely settled with poised men in white, its dispassionate mathematics, seems to me best suited to accommodate, and be ornamented by, a loner. It is essentially a lonely game. No other player visible to my generation has concentrated within himself so much of the sport's poignance, has so assiduously refined his natural skills, has so constantly brought to the plate that intensity of competence that crowds the throat with joy.

What gives this passage its depth is that it's the work of a writer, not a sportswriter. Updike knows there's not much more to say about Williams's matchless ability at the plate: the famous swing, the eyes that could see the stitches on a baseball arriving at ninety miles an hour. But the mystery of the man is still unsolved, even on the final day of his career, and that's where Updike steers our attention, suggesting that baseball was suited to such a reclusive star because it's a lonely game. The very idea takes us by surprise. Baseball lonely? Our great American tribal rite? Think about it, Updike says.

Something in Updike made contact with something in Williams: two solitary craftsmen laboring in the glare of the crowd. Always look for this human contact. Remember that athletes aren't like ordinary mortals in their relationship to your readers. They are men and women who become part of our lives during the season, almost part of the family, acting out our dreams or filling some other need for us, and we want that bond to be honored. Hold the hype and give us heroes who are believable.

Even Babe Ruth was ushered down from the sanitized slopes of Olympus and converted into a real person, with appetites as big as his girth, in Robert Creamer's fine biography *Babe*. The same qualities went into Creamer's later book, *Stengel*. A decade ago readers might have settled for the standard version of Casey Stengel as an aging pantaloon who mangled the language and somehow managed to win ten pennants. Creamer's Stengel is far more interesting: a complex man who was nobody's fool and whose story is very much the story of baseball itself, going back to the nineteenth century.

Honest portraiture is only one of many new realities in what used to be a fairy-tale world. Sport has become a major frontier of social change, and some of the nation's most vexing issues— drug abuse, spectator violence, women's rights, minorities in management—are being played out in our stadiums, grandstands and locker rooms. If you want to write about America, this is one place to pitch your tent. The financial seduction of school and college athletes, for instance, is far more than a sports story. It's the story of our national values—our priorities—in the education of our children. King Football and King Basketball sit secure on their throne; how many college and high school coaches get paid more than the President, the principal and the teachers?

Money is the looming monster in sport, its dark shadow everywhere. When I open a newspaper to the sports pages I often think I've stumbled into the business section by mistake. Multiyear contracts of unimaginable magnitude swim before my eyes. On one December day in 1989, as the old decade slipped away in an orgy of free-agent bidding, five major league ballplayers signed contracts totaling $32.7 million. Big money in turn has brought big emotional trouble; today much of the sports reporting in newspapers and on TV has nothing to do with sports. First we have to be told whose feelings are hurt because he's being booed by fans who feel that a $2.5 million player should bat higher than .225 and run after fly balls hit in his direction. In tennis the pot of gold is enormous and the players are strung as tightly as their high-tech racquets—millionaires quick to whine at the referee and the linesmen. In football and basketball the pay is sky-high, and so are the sulks.

"It wasn't my idea for basketball to become tax-shelter show biz," Bill Bradley writes in *Life on the Run,* a chronicle of his seasons with the New York Knicks. Senator Bradley's book is a good example of the new sportswriting because it ponders the darker forces that are altering the quality of American sport— the greed of entrepreneurs, the worship of stars, the inability to accept defeat:

> After Van's departure I realized that no matter how kind, friendly and genuinely interested the owners may be, in the end most players are little more than depreciable assets to them.
>
> Self-definition comes from external sources, not from

within. While their physical skill lasts, professional athletes are celebrities—fondled and excused, praised and believed. Only toward the end of their careers do the stars realize that their sense of identity is insufficient.

The winning team, like the conquering army, claims everything in its path and seems to say that only winning is important. Yet victory has very narrow meanings and can become a destructive force. The taste of defeat has a richness of experience all its own.

Bradley's book is also an excellent travel journal, catching the fatigue and loneliness of the professional athlete's nomadic life—the countless night flights and bus rides, the dreary days and endless waits in motel rooms and terminals:

> In the airports that have become our commuter stations we see so many dramatic personal moments that we are callused. To some, we live romantic lives. To me, every day is a struggle to stay in touch with life's subtleties.

Amid so much erosion I see one huge gain: the emergence of women as outstanding athletes, often on turf previously monopolized by men, and as respected writers and reporters with equal access to male locker rooms and the other routine rights of journalism. Consider the many kinds of progress—both in performance and in attitude—represented in the following piece by one of these writers, Janice Kaplan, which ran in 1984:

> To understand how good women have become in sports, you have to understand how bad they were just a decade ago. In the early '70s the debate wasn't how much women could do athletically, but whether a normal woman should be athletic at all.

> Marathoning, for example, was said to be bad for children,

for the elderly and for women. The formidable Boston Marathon was officially closed to women until 1972. That year Nina Kuscsik battled sexism and a mid-race bout with diarrhea to become the first winner of the women's division. Those of us who knew about it felt a surge of pride, mixed with a tinge of embarrassment. Pride, because Kuscsik's victory proved that women could run 26 miles after all. Embarrassment, because her time of three hours and ten minutes was more than 50 minutes slower than the best men's times. Fifty minutes. That's an eternity in racing lingo. The obvious explanation was that women had rarely run marathons before and lacked training and experience. An obvious explanation—but who really believed it?

Flash ahead to this year. For the first time, the women's marathon will be an Olympic event. One of the top competitors is likely to be Joan Benoit, who holds the current women's world record—two hours and 22 minutes. In the dozen years since the first woman raced in Boston, the best women's times have improved by about 50 minutes. Another eternity.

Men's times in the marathon have meanwhile improved by only a few minutes, so this dramatic progress should begin to answer the question of training vs. hormones: Are women slower and weaker than men because of built-in biological differences—or because of cultural bias and the fact that we haven't been given a chance to prove what we can do? . . . Whether the gap between men and women will ever be totally closed seems almost beside the point. What matters is that women are doing what they never dreamed they could do—taking themselves and their bodies seriously.

Typical of the sports that have been dominated by men is rock climbing. Yet at the start of the 1990s a twenty-eight-year-old woman, Lynn Hill, was not only one of the top five climbers of both sexes in the United States; she also consistently finishes among the top five men in competitions on the world circuit, according to an article by Trip Gabriel in the *New York Times Magazine.*

Hill's achievements have thrown into question old assumptions about the inequality of men's and women's abilities in rock climbing. In a sport requiring extremely well-developed muscles, very low body fat and an appetite for boldness—all supposedly "masculine" characteristics—how is it possible for a woman to achieve what men can?

Although climbing seems to be all about strength, brute strength is less important than the ratio of strength to weight, the factor that allows an ant to carry a potato chip. Hill is quite small, 5-foot-2 and 100 pounds, but within this tight package is extraordinary power.

A pivotal event in this revolution of altered consciousness was the mid-1970s tennis match between Billie Jean King and Bobby Riggs. "It was billed as the Battle of the Sexes," Janice Kaplan recalls in another article, "and it was."

There has probably never been a sporting event that was less about sports and more about social issues. The big issue in this match was women: where we belonged and what we could do. Forget Supreme Court decisions and ERA votes; we looked to two athletes to settle the issues of equality for women in a way that really mattered. In sports, all is writ large and writ in concrete. There is a winner and a loser; there is no debate.

For many women there was a sense of personal triumph in Billie Jean's victory. It seemed to release an energy in women all over the country. Young women demanded—and got—a greater role in college sports. Prize money for women in many professional sports soared. Little girls began playing Little League, joining boys' teams, proving that the physiological differences between males and females aren't as great as they were once imagined.

American sport has always been interwoven with social history, and the best sportswriters are the men and women who make the connection. One pleasant example of making the connection was a piece by Jean Shepherd about the Indianapolis 500, which explains that the Indy has only one counterpart in American sport—the Kentucky Derby—and that both "can only be understood by the outsider in terms of folklore":

Any horse that wins the Derby enters the pearly gates of history forever. Hundreds of horses have won "classics" over the years, but even non-horseplayers remember Derby winners. So it is with the 500. Who knows or cares what other races Wilbur Shaw might have won in his great career? The fact that he took the 500 three times makes him immortal. . . .

Indiana in the early days was to the automobile as Kentucky was and is to the horse. Some of the truly great machines by any world standard were born and bred on the Indiana flatlands. The stylish and terrifying Dusenbergs created by the almost mythical Dusenberg brothers, Fred and August, were hammered out a few miles from the brick track. The Auburn, the Cord and the great racing Studebakers were all spawned in dusty Indiana hamlets and came together every spring in the dawn of automobiling to battle it out.

The automobile also means much more to the common people of the great plains than it does to the city folk who huddle jammed together in the great urban East. It meant, and still means, freedom, mobility and, above all, a way out for lives that are often as monotonous as the landscape they are lived in.

These are the values to look for when you write about sport—people, places, the link between past and present, the tug of the future. Here's an enjoyable list of the kind of people every sport comes furnished with. It's from the obituary of G.F.T. Ryall, who covered thoroughbred racing for *The New Yorker,* under the pen name Audax Minor, for more than half a century until a few months before he died at the age of ninety-two. The obituary made the point that Ryall "came to know *everyone* connected with racing—owners, breeders, stewards, judges, timers, mutuel clerks, Pinkertons, trainers, cooks, grooms, handicappers, hot-walkers, starters, musicians, jockeys and their agents, touts, high-rolling gamblers and tinhorns."

Hang around the track and the paddock, the ballpark and the rink. Observe closely. Interview in depth. Listen to old-timers. Ponder the changes. Write well.

18

Criticism

Every writer wants at some time to be a critic. The small-town reporter dreams of the moment when his editor will summon him to cover the Russian ballet troupe, the concert pianist, the touring repertory company that has been booked into the local auditorium. Then he will trot out the hard-won words of his college education—"intuit" and "sensibility" and "Kafka-esque"—and show the whole county that he knows a *glissando* from an *entrechat*. He will discern more symbolism in Ibsen than Ibsen ever thought of.

This is part of the urge. Criticism is the stage on which journalists do their fanciest strutting.

It's also where reputations for wit are born. The American vernacular is rich in epigrams ("She ran the gamut of emotions from A to B") minted by people like Dorothy Parker and George S. Kaufman, who became famous partly by minting them, and the temptation to make an instant name at the expense of some talentless ham is too strong for all but the most saintly.

Not that the epigrams aren't enjoyable. I particularly like Kaufman's hint that Raymond Massey in *Abe Lincoln in Illinois* was perhaps overplaying the title role: "Massey won't be satisfied until he's assassinated." But true wit is rare, and a thousand barbed arrows fall at the feet of the archer for every one that flies. It's also too facile an approach if you want to write serious criticism, for, by no accident, the only epigrams that have survived are cruel ones. It's far easier to bury Caesar than to praise him—and that goes for Cleopatra, too. But to say why you think a play is *good,* in words that don't sound banal, is one of the hardest chores in the business.

So don't be deluded that criticism is an easy route to glory. Nor does the job carry as much power as is widely supposed. Probably only the daily drama critic of the *New York Times* can make or break the product—a new play—and a music critic has almost no power, writing, as he does, about a cluster of sounds that have vanished into the air and will never be heard in quite the same way again. As for literary critics, they have never kept the best-seller list from becoming a nesting ground for authors like Sidney Sheldon and Danielle Steel—whose sensibility they don't intuit—and movie critics wield their influence mainly in the case of a foreign film, where a good review can lengthen its run.

A distinction should therefore be made between a "critic" and a "reviewer." In general a reviewer writes for a newspaper or a popular magazine, and what he covers is not primarily an art but an industry—the output of, for instance, the television industry, the motion-picture industry and, increasingly, the publishing industry in its outpouring of "gift books," cookbooks, how-to books, "as told to" books and other such items of merchandise.

As a reviewer your job is more to report than to make an aesthetic judgment. You are the deputy for the average man or woman who wants to know: "What is the new TV series about?" "Is the movie too dirty for the kids?" "Will the book really improve my sex life or tell me how to make a chocolate mousse?" Think what *you* would want to know if *you* had to spend the money for the movie, the babysitter and the long-promised dinner at a good restaurant. Obviously you will make your review simpler and less sophisticated than if you were appraising a new novel by Thomas Pynchon.

And yet I suggest several conditions that apply equally to good reviewing and good criticism.

One is that a critic should like—or, better still, love—the medium he is reviewing. If you think movies are dumb, don't write about them. The reader deserves a lifelong movie buff who will bring along a reservoir of knowledge, passion and prejudice. I don't mean that the critic has to like every film. On the contrary, his prejudices are as important as his passions—criticism, after all, is only one person's opinion and a highly subjective form. But he should go to every movie wanting to like it. If he is more often disappointed than pleased, it's because the film has failed to live up to what he knows are its best possibilities. This is far different from the critic who prides himself on hating everything, who relishes giving us his weekly dose of bile. He becomes tiresome faster than you can say "Kafkaesque."

Another rule is: Don't give away too much of the plot. Tell readers just enough to let them decide whether it's the kind of story they tend to enjoy, but not so much that you will kill their eventual enjoyment. One sentence will often do the trick. "This is a picture about a whimsical Irish priest who enlists the help of three orphan boys dressed as leprechauns to haunt a village where a mean widow has hidden a crock of gold coins." I couldn't be flailed into seeing that movie—I've had my fill of "the little people" on stage and screen. But there are legions who don't share that particular crotchet of mine and would flock to the film. Don't spoil their pleasure by revealing every twist of the narrative—especially the funny part about the troll under the bridge.

A third principle is to use as much specific detail as possible. This avoids dealing in generalities, which, being generalities, mean nothing. "The play is always fascinating" is a typical critic's sentence. But *how* is it fascinating? Your idea of fascinating is different from other people's idea. Cite a few examples and let your readers weigh them on their own fascination scale. Here are excerpts from two separate reviews of a film directed by Joseph Losey. (1) "In its attempts to be civilized and restrained it denies its possibilities for vulgarity and mistakes bloodlessness for taste." The sentence is vague, giving us at the most a whiff of the movie's mood but no image that we can visualize. (2) "Losey pursues a style that finds portents in lampshades and meanings in table settings." The sentence is precise—we know just what kind of arty filmmaking this is. We can almost see the camera lingering with studied sluggishness over the family crystal.

In book reviewing this means allowing the author's words to do their own documentation. Don't say, for instance, that Tom Wolfe's style is gaudy and unusual. Quote a few of his gaudy and unusual sentences and let the reader see how distinctive they are, how quirky. In reviewing a play, don't just tell us that the set is "striking." Describe its various levels, or how it is ingeniously lit, or how it helps the actors to make their entrances and exits as a less imaginative set would not. Put your readers in your theater seat. Help them to see what you saw.

A final caution is to avoid the ecstatic adjectives that occupy such disproportionate space in every critic's quiver—words like "enthralling" and "luminous." Good criticism needs a lean and vivid style to express what you observed and what you think. Florid adjectives smack of the panting prose with which *Vogue* likes to disclose its latest chichi discovery: "We've just heard about the most utterly enchanting little beach at Cozumel."

So much for reviewing and the simpler rules of the game. What, then, is criticism?

Criticism is a serious intellectual act. It tries to appraise serious works of art and to place them in the context of what has been done before in that medium or by that particular artist.

This doesn't mean that the critic must limit himself to the work of men and women whose aims are high; he may select some commercial product like *Miami Vice* to make a point about American taste and values. But on the whole he doesn't want to waste his time on peddlers. He sees himself as a scholar, and what interests him is the play of ideas in his field.

Therefore if you want to be a critic, steep yourself in the literature of the medium that you hope to make your province. If your goal is to be a theater critic, see every possible play—the good and the bad, the old and the new. Catch up on the past by reading the classics or seeing them in revival. Know your Shakespeare and Shaw, your Chekhov and Molière, your Arthur Miller and Tennessee Williams, and know what they meant to audiences of their era and how they broke new ground. Learn everything you can about the great actors and directors and how their methods differed, and about the great clowns, like Bert Lahr. Know the history of the American musical: the distinctive contribution of Jerome Kern and the Gershwin brothers, of Cole Porter, of Rodgers and Hart and Hammerstein, of Frank Loesser and Stephen Sondheim, of Agnes de Mille and Jerome Robbins. Only then can you place every new play or musical within an older tradition, recognize genius when it comes along and tell the pioneer from the imitator.

I could make the same kind of list for every art. A film critic who reviews a new Fellini picture without having seen Fellini's earlier films is not much help to the serious moviegoer. A music critic should know not only his Bach and Palestrina, his Mozart and Beethoven, but his Schoenberg and Satie, his Ives and Varèse—the theoreticians and mavericks and experimenters.

Obviously I'm now also assuming a more urbane body of readers. As a critic you can presuppose certain shared areas of knowledge with the men and women you are writing for. You don't have to tell them that William Faulkner was a Southern novelist. What you *do* have to do, if you are assessing the first novel of a Southern author and weighing Faulkner's influence, is to generate a provocative idea and to throw it onto the page, where your fellow scholars can savor it. They may disagree with your point—that's part of their intellectual fun. But at least they have enjoyed the turn of your mind and the journey that took you to your conclusion. We like good critics as much for their personality as for their opinions.

There's no medium like the movies to give us the pleasure of traveling with a good critic. The shared territory is so vast. Movies are intertwined with our daily lives and attitudes, with our memories and myths, and we count on the critic to make those connections for us—to bring us the news not only about the latest film but about ourselves and the country we live in.

One critic I like to have doing this work for me is Molly Haskell. The movie *Big,* for instance, in which Tom Hanks plays a thirteen-year-old boy who suddenly finds himself in the body of a man, got Haskell thinking about the "epidemic" of recent films—like Steven Spielberg's fantasies and Rob Reiner's *Stand By Me*—made by men who are "taking refuge" in enchanted childhoods, "embracing not only younger but wiser and more morally precocious versions of their adult selves."

> The idea, made literal in *Big,* is that there's a little boy in all of us, an unjaded innocent who is full of wonder and idealism. Men who are pulling down six figures can assuage their guilt: inside every workaholic corporate yuppie is a little tyke who thinks in pennies rather than millions and dreams of toys rather than mergers or real estate coups.

Noting that these rite-of-passage movies are always about boys, never about girls, Haskell says, "Boys *have* rites of passage; girls *are* rites of passage." It's a typically wise perception—and a reminder that good movie critics must also be part social historian and part psychologist.

Another function of the movie critic is to freeze briefly for our inspection the stars who shoot across the screen in film after film, sometimes arriving from a galaxy previously unknown to stargazers. Reviewing *A Cry in the Dark,* in which Meryl Streep plays an Australian woman convicted of killing her baby on a camping trip, Haskell ponders Streep's "delight in disguise—in bizarre wigs, unorthodox getups and foreign accents—and in playing women who are outside the normal range of audience sympathy." Putting this in a historical context, as good critics should, she writes:

> The aura of the old stars radiated out of a sense of self, a core identity projected into every role. However varied the performances of Bette Davis, or Katharine Hepburn, or Margaret Sullavan, we always felt we were in the presence of something knowable, familiar, constant. They had recognizable voices, ways of reading a line, even certain expressions that remained constant from film to film. Comics could do imitations of them, and you either responded to them, unambivalently, or you didn't. Streep, chameleon-like, undercuts this response by never staying in one place long enough for you to get a fix on her.
>
> Bette Davis, stretching the bounds of type, went in for costume *(The Virgin Queen)* and period *(The Old Maid),* but she was always Bette Davis, and no one would have thought to want it otherwise. Like Streep, she even dared to play unlikable, morally ambiguous heroines, her greatest being the wife of the plantation owner in *The Letter* who murders her treacherous lover in cold blood, then refuses to repent. The difference is that Davis fused with the role, poured her own passion and intensity into it. Her heroine is as icily proud and implacable as Medea—which may be why members of the Academy denied her the Oscar she deserved in favor of sweeter and tamer Ginger Rogers for *Kitty Foyle*—but Davis

makes us respond to the fire within. It's hard to imagine an actress like Streep, who remains at a safe distance from her roles, rising to such heights . . . or falling to such depths.

The passage deftly connects Hollywood past and Hollywood present, leaving us to fathom the postmodern cool of Meryl Streep but also telling us everything we need to know about Bette Davis. By extension it tells us about a whole generation of grand dragons who reigned with Davis in the golden age of the star system—the likes of Joan Crawford and Barbara Stanwyck—and who didn't mind being hated on the screen as long as they were loved at the box office.

Another new specimen thrown up by the Hollywood surf was James Dean. Hearing in 1988 that a museum memorializing the actor was going to be built in his home town of Fairmount, Indiana, Molly Haskell wrote:

> I was never drawn to candle-burning, but the fanaticism surrounding Dean I can understand. *East of Eden* was released in 1955, just before he died [in a car crash], *Rebel Without a Cause* soon after, and *Giant* the following year. For those of us who were teenagers when we saw and were stunned by his three great performances, a new star had appeared in the firmament. Here was a young person for whom youth itself was torture; someone who was beautiful, and baffled and "bad" in ways we felt ourselves to be. As the patron saint of teenagers, he had put us on the map and altered the balance of power forever. And as an androgynous new male icon, he presided over the first slippage of sexual roles. . . .
>
> Dean shared with some of the greatest stars of the past— Olivier, Garbo, Gary Cooper, Dietrich, Mae West, Katharine Hepburn—an androgynous image. But Dean took it a step further, blurring the boundaries not only between male and

female but between adult and child. . . . [He] seems to have defined a generation, and indeed, male "softness" has become commonplace, so much so that stoicism may be making a comeback in such refreshingly stiff-upper-lipped types as Kevin Costner and Harrison Ford. But "soft" may be the wrong word for Dean. Vulnerable, yes, but shrewd and tyrannical with his genius. He knew how to keep everyone off balance, to reach into the depths of his psyche, and to get the last word, as the actors he upstaged can tell you.

Turning to another medium, here's an excerpt from *Living-Room War* by Michael J. Arlen, a collection of the critical columns on television that Arlen wrote in the mid-1960s.

Vietnam is often referred to as "television's war," in the sense that this is the first war that has been brought to the people preponderantly by television. People indeed look at television. They really look at it. They look at Dick Van Dyke and become his friend. They look at thoughtful Chet Huntley and find him thoughtful, and at witty David Brinkley and find him witty. They look at Vietnam. They look at Vietnam, it seems, as a child kneeling in the corridor, his eye to the keyhole, looks at two grownups arguing in a locked room— the aperture of the keyhole small; the figures shadowy, mostly out of sight; the voices indistinct, isolated threats without meaning; isolated glimpses, part of an elbow, a man's jacket (who is the man?), part of a face, a woman's face. Ah, she is crying. One sees the tears. (The voices continue indistinctly.) One counts the tears. Two tears. Three tears. Two bombing raids. Four seek-and-destroy missions. Six administration pronouncements. Such a fine-looking woman. One searches in vain for the other grownup, but, ah, the keyhole is so small, he is somehow never in the line of sight. Look! There is General Ky. Look! There are some planes returning safely to the *Ticonderoga*. I wonder (sometimes) what it is that the people who run television think about the war, because *they* have given us this keyhole view; we have given them the airwaves, and now, at this crucial time, they have given back to us this keyhole view—and I wonder if they truly think that those isolated glimpses of elbow, face, a swirl of dress (who *is* that other person anyway?) are all that we children can stand to see of what is going on inside the room.

This is criticism at its best: stylish, allusive, disturbing. It disturbs us—as criticism often should—because it jogs a set of beliefs and forces us to reexamine them. What holds our attention here is the metaphor of the keyhole, so exact and yet so mysterious. But what remains is a fundamental question about how a country's most powerful medium was telling the country's people about the war that they were fighting—and escalating. The column ran in 1966, when most Americans still supported the Vietnam war. Would they have turned against it sooner if TV had widened the keyhole, had shown us not only the "swirl of dress" but the severed head and the burning child? It's too late now to know. But at least one critic was keeping watch. Critics should always be among the first to notify us when the truths we hold to be self-evident cease to be true.

Some arts, of course, are harder to catch in print than others. One is dance, which consists of movement. How can a writer freeze all the graceful leaps and pirouettes? Another is music. It's an art that we receive through our ears, yet the writer is stuck with describing it in words that we will see. At best he can only partly succeed, and many a music critic has built a long career by hiding from his readers behind a hedge of Italian technical terms. He will find just a shade too much *rubato* in a pianist, a tinge of shrillness in a soprano's *tessitura*.

But even in this world of evanescent notes a good critic can make sense of what happened by writing good English and by using references that mere mortals can understand. Virgil Thomson, the music critic of the *New York Herald Tribune* from 1940 to 1954, was an elegant practitioner. A composer himself, an erudite and cultivated man, he never forgot that his readers were real people, and he wrote with a zest that swept them along, his style alive with pleasant surprises. He also never forgot that musicians are real people, and he didn't hesitate to shrink the giants to human scale. What other critic would dare to secularize the sainted Toscanini?

> It is extraordinary how little musicians discuss among themselves Toscanini's rightness or wrongness about matters of speed and rhythm and the tonal amenities. Like other musicians, he is frequently apt about these and as frequently in error. What seems to be more important is his unvarying ability to put over a piece. He quite shamelessly whips up the tempo and sacrifices clarity and ignores a basic rhythm, just making the music, like his baton, go round and round, if he finds his audience's attention tending to waver. No piece has to mean anything specific; every piece has to provoke from its hearers a spontaneous vote of acceptance. This is what I call the "wow technique."

No *rubatos* or *tessituras* there, and no blind hero worship. Yet the paragraph catches the essence of what made Toscanini great—an extra helping of show biz. If his worshipers are offended to think that the essence contained so coarse an ingredient, they can continue to admire the Maestro for his "lyrical colorations" or "orchestral *tuttis.*" I'll go along with Thomson's diagnosis, and so, I suspect, would the Maestro.

Here, on the other hand, is Thomson analyzing pure musicianship, telling us why a piano recital by Josef Lhevinne was not only perfect in itself but significantly better than the work of other major artists:

Any authoritative execution derives as much of its excellence from what the artist does not do as from what he does. If he doesn't do anything off color at all, he is correctly said to have taste. Mr. Lhevinne's taste is as authoritative as his technical method. Not one sectarian interpretation, not one personal fancy, not one stroke below the belt, not a sliver of ham, mars the universal acceptability of his readings. Everything he does is right and clear and complete. Everything he doesn't do is the whole list of all the things that mar the musical executions of lesser men.

How should a good piece of criticism start? You must make an immediate effort to orient your readers to the special world they are about to enter. Even if they are broadly educated men and women they need to be told or reminded of certain facts. You can't just throw them in the water and expect them to swim easily; the water needs to be warmed up.

This is particularly true of literary criticism. So much has gone before: all writers are part of a long stream, whether they decide to swim with the current or to hurl themselves against it and try something new. No poet of this century was more innovative and influential than T. S. Eliot. Yet his one hundredth birthday in 1988 passed with surprisingly little public attention, as Cynthia Ozick noted at the start of a long critical essay, pointing out that college students today have almost no knowledge of Eliot's "mammoth prophetic presence":

To anyone who was an undergraduate in the forties or the fifties (or possibly even in the first years of the sixties), all that is inconceivable—as if a part of the horizon had crumbled away. When, four decades ago, in a literary period that resembled eternity, T. S. Eliot won the Nobel Prize in Literature, he seemed pure zenith, a colossus, nothing less than a permanent luminary, fixed in the firmament like the sun and the moon. . . .

How adroitly Ozick warms up the waters, beckoning us to return to the literary landscape of her own college years—and thereby to understand her amazement at the tale of near oblivion she is about to unfold.

> The doors to Eliot's poetry were not easily opened. His lines and themes were not readily understood. But the young flung themselves through those portals, lured by unfamiliar enchantments and bound by pleasurable ribbons of ennui. "April is the cruel-lest month"—Eliot's voice, with its sepulchral cadences, came spiraling out of student phonographs— "breeding/ Lilacs out of the dead land, mixing/ Memory and desire." That tony British accent—flat, precise, steady, unemotive, surprisingly high-pitched, bleakly passive— coiled through awed English Departments and worshipful dormitories, rooms where the walls had pinup Picassos, and where Pound and Eliot and *Ulysses* and Proust jostled one another higgledy-piggledy in the rapt late adolescent breast. The voice was, like the poet himself, nearly sacerdotal; it was impersonal, winding and winding across the country's campuses like a spool of blank robotic woe. "Shantih shantih shantih," "not with a bang but a whimper," "an old man in a dry month," "I shall wear the bottoms of my trousers rolled": these were the devout chants of the literarily passionate in the forties and fifties, who in their own first verses piously copied Eliot's tone—its restraint, gravity, mystery, its invasive remoteness and immobilized, disjointed despair.

The paragraph is brilliant in its remembered detail, its scholarly fastidiousness, its conjuring back of Eliot himself as a physical presence on campuses from one coast to the other. As readers we are transported back to the high priest's highest moment—a perfect launch for the long descent that lies ahead. We may not like everything Ozick says about Eliot—in fact, when her essay was published in *The New Yorker,* many scholars didn't. They thought she had exaggerated the poet's fall from renown. But for me that just validated the piece. Literary criticism that doesn't stir a few combative juices is hardly worth writing, and there are few spectator sports so enjoyable as a good academic brawl.

Today criticism has many first cousins in journalism: the newspaper or magazine column, the essay, the editorial, and the essay-review, in which a critic digresses from a particular book or cultural phenomenon into a larger point. (Gore Vidal has brought a high impudence to the form.) Many of the same principles that govern good criticism go into these columns. A political columnist, for instance, must love politics and know its ancient, tangled threads.

But what is common to all the forms is that they consist of personal opinion. Even the editorial that uses "we" was obviously written by an "I." And what is crucial for you as the writer is to express your opinion firmly. Don't cancel its strength with last-minute evasions and escapes. The most boring sentence in the daily newspaper is the last sentence of the editorial that says "it is still too early to tell whether the new policy will work" or "the effectiveness of the decision remains to be seen." If it's still too early to tell, don't bother us with it at all, and as for what remains to be seen, *everything* remains to be seen, including what you'll be doing ten minutes from now. Take your stand with conviction.

Many years ago when I was writing editorials for the *New York Herald Tribune,* the editor of the page was a huge and ungainly man from Texas. I respected him because he had no pretense and hated any undue circling around a subject. Every morning we would all meet to discuss what editorials we would like to write for the next day and what position on the issues we would take. Frequently we weren't quite sure, especially the writer who was an expert on Latin America.

"What about that coup in Uruguay?" the editor would ask.

"It could represent progress for the economy," the writer would reply, "or then again it might destabilize the whole political situation. I suppose I could mention the possible benefits and then—"

"Well," the man from Texas would break in, "let's not go peeing down both legs."

It was a plea he made often, and it was the most inelegant advice I ever received. But over a long career of writing reviews and columns and books and trying to make a point that I felt strongly about, it was also probably the best.

19

Humor

Humor is the secret weapon of the nonfiction writer. It's secret because so few writers realize that humor is often their best tool—and sometimes their only tool—for making an important point.

If this strikes you as a paradox, you're not alone. The professional writer of humor lives with the knowledge that half of his readers never know what he is trying to do. I remember a reporter calling to ask how I happened to write a certain parody in *Life*. At the end he said, "Should I refer to you as a humorist? Or have you also written anything serious?"

The answer is that if you're trying to write humor, almost everything you do is serious. Few Americans understand this. We dismiss our humorists as triflers because they never settled down to "real" work. So the Pulitzer Prizes go to authors like Ernest Hemingway and William Faulkner, who are (God knows) serious and are therefore certified as men of literature. The prize has never gone to people like George Ade, H. L. Mencken, Ring Lardner, Robert Benchley, S. J. Perelman, Art Buchwald, Jules Feiffer, Woody Allen and Garrison Keillor, who seem to be just fooling around.

They're not just fooling around. They are as serious in purpose as Hemingway or Faulkner—in fact, they are a national asset in forcing the country to see itself clearly. To them, humor is urgent work. It's an attempt to say important things in a special way that regular writers aren't getting said in a regular way—or if they are, it's so regular that nobody is reading it.

One cartoon by Herblock or Bill Mauldin is worth a hundred solemn editorials. One *Doonesbury* comic strip by Garry Trudeau—on the tendency of voters to reelect convicted congressmen, or the tendency of Reagan's environmental agency to not protect the environment—is worth a thousand words of moralizing. One *Catch-22* or *Dr. Strangelove* is more powerful than all the books and movies that try to show war "as it is." They are two works of comic imagination, but they are still the standard points of reference for anyone trying to warn us about the military mentality that could blow us all up tomorrow. Joseph Heller and Stanley Kubrick heightened the truth about war just enough to catch its essential lunacy, and we recognize it as lunacy. The joke is no joke.

This heightening of some crazy truth—to a level where it will be seen as crazy—is the essence of what the serious humorist is trying to do. I'll give you an example that may help to explain how he goes about his mysterious work.

One day in the 1960s I realized that half the girls and women in America were suddenly wearing hair curlers. It was of course an incredible new blight, and it was puzzling because I couldn't imagine when the women took the curlers out. There was no evidence that they ever did. They wore them to the supermarket and to church and on dates, and quite possibly to their own weddings, and to many other places where they would be seen by many people. So what was the wonderful event they were saving the wonderful hairdo for?

I tried for a year to think of a way to write about this phenomenon. I could have come right out and said "It's an outrage," "It's a national disgrace" and "Have these women no pride?" But that would have been a sermon, and sermons are the death of humor. The writer must find some comic device—satire, parody, irony, lampoon, nonsense—that he can use to disguise his serious point. Very often he never finds it, because it's hard to find, and the point doesn't get made.

Luckily, my vigil was at last rewarded. I was browsing at my local newsstand and saw four magazines side by side: *Hairdo, Celebrity Hairdo, Combout* and *Pouf*. I bought all four—to the alarm of my news dealer—and found that there's a whole thriving world of journalism devoted solely to hair: life from the neck up, but not including the brain. The magazines had hundreds of diagrams of elaborate roller positions, and they also had lengthy columns in which a girl could send her roller problem to the editors for their advice. This was what I needed. I invented a magazine called *Haircurl* and wrote a series of parody letters and replies. The piece ran in *Life* and it began like this:

Dear Haircurl:

I am 15 and am considered pretty in my group. I wear baby pink rollers, jumbo size. I have been going steady with a certain boy for 2½ years and he has never seen me without my rollers. The other night I took them off and we had a terrible fight. "Your head looks small," he told me. He called me a dwarf and said I had misled him. How can I win him back?

HEARTSICK
Speonk, N.Y.

Dear Heartsick:

You have only yourself to blame for doing something so stupid. The latest "Haircurl" survey shows that 94% of American girls now wear rollers in their hair 21.6 hours a day and 359 days a year. You tried to be different and you lost your fella. Take our advice and get some super-jumbo rollers (they come in your favorite baby pink shade, too) and your head will look bigger than ever and twice as lovely. Don't ever take them off again.

Dear Haircurl:

My boyfriend likes to run his fingers through my hair. The trouble is he keeps getting them pinched in my rollers. The other night a terribly embarrassing episode happened. We were at the movies and somehow my boyfriend got two of his fingers caught (it was right where the medium roller meets the clip-curl) and couldn't get them out. I felt very conspicuous leaving the theater with his hand still in my hair, and going home on the bus several people gave us "funny looks." Fortunately I was able to reach my stylist at home and he came right over with his tools and got poor Jerry loose. Jerry was very mad and said he's not going to date me again until I get some rollers that don't have this particular habit. I think he is being unfair, but he "means business." Can you help me?

FRANTIC
Buffalo

Dear Frantic Buffalo:

We're sorry to have to tell you that no rollers have yet been developed that do not occasionally catch the fingers of boys who tousle. The roller industry, however, is working very hard on the problem, as this complaint frequently comes up. Meanwhile why not ask Jerry to wear mittens? That way you'll be happy and he'll be safe.

There were many more, and perhaps the article even made a small contribution to Lady Bird Johnson's "beautification" program. But the point is this: once you've read that article you

can never look at hair curlers again in quite the same way.
You've been jolted by humor into looking with a fresh eye at
something bizarre in our daily environment that was previously
taken for granted. This is what the serious humorist is trying to
do. The subject here isn't important—hair curlers certainly
won't be the ruin of our society. But the method will work for
subjects that *are* important, or for almost any subject, if you can
find the right comic frame.

Over the last five years of the old *Life,* 1968–1972, I used
humor to get at all kinds of improbable subjects. Quite a few
columns were on the excesses of military power and nuclear
testing. One was on the petty squabbling over the shape of the
table at the Vietnam peace conference in Paris. The situation
had become so outrageous after nine weeks that it could only
be approached through high ridicule, and I described various
efforts to get peace at my own dinner table by changing its
shape every night, or by lowering the chairs of different people
to give them less "status," or by turning their chairs around so
the rest of us wouldn't have to "recognize" them. It was absurd,
but it was exactly what was happening in Paris.

What made the pieces work as parody was that they stuck
close to the form they were parodying. Humor may seem to be
an act of gross exaggeration. But the hair curler letters wouldn't
succeed if we didn't recognize them as a specific journalistic
form, both in their style and in their mentality. Control is vital
to humor. Don't use comical names like Throttlebottom. Don't
repeat the same kind of joke two or three times—readers will
enjoy themselves more if you make it only once. Trust the
sophistication of readers who *do* know what you're doing, and
don't worry about the rest.

The columns that I wrote for *Life* made people laugh. But
they had a serious purpose, which was to say: "Something gro-
tesque is going on here—some erosion in the quality of life, or
some threat to life itself, and yet everyone assumes that it's

normal." Today in America the outlandish becomes routine overnight. The humorist is trying to say that it really is still outlandish.

I remember a cartoon by Bill Mauldin during the student turmoil of the late 1960s, when infantrymen and tanks were summoned to keep peace at a college in North Carolina and undergraduates at Berkeley were dispersed by a helicopter spraying them with Mace. The cartoon showed a mother pleading with her son's draft board: "He's an only child—please get him off the campus." It was Mauldin's way of pinning down this particular lunacy, and he was right on target. In fact, he was at the center of the bull's-eye, as Kent State proved not long after his cartoon appeared.

The targets will change from week to week and from year to year. But there will never be a dearth of new lunacies—and dangers—for the humorist to detect and to fight. Lyndon Johnson in the years of his Vietnamization was brought down partly by Jules Feiffer and Art Buchwald. Joseph McCarthy and Spiro Agnew were brought down partly by Walt Kelly in the comic strip *Pogo*. H. L. Mencken brought down a whole galaxy of hypocrites in high places, and "Boss" Tweed was partly toppled by the cartoons of Thomas Nast. Mort Sahl, a comic, was the only person who stayed awake during the Eisenhower years, when all of America was under sedation and didn't want to be roused. Many people regarded Sahl as a cynic, but he thought of himself as an idealist. "If I criticize somebody," he said, "it's because I have higher hopes for the world, something good to replace the bad. I'm not saying what the Beat Generation says: 'Go away because I'm not involved.' I'm here and I'm involved."

"I'm here and I'm involved"—make this your creed if you seriously want to write serious humor. The humorist operates on a deeper current than most people suspect. He must not only make a strong point; he must be willing to go against the grain, to say what the populace and the Presidents may not want to hear. Art Buchwald and Garry Trudeau perform an act of courage at least once a week. They say things that need to be said but that a regular columnist couldn't get away with. What saves them is that politicians are not known for humor and are therefore even more befuddled by it than the citizenry. No other kind of writer risks his neck so visibly on the high wire of public approval. Yet he is in dead earnest, this acrobat bobbing over our heads, trying to startle us with nonsense into seeing our lives with sense.

*

But humor has many uses besides the topical. They aren't as urgent because they don't address problems of the day, but they are equally important because they help us to look at far older problems of the heart, the home, the family, the job and all the other frustrations of just getting from morning to night. In 1970 I interviewed the late Chic Young, creator of *Blondie,* when he had been writing and drawing that strip, daily and Sunday, for forty years—14,500 strips. It was the most popular of all comic strips, reaching sixty million readers in every corner of the world and in many languages, and I asked him why it was so durable.

"It's durable because it's simple," he said. "It's built on four things that everybody does: sleeping, eating, raising a family and making money." The comic twists on these four themes are as various in the strip as they are in life. Dagwood's efforts to get money from his boss, Mr. Dithers, have their perpetual counterweight in Blondie's efforts to spend it. "I try to keep Dagwood in a world that people are used to," Young said. "He never does anything as special as playing golf, and the people who come to the door are just the people that an average family has to deal with." The person who turns up most often at the Bumsteads' door is the mailman.

I cite Young's four themes as a reminder that most humor, however freakish it may seem, is based on fundamental truths. Humor is not a separate organism that can survive on its own frail metabolism. It's a special angle of vision granted to certain writers who already write good English. They aren't writing about life that's essentially ludicrous. They are writing about life that's essentially serious, but their vision focuses on the areas where serious hopes are mocked by some ironic turn of fate— "the strange incongruity," as Stephen Leacock put it, "between our aspiration and our achievement." E. B. White also emphasized that the humor writer is not some sort of maverick. "I don't like the word 'humorist,'" he said. "It seems to me misleading. Humor is a by-product that occurs in the serious work of some and not others. I was more influenced by Don Marquis than by Ernest Hemingway, by Perelman than by Dreiser."

Therefore I would suggest several principles for the writer of humor. Master the craft of writing good "straight" English; humorists from Mark Twain to Russell Baker are, first of all, superb writers. Don't search high and low for the outlandish and scorn what seems too ordinary; you will touch more chords by finding what's funny in what you know to be true. Finally, don't strain for laughs; humor is built on surprise, and you can surprise the reader only so often.

Unfortunately for the writer, humor is elusive and subjective. No two people think the same things are funny, and an article that one magazine will reject as a dud is often published by another that finds it hilarious. The reasons for rejection are equally elusive. "It just doesn't work," editors say, and there's not much they can add. Occasionally such a piece can be made to work—it has some flaw that can be repaired. Mortality, however, is high. "Humor can be dissected, as a frog can," E. B. White once wrote, "but the thing dies in the process and the innards are discouraging to any but the pure scientific mind."

I'm no fancier of dead frogs, but I wanted to see if at least a few lessons could be learned by poking about in the innards, and one year when I was at Yale I decided to teach a course in humor writing. I warned my students that quite possibly it couldn't be done and that we might end up killing the thing we loved. Luckily, humor not only didn't die; it bloomed in the encircling desert of solemn term papers, and I subsequently repeated the course. Let me briefly reconstruct our journey.

"I hope to point out that American humor has an honorable literature," I wrote in a memo for prospective students, "and to consider the influence of certain pioneers on their successors. . . . Though the line between 'fiction' and 'nonfiction' is often fuzzy in humor, I see this as a nonfiction course—what you write will be based on external events. I'm not interested in 'creative writing,' flights of pure imagination and pointless whimsy."

I began by reading excerpts from early writers to show that a humorist can use a wide range of literary forms, or invent new ones. We started with George Ade's "Fables in Slang," the first of which appeared in 1897 in the *Chicago Record,* where Ade was a reporter. "He was just sitting unsuspectingly in front of a sheet of paper," Jean Shepherd writes in a fine introduction to his anthology, *The America of George Ade,* "when the innocent idea came to him to write something in fable form using the language and the clichés of the moment. In other words, slang. He said that to let people know that he knew better than to use slang in writing, he decided to capitalize all suspicious words and phrases. He was mortally afraid people would think he was illiterate."

He needn't have worried; by 1900 the Fables were so popular that he was earning one thousand dollars a week. Here, for instance, is "The Fable of the Subordinate Who Saw a Great Light":

Once there was an Employé who was getting the Nub End of the Deal. He kicked on the long Hours and the small Salary, and helped to organize a Clerks' Protective Association. He was for the Toiler as against the Main Squeeze.

To keep him simmered down, the Owners gave him an Interest. After that he began to perspire when he looked at the Pay-Roll, and it did seem to him that a lot of big, lazy Lummixes were standing around the shop doing the Soldier Act. He learned to snap his Fingers every time the Office Boy giggled. As for the faithful old Book-Keeper who wanted an increase to $9 and a week's Vacation in the Summer, the best he got was a little Talk about Contentment being a Jewel.

The saddest moment of the Day for him was when the whole Bunch knocked off at 6 o'clock in the Evening. It seemed a Shame to call 10 Hours a Full Day. As for the Saturday Half-Holiday Movement, that was little better than Highway Robbery. Those who formerly slaved alongside of him in the Galleys had to address him as Mister, and he had them numbered the same as Convicts.

One Day an Underling ventured to remind the Slave-Driver that once he had been the Friend of the Salaried Minion.

"Right you are," said the Boss. "But when I plugged for the lowly Wage-Earner I never had been in the Directors' Office to see the beautiful Tableau entitled 'Virtue copping out the Annual Dividend.' I don't know that I can make the situation clear to you, so I will merely remark that all those who get on our side of the Fence are enabled to catch a new Angle on this Salary Question."

Moral: *For Educational Purposes, every Employé should be taken into the Firm.*

The universal truth in that brief gem is still true a hundred years later, as it is in almost all the Fables. "Ade was my first influence as a humorist," Perelman once said. "He had a social sense of history. His pictures of Hoosier life at the turn of the century are more documentary than any of those studies on how much people paid for their coal. His humor was rooted in a perception of people and places. He had a cutting edge and an acerbic wit that no earlier American humorist had."

Next I dipped into Ring Lardner, partly to demonstrate that dramatic dialogue, or the playlet, is another form that can serve the humorist. I'm a pushover for Lardner's nonsense plays, which he must have written just to amuse himself. But I suspect that he was also lampooning the holy conventions of playwriting, in which yards of italic type are used presumably to explain what's happening on stage. I share Lardner's obvious doubt that these stage directions are meant for anyone to read or to fathom.

My favorite Lardner play, *I Gaspiri (The Upholsterers)*, begins with the usual list of "Characters." I mean it's the usual list; they aren't the usual characters:

Ian Obri, *a Blotter Salesman*
Johan Wasper, *his wife*
Greta, *their daughter*
Herbert Swope, *a nonentity*
Ffena, *their daughter, later their wife*
Egso, *a Pencil Guster*
Tono, *a Typical Wastebasket*

Act I consists of ten lines of dialogue, none of it involving these characters, and nine lines of irrelevant italic, concluding with: "The curtain is lowered for seven days to denote the lapse of a week." This leads into Act III, which, we are told, takes place on the Lincoln Highway, with "two bearded glue lifters seated at one side of the road." This is followed by a long italic translator's note explaining the principal industry in Phlace, which is hoarding hay, whereupon the play concludes:

> FIRST GLUE LIFTER: Well, my man, how goes it?
> SECOND GLUE LIFTER: *(Sings "My Man," to show how it goes.)*

We savored this for the pleasure of nonsense as a humor form in itself, often masking some deeper annoyance on the part of the writer. Then I resurrected *Archy and Mehitabel,* by Don Marquis, to show that this influential humorist also used an unlikely medium—doggerel—for his message. Marquis, a columnist for the *New York Sun,* stumbled on a novel solution to the newspaperman's brutal problem of meeting a deadline and presenting his material in an orderly form, just as Ade stumbled on the fable. In 1916 he created the cockroach Archy, who banged out free verse on Marquis's typewriter at night, minus capital letters because he wasn't strong enough to press the shift key.

Archy's poems, describing his friendship with a cat named Mehitabel, are of a philosophical bent that one wouldn't guess from their ragged appearance. No formal essay could more thoroughly deflate all the aging actors who bemoan the current state of the theater than Marquis does in "The Old Trouper," a long poem in which Archy describes Mehitabel's meeting with an old theater cat named Tom:

> i come of a long line
> of theatre cats
> my grandfather
> was with forrest
> he had it he was a real trouper . . .
> once he lost his beard
> and my grandfather
> dropped from the

fly gallery and landed
under his chin
and played his beard
for the rest of the act
you don t see any theatre
cats that could do that
nowadays
they haven t got it they
haven t got it
here . . .

Marquis was using the cat to leaven his impatience with a type
of bore he knew well. It's a universal impatience, whatever the
category of old-timer, just as it's a universal trait of old-timers
to complain that their profession has gone to the dogs. Marquis
achieves one of the classic functions of humor: to deflect anger
into a channel where we can laugh at frailty instead of railing
against it.

To illustrate parody I chose Thurber's nudge at Fowler's
Modern English Usage, a book which, for all its eminence, can
get (as Fowler would never allow me to say) mighty tiresome.
Thurber expressed with parody what I have often felt myself.
Like Marquis, he provided the humorist's gift of catharsis:

The number of people who use "whom" and "who"
wrongly is appalling. Take the common expression, "Whom
are you, anyways?" That is of course, strictly speaking, correct—and yet how formal, how stilted! The usage to be preferred in ordinary speech and writing is "Who are you, anyways?" "Whom" should be used in the nominative case only
when a note of dignity or austerity is desired. For example,
if a writer is dealing with a meeting of, say, the British Cabinet, it would be better to have the Premier greet a new
arrival, such as an under-secretary, with a "Whom are you,
anyways?" rather than a "Who are you, anyways?"—always

granted that the Premier is sincerely unaware of the man's identity. To address a person one knows by a "Whom are you?" is a mark either of incredible lapse of memory or inexcusable arrogance.

The next writers on my tour were Donald Ogden Stewart and Robert Benchley, two men who greatly broadened for their successors the possibilities of "free association" humor. Benchley added a dimension of warmth and vulnerability that wasn't present in humorists like Ade and Marquis, who ducked into impersonal forms such as fable and doggerel. Nobody has ever been better at diving headlong into his subject:

> St. Francis of Assisi (unless I am getting him mixed up with St. Simeon Stylites, which might be very easy to do as both their names begin with "St.") was very fond of birds, and often had his picture taken with them sitting on his shoulders and pecking at his wrists. That was all right, if St. Francis liked it. We all have our likes and dislikes, and I have more of a feeling for dogs.

Perhaps they were all just paving the way for S. J. Perelman. In any case, Perelman gratefully acknowledged these debts. "You must learn by imitation," he said. "I could have been arrested for imitating Lardner in my pieces in the late 1920s— not the content, but the manner. These influences gradually fall away."

His own influence, however, hasn't been easily shed. At his death in 1979 he had been writing steadily for more than half a century, putting the language through some of its most breathtaking loops, and in both America and England the woods are still full of writers and comics who were drawn into the gravitational pull of his style and never quite got back out. It doesn't take a detective to see Perelman's hand not only in such brilliant modern writers as Woody Allen but in the BBC's *Goon Show* and *Monty Python,* in the radio skits of Bob and Ray, and in the glancing wit of Groucho Marx—an influence more easily traceable because Perelman wrote several of the Marx Brothers' early movies.

What he created was an awareness that when the writer's mind works by free association it can ricochet from the normal to the absurd and, by the unexpectedness of its angle, demolish whatever trite idea had been there before. Onto this element of perpetual surprise—Perelman's readers never knew what was coming next—he grafted the dazzling wordplay that was his trademark, a vocabulary incredibly rich and recondite, and an erudition based on constant reading and travel. Still, even so rare a mixture wouldn't have sustained him if he hadn't always had a target.

"All humor must be *about* something—it must touch concretely on life," he said, and though readers in their enjoyment of his style may lose sight of his motive, some form of pomposity usually lies in ruins at the end of a Perelman piece, just as grand opera never quite recovered from the Marx Brothers' *A Night at the Opera* or banking from W. C. Fields's *The Bank Dick.* In the 1930s, Perelman recalled, "advertisers were giving themselves the most colossal airs, bombinating away about the creative importance of what they were doing," and many of his early parodies lanced the fatuous ad campaigns of that era. But he was never at a loss for charlatans and knaves, especially in the worlds of Broadway, Hollywood, merchandising, health, medicine, food, fashion, publishing and travel. He had a sure instinct for pretension and avarice.

I still remember the moment—I was about sixteen—when I first got hit by one of Perelman's sentences. His sentences were unlike any that I had ever seen, or even imagined, and they fractured me:

The whistle shrilled and in a moment I was chugging out of Grand Central's dreaming spires. I had chugged only a few feet when I realized that I had left without the train, so I had to run back and wait for it to start. . . . With only two hours in Chicago I would be unable to see the city, and the thought drew me into a state of composure. I noted with pleasure that a fresh coat of grime had been given to the Dearborn Street station, though I was hardly vain enough to believe that it had anything to do with my visit.

From the ostermoor where I was stretched out lazily, I murmured an inviting "Come in!"
"Come in!" I murmured invitingly. He entered shaking himself vigorously. There had been a heavy fall of talcum several hours before and as far as the ground could see the eye was white.

Women loved this impetual Irish adventurer who would rather fight than eat and vice-versa. One night he was chafing at The Bit, a tavern in Portsmouth, when he overheard a chance remark from a brawny gunner's mate in his cups. . . . The following morning the "Maid of Hull," a frigate of the line mounting 36 guns, out of Bath and into bed in a twinkling, dropped downstream on the tide, bound for Bombay, object matrimony. On her as passenger went my great-grandfather. . . . Fifty-three days later, living almost entirely on cameo brooches and the ptarmigan which fell to the ptrigger of his pfowling piece, he at last sighted the towers of Ishpeming, the Holy City of the Surds and Cosines, fanatical Mohammedan warrior sects.

Obviously I could go on (and on), just as I could quote at length from all the writers I introduced to my class, ending with Woody Allen, the most cerebral humorist around today. Allen's

magazine pieces, since collected in *Getting Even* and several
other books, constitute a body of written humor unique for
being both intellectual and hilarious, probing not only his well-
known themes of death and anxiety but such overbearing academic disciplines and literary forms as philosophy, psychology,
drama, Irish poetry and the explication of texts ("Hassidic
Tales"). Nor is he buried solely in an interior world. "A Look at
Organized Crime," a parody of all the articles ever written
explaining the Mafia, is one of the funniest pieces I know, and
"The Schmeed Memoirs"—the recollections of Hitler's barber—is the ultimate jab at the "good German" who was just
doing his job:

> I have been asked if I was aware of the moral implications
> of what I was doing. As I told the tribunal at Nuremberg, I
> did not know that Hitler was a Nazi. The truth was that for
> years I thought he worked for the phone company. When I
> finally did find out what a monster he was, it was too late to
> do anything, as I had made a down payment on some furni-
> ture. Once, toward the end of the war, I did contemplate
> loosening the Führer's neck-napkin and allowing some tiny
> hairs to get down his back, but at the last minute my nerve
> failed me.

None of the brief excerpts in this chapter can convey more
than a glimmer of the immense output and artistry of these
writers. But I wanted my students to know that they were
operating within a long tradition of serious intent and considerable nerve—a tradition that's still alive today in the work of
writers like Garrison Keillor, Ian Frazier and Calvin Trillin, of
columnists like Erma Bombeck, and in magazines like *Spy*.
Keillor probably has the surest eye for social change and the
most inventive mind for making his point obliquely. Again and
again he gives us the pleasure of finding an old genre dressed

up in new clothes. America's current hostility to cigarette smokers, for instance, is a trend that any alert writer might have noticed and written about with due sobriety. This approach, however, is pure Keillor:

> The last cigarette smokers in America were located in a box canyon south of Donner Pass in the High Sierra by two federal tobacco agents in a helicopter who spotted the little smoke puffs just before noon. One of them, the district chief, called in the ground team by air-to-ground radio. Six men in camouflage outfits, members of a crack anti-smoking joggers unit, moved quickly across the rugged terrain, surrounded the bunch in their hideout, subdued them with tear gas, and made them lie face down on the gravel in the hot August sun. There were three females and two males, all in their mid-forties. They had been on the run since the adoption of the Twenty-eighth Amendment.

The genre that's in Keillor's head has been a staple of American newspapers since the Dillinger era of the '30s, and his enjoyment of that journalistic form, with all its echoes of gangsters and G-men, of stakeouts and shootouts, is obvious in his writing.

Another situation that Keillor obviously enjoyed having found a perfect framework for was the Bush administration's bailout of the savings-and-loan industry. This is how his piece "How the Savings and Loans Were Saved" begins:

> The President was playing badminton in Aspen the day vast hordes of barbaric Huns invaded Chicago, and a reporter whose aunt lives in Evanston shouted to him as he headed for the clubhouse, "The Huns are wreaking carnage in Chicago, Mr. President! Any comment?"
>
> Mr. Bush, though caught off guard by news of the invasion, said, "We're following that whole Hun situation very closely, and right now it looks encouraging, but I'm hoping we can

get back to you in a few hours with something more definite."
The President appeared concerned but relaxed and definitely chins-up and in charge.

The piece goes on to describe how rapacious barbarians
swarmed into the city, "burned churches and performing-arts
centers and historic restorations, and dragged away monks, vir-
gins and associate professors . . . to be sold into slavery" and
seized the savings-and-loan offices, provoking no action by President Bush, however, because "exit polling at shopping malls
showed that people thought he was handling it O.K."

> The President decided not to interfere with the takeover
> attempts in the savings-and-loan industry and to pay the hun-
> dred and sixty-six billion dollars, not as a ransom of any type
> but as ordinary government support, plain and simple, noth-
> ing irregular about it, and the Huns and the Vandals rode
> away, carrying their treasure with them, and the Goths sailed
> away up Lake Michigan.

Keillor's satire left me full of admiration—first, for an act of
humor so original, but also for expressing the outrage that I
myself hadn't found a way to express. All I had been able to
muster was helpless anger that my grandchildren in their old
age would still be paying for Bush's rescue of the industry that
the greedy hordes had plundered.

Enjoyment, finally, is what all humorists must convey—the
sense that they are having a terrific time (even if they're feeling
lousy)—and this notion of cranked-up audacity is what I wanted
the students in my humor class at Yale to grapple with. I wanted
them to try their wings and to fly high.

At first I told them to write in one of the existing humor
forms—satire, parody, lampoon, etc.—and not to use "I" or to
write from their own experience. I assigned the same topic to
the whole class, bringing in some absurdity I had noticed in the

newspaper. My best hopes were realized. What the students wrote was funny and often surrealistic. They jumped boldly into free association and nonsense. They learned that it was possible to break out of the chains of logic and to have fun making a serious point within a given humor form. They were heavily under the influence of Woody Allen's off-the-wall non sequiturs ("For this the Rabbi bashes his head in, which, according to the Torah, is one of the most subtle methods of showing concern").

After about four weeks, fatigue set in. The students had found that they were capable of writing humor. But they had also found how tiring it is to sustain a weekly act of comic invention, writing in other voices. It was time to slow down their metabolism—to start them writing in their own voice and about their own experience. I declared a moratorium on Woody Allen and said I would tell them when they could read him again. That day never came.

I adopted the Chic Young principle—stick to what you know—and began to read from writers who use humor as a vein that runs quietly through their work and leaves a cumulative pleasure. One piece was E. B. White's "The Eye of Edna," in which White recalls waiting on his Maine farm for the actual arrival of Hurricane Edna while listening for several days to inane radio reports of its progress. It's a perfect essay, full of wisdom and gentle wit. Another writer whose work I excavated was Stephen Leacock, a Canadian. I remembered him from my boyhood as hilarious, but was afraid that, as often happens in looking up old friends, he would turn out to be "comical" but not funny. His pieces, however, had survived the erosion of time, and one that I particularly remembered—"My Financial Career," in which he tries to open a bank account with $56— still seems the model piece of humor on how rattled we all become when dealing with banks, libraries and other institutions. Rereading Leacock reminded me that still another function of the humorist is to represent himself as the victim or the dunce, helpless in most situations. This is pure therapy for readers, enabling them to feel superior to the writer, or at least to identify with a fellow victim.

So that was the direction in which our class began to move, the students trying to find their voice and to write about their own lives. Many of them wrote about their families. We ran into problems, mainly of exaggeration, and gradually solved them, trying to achieve control—cutting the extra sentence, for instance, which explains a funny point that is already implicit. A hard decision was to know how much exaggeration was allowable and how much was too much. One student wrote a funny piece about what a terrible cook his grandmother was. When I praised it he said she was really a very good cook. I said I was sorry to hear it—somehow the piece now seemed less funny. He asked if this made a difference. I said it didn't make a difference in this piece, since I had enjoyed it without knowing it was untrue, but that I thought he would last longer as a humorist if he started from the truth rather than from invention. In Thurber's story "The Night the Bed Fell," we know that he has slightly enlarged the facts; but we also know that *something* happened to the bed that night in the attic.

In short, our class began by striving first for humor and hoping to wing a few truths along the way. We ended by striving for truth and hoping to add humor along the way. Ultimately we realized that the two are intertwined.

Near the end of the term Perelman came and talked to the class. "When you endeavor to be funny in every line," he told us, "you place an intolerable burden not only on yourself but on the reader. You have to allow the reader to breathe. Whenever George S. Kaufman saw three straight funny lines in a play he was directing, he cut the first two. The fact is that all of us have only one personality, and we wring it out like a dish towel. I don't think you can constantly create a new identity if you're a comic writer. You are who you are."

20

Writing About Yourself

Of all the subjects available to you as a writer, the one you know best is yourself: your past and your present, your thoughts and your emotions. Yet it's probably the subject you try hardest to avoid.

Whenever I'm invited to visit a writing class in a school or a college, the first thing I ask the students is: "What are your problems? What are your concerns?" Their answer, from Maine to California, is the same: "We have to write what the teacher wants." It's a depressing sentence.

"That's the last thing any good teacher wants," I tell the students. "No teacher wants twenty-five copies of the same person writing about the same topic. What we're all looking for—what we want to see pop out of your papers—is individuality. We're looking for whatever it is that makes each of you unique. Write about what you know and what you think."

They can't. They don't think they have permission. I think they get that permission by being born.

Middle age brings no release. At writers' conferences I meet women whose children have grown up and who now want to sort out their lives through writing. I urge them to write in personal detail about what is closest to them. They protest. They say, "We have to write what editors want." In other words, "We have to write what the teacher wants." Why do they think they need permission to write about the experiences and feelings they know best—their own?

Jump still another generation. I have a journalist friend who has spent a lifetime writing honorably, but always out of second-hand sources, explicating other people's events. Over the years I've often heard him mention his father, a minister who took many lonely liberal stands in a conservative Kansas town, and obviously that's where my friend got his own strong social conscience. A few years ago I asked him when he was going to start writing about the elements in his life that were truly important to him, including his father. One of these days, he said. But the day was always carefully avoided.

When he turned sixty-five I began to pester him. I sent him some memoirs that had moved me, and finally he agreed to spend his mornings writing in that vein. Now he can hardly believe what a liberating journey he is embarked on: how much he is discovering about his father, and about what his own life adds up to, that he never knew. But when he describes it he always says, "I never had the nerve before," or "I was always afraid to try." In other words, "I didn't think I had permission."

Why not? Wasn't America always the land of the "rugged individualist"? Let's get that lost land and those lost individualists back. If you're a writing teacher, make your students believe in the validity of their lives. If you're a writer, give yourself permission to tell us who you are.

By "permission" I don't mean "permissive." I have no patience with sloppy workmanship—with the let-it-all-hang-out verbiage of the '60s. To have a decent career in America it's important to be able to write a clear English sentence. But on the question of who you're writing *for,* don't be eager to please. If you consciously write *for* a teacher or *for* an editor, you'll end up not writing for anybody. If you write for yourself, you'll reach all the people you want to write *for.*

Writing about one's life is naturally related to how long one has lived. When students say they have to write what the teacher wants, what they often mean is that they don't have anything to say—so meager is their after-school existence, bounded largely by television and the mall, two wholly artificial versions of reality. Still, at any age, memory is a powerful writer's tool and the physical act of writing is a powerful search mechanism. I'm often amazed, dipping into my past, to find some wholly forgotten incident clicking into place just when I need it. Your memory is almost always good for material when your other wells go dry.

What memory also does is to plug you into narrative—pure gold for a writer. I was taught this lesson by a recent book of my own, *Writing to Learn*. Its premise was that writing is a major component of learning and that writing should be a required part of all school and college courses. I saw the book as a kind of anthology: I would collect examples of good writing in various academic disciplines that students and teachers could use as a model.

But when I started to write, the book told me how it wanted to be written. In almost every chapter I found myself recalling some experience in my past as the most helpful way (I thought) of introducing a particular discipline. The anthology emerged from its cocoon looking like a memoir. I didn't throw it back. On the contrary, I was grateful to the process of writing for teaching me how to animate an academic subject. Later several professors wrote to give me similar news. They said they had been "blocked" on books that they were unable to bring to life; the gravity of their research, they felt, obliged them to write in an impersonal expository style. "Then I saw in *Writing to Learn*," they told me, almost in the same words, "that you let yourself become part of the story. I didn't know that was allowed." (Translation: "I didn't think I had permission.") "I went back to my book and recast it in a form that was more personal and natural, and everything fell into place."

Permission, of course, is a two-edged instrument, and nobody should use it without posting in full view a surgeon general's warning: EXCESSIVE WRITING ABOUT YOURSELF CAN BE HAZ-

ARDOUS TO THE HEALTH OF THE WRITER AND THE READER. A thin line separates ego from egotism. Ego is healthy; no writer can go far without it. Egotism, however, is a bore, and this chapter is not intended as a license to prattle just for therapy. Again, a rule I suggest is: Make sure every component in your memoir is doing useful work. Write about yourself, by all means, with confidence and pleasure. But see that all the details—people, places, events, anecdotes, ideas, emotions—are moving your story steadily along, taking you where you want to go.

*

Which brings us to memoir as a form. I will read almost anybody's memoir. For me, no other nonfiction form goes so deeply to the roots of personal experience—to all the drama and humor and unexpectedness of life. The books I remember most vividly from my first reading of them are memoirs: books such as Michael J. Arlen's *Exiles,* Russell Baker's *Growing Up,* Vivian Gornick's *Fierce Attachments,* Moss Hart's *Act One,* John Houseman's *Run-Through,* Vladimir Nabokov's *Speak, Memory* and V. S. Pritchett's *A Cab at the Door.*

What gives them their power is the narrowness of their focus. Unlike autobiography, which spans an entire life, memoir assumes the life and ignores almost all of it. The memoir writer takes us back to some corner of his or her past that was unusually intense—childhood, for instance—or that was framed by war or some other upheaval. Baker's *Growing Up* is a box within a box: it's the story of a boy growing up, placed inside the story of a family being battered by the Depression; it takes much of its strength from its historical context. Nabokov's *Speak, Memory,* the most elegant memoir I know, invokes a golden boyhood in czarist Saint Petersburg, a world of private tutors and summer houses that the Russian Revolution would end forever. It's an act of writing frozen in a unique time and place. Pritchett's *A Cab at the Door* recalls a childhood that was

almost Dickensian; his grim apprenticeship to the London
leather trade seems to belong to the nineteenth century. Yet
Pritchett describes it without self-pity and even with merri-
ment. We see that his childhood was inseparably joined to the
particular moment and country and class he was born into—and
was an organic part of the wonderful writer he grew up to be.

Think narrow, then, when you try the form. Memoir isn't the
summary of a life; it's a window into a life, very much like a
photograph in its selective composition. It may look like a casual
and even random calling up of bygone events. It's not; it's a
deliberate construction. Ask Thoreau: he wrote seven different
drafts of *Walden* in eight years; no American memoir was more
painstakingly pieced together. To write a good memoir you
must become the editor of your own life, imposing on an untidy
sprawl of half-remembered events a narrative shape and an
organizing idea. Memoir is the art of inventing the truth.

The secret of the art is detail. Any kind of detail will work—a
sound or a smell or a song title—as long as it played a shaping
role in the portion of your life you have chosen to distill. Consider sound. Here's how Eudora Welty begins her memoir, *One
Writer's Beginnings,* a deceptively slender book packed with
rich remembrance:

> In our house on North Congress Street, in Jackson, Missis-
> sippi, where I was born, the oldest of three children, in 1909,
> we grew up to the striking of clocks. There was a mission-style
> oak grandfather clock standing in the hall, which sent its
> gong-like strokes through the living room, dining room,
> kitchen, and pantry, and up the sounding board of the stair-
> well. Through the night, it could find its way into our ears;
> sometimes, even on the sleeping porch, midnight could wake
> us up. My parents' bedroom had a smaller striking clock that
> answered it. Though the kitchen clock did nothing but show
> the time, the dining room clock was a cuckoo clock with
> weights on long chains, on one of which my baby brother,

after climbing on a chair to the top of the china closet, once succeeded in suspending the cat for a moment. I don't know whether or not my father's Ohio family, in having been Swiss back in the 1700s before the first three Welty brothers came to America, had anything to do with this; but we all of us have been time-minded all our lives. This was good at least for a future fiction writer, being able to learn so penetratingly, and almost first of all, about chronology. It was one of a good many things I learned almost without knowing it; it would be there when I needed it.

My father loved all instruments that would instruct and fascinate. His place to keep things was the drawer in the "library table" where lying on top of his folded maps was a telescope with brass extensions, to find the moon and the Big Dipper after supper in our front yard, and to keep appointments with eclipses. There was a folding Kodak that was brought out for Christmas, birthdays, and trips. In the back of the drawer you could find a magnifying glass, a kaleidoscope, and a gyroscope kept in a black buckram box, which he would set dancing for us on a string pulled tight. He had also supplied himself with an assortment of puzzles composed of metal rings and intersecting links and keys chained together, impossible for the rest of us, however patiently shown, to take apart; he had an almost childlike love of the ingenious.

In time, a barometer was added to our dining room wall; but we really didn't need it. My father had the country boy's accurate knowledge of the weather and its skies. He went out and stood on our front steps first thing in the morning and took a look at it and a sniff. He was a pretty good weather prophet.

"Well, I'm *not,*" my mother would say with enormous self-satisfaction. . . .

So I developed a strong meteorological sensibility. In years ahead when I wrote stories, atmosphere took its influential role from the start. Commotion in the weather and the inner feelings aroused by such a hovering disturbance emerged connected in dramatic form.

Notice how much we learn instantly about Eudora Welty's beginnings—the kind of home she was born into, the kind of man her father was. She has rung us into her Mississippi girlhood with the chiming of clocks up and down the stairs and even out onto the sleeping porch.

For Alfred Kazin, smell is a thread that he follows back to his boyhood in the Brownsville section of Brooklyn. From my first encounter with Kazin's *A Walker in the City* I remember it as a sensory memoir. The following passage is not only a good example of how to write with your nose; it also shows how memoir is nourished by a writer's ability to create a sense of place: what it was that made his neighborhood and his heritage distinctive:

> It was the darkness and emptiness of the streets I liked most about Friday evening, as if in preparation for that day of rest and worship which the Jews greet "as a bride"—that day when the very touch of money is prohibited, all work, all travel, all household duties, even to the turning on and off of a light—Jewry had found its way past its tormented heart to some ancient still center of itself. I waited for the streets to go dark on Friday evening as other children waited for the Christmas lights. . . . When I returned home after three, the warm odor of a coffee cake baking in the oven, and the sight of my mother on her hands and knees scrubbing the linoleum on the dining room floor, filled me with such tenderness that I could feel my senses reaching out to embrace every single object in our household. . . .
>
> My great moment came at six, when my father returned from work, his overalls smelling faintly of turpentine and

shellac, white drops of silver paint still gleaming on his chin. Hanging his overcoat in the long dark hall that led into our kitchen, he would leave in one pocket a loosely folded copy of the New York *World;* and then everything that beckoned to me from that other hemisphere of my brain beyond the East River would start up from the smell of fresh newsprint and the sight of the globe on the front page. It was a paper that carried special associations for me with Brooklyn Bridge. They published the *World* under the green dome on Park Row overlooking the bridge; the fresh salt air of New York harbor lingered for me in the smell of paint and damp newsprint in the hall. I felt that my father brought the outside straight into our house with each day's copy of the *World.*

Kazin would eventually cross the Brooklyn Bridge and become the dean of American literary critics. But the literary genre that has always been central to his life is not the usual stuff of literature—the novel or the short story or the poem. It's what he calls "personal history": specifically, such "personal American classics," discovered when he was a boy, as Walt Whitman's Civil War diary *Specimen Days* and his *Leaves of Grass,* Thoreau's *Walden* and especially his Journals, and *The Education of Henry Adams.* What excited Kazin was that Whitman, Thoreau and Adams wrote themselves into the landscape of American literature by daring to use the most intimate forms—journals, diaries, letters and memoirs—and that by writing personal history himself he could make the same "cherished connection" to America and could thereby place himself, the son of Russian Jews, in the same landscape. You can use your own personal history to cross your own Brooklyn Bridge.

Another shaping element in every recollected life is the part of the country where we grew up—the topography, the climate, the attitudes of the place known as home. "Our cold was our pride," writes Patricia Hampl, recalling her Minnesota childhood in her memoir *A Romantic Education*. It was a fact of family life, she says, that "we were not to speak against the winter."

We watched the *Today* show weather report and a shiver—not of cold but entirely of civic pride—ran through us as, week after week, some aching Minnesota town came in with the lowest temperature in the country. We did not delight in the admittance of Alaska, our icy rival, into the Union. We said nothing against it, but it was understood that it didn't really count, it had an unfair advantage which caused us to ignore it. "Didn't Alaska belong to Russia?" my mother said. "I mean, isn't it strictly speaking part of Siberia?" . . .

"If you stepped outside right now without any clothes on," my brother said one day when we had not been allowed to go skating because the temperature was 25° below zero, "you'd be dead in three minutes." He sounded happy, the Minnesota pride in the abysmal statistic—which, for all I know, he had made up on the spot. We looked out the dining room window to the forbidden world. The brilliant, mean glare from the mounds of snow had no mercy on the eye and was a mockery of the meaning of sun. "You'd be *stiff*. Like frozen hamburger," he said. "Or a frozen plucked chicken," regarding me and finding a better simile. "And when you thawed out, you'd turn green." The pleasure of being horrified, standing there by the hot radiator with my ghoulish brother.

We shared the pride of isolation, the curious glamour of hermits. More than any other thing I can name, the winter made me want to write.

The crucial ingredient in memoir is, of course, people. Sounds and smells and sleeping porches will take you just so far; finally you must summon back the men and women and children who notably crossed your life. What was it that made them memorable—what turn of mind, what crazy habits? A typical odd bird from memoir's vast aviary is John Mortimer's father, a blind barrister, as recalled by the son in *Clinging to the Wreckage,* a memoir that manages the feat of being both tender and hilarious. Mortimer, a lawyer himself and a prolific author and playwright, best known for *Rumpole of the Bailey,* writes that when his father became blind he "insisted on continuing with his legal practice as though nothing had happened" and that his mother thereupon became the person who would read his briefs to him and make notes on his cases.

She became a well-known figure in the Law Courts, as well known as the Tipstaff or the Lord Chief Justice, leading my father from Court to Court, smiling patiently as he tapped the paved floors with his clouded malacca cane and shouted abuse either at her or at his instructing solicitor, or at both of them at the same time. From early in the war, when they settled permanently in the country, my mother drove my father fourteen miles a day to Henley Station and took him up in the train. Ensconced in a corner seat, dressed like Winston Churchill, in a black jacket and striped trousers, bow-tie worn with a wing-collar, boots and spats, my father would require her to read in a loud and clear voice the evidence in the divorce case that would be his day's work. As the train ground to a halt around Maidenhead the first-class carriage would fall silent as my mother read out the reports of Private Investigators on adulterous behavior which they had observed in detail. If she dropped her voice over descriptions of stained bed-linen, male and female clothing found scattered about, or misconduct in motor cars, my father would call out, "Speak up, Kath!" and their fellow travelers would be treated to another thrilling installment.

But the most interesting character in a memoir, we hope, will turn out to be the person who wrote it. What did that man or

woman learn from the hills and valleys of life? How did he or
she change or grow? One book that takes us on such a journey
of rediscovery is Leonard Woolf's five-volume autobiography—
actually, five memoirs recalling five successive periods in a
richly varied life. My favorite is the second volume, *Growing,*
which covers Woolf's seven years as a young British civil servant
in Ceylon. By its compression into a tight unit of time—1904 to
1911—the memoir captures the dailiness of a highly exotic assignment. But by extension it also tells the story of all the earnest British colonials who have found themselves trying to ad-
minister justice in an alien and bewildering land.

> In October 1904, I sailed from Tilbury Docks in the P. & O.
> *Syria* for Ceylon. I was a Cadet in the Ceylon Civil Service.
> To make a complete break with one's former life is a strange,
> frightening, and exhilarating experience. It has upon one, I
> think, the effect of a second birth.

That's how *Growing* begins, and it couldn't begin more simply and strongly. Woolf goes on to say that "to be born again in
this way at the age of twenty-four imprints a permanent mark
upon one's character and one's attitude to life." Thus alerted,
we read on in the expectation of being told what Leonard Woolf
found out that permanently stamped his character and his attitude, for we also know that in his subsequent marriage and
distinguished public career the husband of Virginia Woolf
brought with him deep reserves of patience, intellect and com-
passion.

Here's a paragraph from the middle of the book that tells us
how one lifelong attitude was imprinted:

> I was the only white man in the 400 square miles of the
> District, and here for the first time I learned the profound
> happiness of complete solitude. For a month I never spoke to
> anyone except clerks, headmen, Tamil villagers, and my own

Tamil servants. My life and my work were entirely my own
responsibility and there was no one whom I could consult
about anything connected with either. I think this kind of
complete solitude, with the necessity of relying absolutely
upon oneself and one's own mind, is, when one is young,
extremely good for one. I experienced it again during my
three years in the Hambantota District. I acquired a taste for
it which I have never lost, not for the permanent solitude of
the hermit, or even for long periods of it, but for interludes
of complete isolation. Even today, when evening falls and the
door is shut in the street or in the village, and all life except
my own and my dog's and my cat's is for the moment ex-
cluded, and for the moment there is cessation of the incessant
fret and interruption of other people and outside existence,
I enjoy the wordless and soundless meditation and the savor
of one's own unhurried existence, and psychologically I am
almost back again in the empty silent Residencies of Mannar
and Hambantota or camping in the thick uninhabited jungles.

Thinking of Virginia Woolf, I'm reminded that she was an
avid writer of journals, diaries and letters, and that this highly
personal writing helped her to clarify her thoughts and emotions. (How often we start writing a letter out of obligation and
only find out in the third paragraph that we have something we
really want to say to the person we're writing to.) What Virginia
Woolf intimately wrote during her lifetime has been immensely
helpful to other women wrestling with similar angels and demons. Acknowledging that debt in a 1989 review of a book
about Woolf's abused girlhood, Kennedy Fraser begins with a
memoir of her own that seizes our attention with its honesty
and vulnerability:

There was a time when my life seemed so painful to me
that reading about the lives of other women writers was one

of the few things that could help. I was unhappy, and
ashamed of it; I was baffled by my life. For several years in
my early thirties, I would sit in my armchair reading books
about these other lives. Sometimes when I came to the end,
I would sit down and read the book through from the beginning again. I remember an incredible intensity about all this,
and also a kind of furtiveness—as if I were afraid that someone might look through the window and find me out. Even
now, I feel I should pretend that I was reading only these
women's fiction or their poetry—their lives as they chose to
present them, alchemized as art. But that would be a lie. It
was the private messages I really liked—the journals and
letters, and autobiographies and biographies whenever they
seemed to be telling the truth. I felt very lonely then, self-
absorbed, shut off. I needed all this murmured chorus, this
continuum of true-life stories, to pull me through. They were
like mothers and sisters to me, these literary women, many
of them already dead; more than my own family, they
seemed to stretch out a hand. I had come to New York when
I was young, as so many come, in order to invent myself. And,
like many modern people—modern women, especially—I
had catapulted out of my context. . . . The successes [of the
writers] gave me hope, of course, yet it was the desperate bits
I liked best. I was looking for directions, gathering clues. I was
especially grateful for the secret, shameful things about these
women—the pain: the abortions and misalliances, the pills
they took, the amount they drank. And what had made them
live as lesbians, or fall in love with homosexual men, or men
with wives?

One of the best gifts you have to offer when you write personal history is the gift of yourself. Don't forget that it's there
and that it has great power. Give yourself permission to write
about yourself, and have a good time doing it.

PART III

Attitudes

21

Writing with a Word Processor

There are no writers more evangelistic than writers who use a word processor. Like all evangelists, they have been given the good news, which is that a word processor not only frees writers from the drudgery of writing and rewriting and typing and retyping. It also makes them better and more productive writers. Not since the typewriter replaced the pen has such a liberating tool come along. I've never met a writer with a word processor who can even imagine going back to the way he or she wrote before.

What does a word processor do that's so helpful? It puts your words right in front of your eyes for your instant consideration—and reconsideration. Most writers don't initially say what they want to say, or say it as well as they could. The typical sentence as it first emerges almost always has something wrong with it: it's not clear; it's not logical; it's too long; it's full of clutter; it's awkward; it's pretentious; it's boring; it lacks rhythm; it could be read in several different ways; it doesn't follow and develop the previous sentence. As a writer you're half aware of this blunt truth and you know how to go back and make repairs. But you also know how tiring it is just to *think* about going back and making repairs. All of us have an emotional equity in our first draft—we can hardly believe that it wasn't born perfect. Beyond that, there's the fatigue of retyping the manuscript over and over. The tendency is to say, "It's good enough." Or you just run out of time.

But with a word processor you can play with your writing on the screen until you get it right, and the paragraphs will keep rearranging themselves, no matter how many words you change or add or cut, and you don't have to print your article until it's just the way you want it.

Imagine, for example, that you've written a paragraph. When you read it over, you realize that there's something you'd like to add after the second sentence that hadn't occurred to you before. You just type it in. The existing sentences will move to the right to make room for it, and the paragraph will regroup itself with the new material added. Then let's say you read the new paragraph and find that you don't need the new sentence after all. Press the DELETE key. The sentence will vanish and the gaps will close up. You can add or delete or move anything at all—words, phrases, sentences, paragraphs, whole pages. There's no kind of tinkering that you can't do—and undo—instantly.

To me this is God's gift, or technology's gift, to good writing, because the essence of writing is rewriting. I've never regarded rewriting as an unfair burden—extra homework that I don't deserve or some kind of penalty. On the contrary, I consider it a privilege to be able to shape my writing until it's as clean and strong as I can make it. Like a good watch, it should run smoothly and have no extra parts.

Nevertheless, all this rewriting is a chore. I happen to be a slow writer, and I can't write the second paragraph until I've got the first one right, or the third one until I've got the second one right. The floor around my old Underwood typewriter used to be littered with crumpled balls of paper—earlier efforts that didn't work. I consoled myself with the truism that in the act of retyping I was also rewriting. But now I see that the truism is only about 10 percent true: I've spent much of my life retyping, just as I spent a lot of time washing dishes before the dishwasher was invented. The word processor is the writer's dishwasher: it liberates you from a chore that's not creative and that saps your energy.

Of course all writers write differently. My method of writing one paragraph at a time is totally unlike that of the person who writes the whole first draft in one burst. Still, however you write, there's no escape from rewriting.

What do I mean by "rewriting"? I don't mean writing one draft and then writing a whole new version from scratch, and then a third. Most rewriting consists of reshaping and polishing the raw material you wrote on your first try. This means that a certain amount of your typing has already been done. Let's look at a typical paragraph and imagine that it's the writer's first draft. There's nothing really wrong with it—it's clear and it's grammatical. But it's full of ragged edges: failures of the writer to keep the reader notified of changes in time, place and mood, or to animate his style. What I've done is to add, in bracketed italics after each sentence, some of the thoughts that might occur to a careful writer taking a first look at this draft. After that the revised paragraph appears.

There used to be a time when neighbors took care of one another, he remembered. [*Put "he remembered" first to establish reflective tone.*] It no longer seemed to happen that way, however. [*The contrast supplied by "however" must start the sentence. Also establish place.*] He wondered if it was because everyone in the modern world was so busy. [*All these opening sentences are the same length and have the same dreary rhythm; turn this one around.*] It occurred to him that people today had so many things to do that they didn't have time anymore for old-fashioned friendship. [*Sentence essentially repeats previous sentence; give it specific detail or kill it.*] Things didn't work that way in America in previous eras. [*Reader is still in the present; reverse the sentence to tell him he's now in the past. "America" no longer needed here if inserted earlier.*] And he knew that the situation was very different in other countries of the world, as he recalled from the years when he lived in villages in such places as Spain and Italy. [*Reader is still in America; start with a negative transition word. Sentence also too flabby. "Countries of the world" redundant.*] It almost seemed to him that as people got richer and built their houses farther apart they isolated themselves from the essentials of life. [*Plant irony early? Sharpen the paradox about richness.*] And there was another thought that troubled him. [*This is the real point of the paragraph; signal the reader that it's important. Avoid weak "there was" construction.*] His friends had deserted him when he needed them most during his recent illness. [*Reshape the sentence so the last word is "most"; the last word is the one that lingers in the reader's ear. Hold sickness for next sentence.*] It was almost as if they found him guilty of doing something shameful. [*Introduce sickness here as the reason. Is "guilty" necessary? Implicit?*] He recalled reading somewhere about societies in primitive parts of the world in which sick people were shunned, though he had never heard of any such ritual in America. [*Sentence starts slowly and stays very windy. Break it into shorter units. Snap off the point.*]

He remembered that neighbors used to take care of one another. But that no longer seemed to happen in America. Was it because everyone was so busy? Were people really so preoccupied with their TV sets and their cars and their fitness programs that they had no time for friendship? In previous eras that was never true. Nor was it how families lived in other parts of the world. Even in the poorest villages of Spain and Italy, he recalled, people would drop in with a loaf of bread. An ironic idea struck him: as people got richer they cut themselves off from the richness of life. But what really troubled him was an even more shocking fact. The time when his friends deserted him was the time when he needed them most. By getting sick he almost seemed to have done something shameful. He knew that other societies had a custom of "shunning" people who were very ill. But that ritual only existed in primitive cultures. Or did it?

My revisions aren't the best ones that could be made, or the only ones. They're mainly matters of carpentry: fixing the structure and the flow. Much could still be done in such areas as cadence, detail and freshness of language. But my point is that most rewriting is a process of juggling elements that already exist. And I'm not just talking about individual sentences. The total construction is equally important. Read your article aloud from beginning to end and put yourself in the reader's mind. You might find, for instance, that you had written two sentences like this:

The tragic hero of the play is Othello. Small and malevolent, Iago feeds his jealous suspicions.

In itself there's nothing wrong with the Iago sentence. But as a sequel to the previous sentence it's very wrong. The name lingering in the reader's ear is Othello; the reader naturally assumes that Othello is small and malevolent.

When you read your writing aloud with these connecting links in mind you'll hear a dismaying number of places where you have lost or confused the reader, or failed to tell him the one fact he needs to know, or told him too much. With a word processor you can move through your piece easily, patching all these trouble spots. After every patch, read aloud what you've done and decide whether you like it. If you don't, try something else. When you finish your revisions, the machine will paginate your entire article and the printer will type it while you go and have a beer. Sweeter music could hardly be sung to a writer than the sound of his article being typed exactly the way he wants it—but not by him.

Later you may decide that you want to add a few paragraphs of new information on, say, page 8. Just call page 8 back to the screen, add the new material, and tell the machine to repaginate the article from that point forward. If you've forgotten a footnote—and what dissertation writer hasn't?—just type it in its proper place and let the machine do the dirty work of redistributing the lines, renumbering the pages and making a clean copy. Why should Ph.D. candidates waste their intellect on such slave labor? Their thesis is two years late anyway.

In short, the word processor can concentrate your mind on the craft of writing, revising and editing—much more powerfully than this has ever been possible, because your words are right in front of you in all their infinite possibility, waiting to be infinitely reshaped. Technology, the great villain, turns out to be your friend. I can't agree with people who say that writing at a terminal will make our writing mechanical, or turn our children into robots. What we write still has to come out of our heads; no machine is going to do that for us.

For children, in fact, the word processor strikes me as an ideal tool for learning to write. Children are natural writers—their heads are full of images and wonder and wordplay. Their motor skills, however, are too slow to get all the wonderful words onto paper, and the words that they *do* get on paper look childish and clumsy; children, no less than adults, deserve the dignity of having their writing look decent. Pleasure turns to frustration and is often lost forever. This wouldn't happen if children could tap out their words on a keyboard and see them on a screen, and move the words around, and substitute one word for another, and then have a machine print their composition neatly. *That's* the joy of writing, as every poet knows—to make words dance for us in all their possible patterns.

When I started using a word processor, bringing to it a life-long fear of machines, I was comforted by the thought that I could always make a printout of what I had written. Then I would be able to edit it with my sacred pencil. But very soon I realized that I was editing my writing on the screen more quickly and competently than I had edited it on paper. Visually, the words seemed clearer when they were right in front of my eyes than when they were on a piece of paper viewed from a 45-degree angle. And to be able to change those words instantly was a miracle. Every morning I would just call up what I had written the previous day, read it aloud, make the usual improvements that hadn't occurred to me earlier, and keep going. I weaned myself from paper almost immediately.

But (I hear you saying) what if you decide after revising a paragraph that you liked the first version better? Especially that long opening sentence that caught the energy you were feeling at the time. And what was that elegant phrase—something about the clouds scudding at dusk—that now seems so absolutely right, if not downright luminous? All those gems have vanished into the electricity. This question about the loss of material is the biggest factor—after the primordial fear of the machine itself—that keeps writers from even trying a word processor.

The question has various answers, depending on how you work. In my case, editing and revising as I go along, I almost always prefer my improvements to what they replaced. I love to see an unnecessary word or phrase evaporate at the flick of a key. I love to replace a humdrum word with one that has more precision or color. I love to strengthen the transition between one sentence and another, or replace an ungainly phrase with one that has a more graceful rhythm. With every change, I feel that I'm getting nearer to where I would finally like to arrive, and as I see the piece growing in strength, literally before my eyes, I feel a purer pleasure than I've ever had in rewriting.

But most writers work in a more spacious manner, freely pouring out ideas and sentences with the knowledge that they can come back later and clean up the mess. If you are this kind of writer you don't want to keep erasing what you've written; you want to save all your drafts. You can do this by making a printout of everything you write, and you can also do it on the screen. The machine requires you to give a different name to every item you create. This is the storage system that enables you to file your work on a disk and to summon it back as often as you need it.

Assume that you're writing an article about automobiles. You might name your first draft CAR. It will exist for you on a disk in that form, with all its raw virtues and flaws. You can also make a printout so that you have a copy of it on paper. Then you might write a second draft and name it CAR2 and make a printout of that. Then you might write a third draft, CAR3, by working from the printout of CAR and CAR2, combining the best features of both. Or you might decide that your well-meant revisions have lost the freshness of the original and that CAR is the version that's truest to your intentions. Just call CAR back to the screen and make it your working version, perhaps borrowing some refinements from CAR2 and CAR3. But whatever you do, the work will be much easier and faster because the words are only images of light, instantly changeable.

In certain kinds of writing you'll save incredible amounts of time and energy. I'm thinking especially of interviews and other articles that make extensive use of quotes. The people you interview may be highly articulate; nevertheless they will ramble and repeat themselves. Even if they give you all the material you need, they will never give it to you in the form in which you'll finally need it. You're stuck with the hard job of imposing a shape on your material, distilling the quotes and creating a narrative flow.

This can involve hours of fiddling with the quotes: putting them in and taking them back out and trying them somewhere else and substituting new ones. Often, for instance, you'll write an entire page incorporating a set of quotes that you thought were perfect for a particular moment. Later you find in your notes a quote that makes the same point in a better way—it's more vivid, perhaps, or more idiosyncratic, or more exact. On a typewriter it would take twenty minutes to replace one quote with the other and retype the whole page. On a word processor you can do it painlessly in a minute or two.

Equally important are such matters as variety and pace. An article that just strings together long chunks of quotes will soon become tiresome. You must periodically alter its rhythm by converting what the speaker said into a sentence of your own, explaining his point in your words. But often the only way to get a sense of the momentum of a piece is to write several paragraphs of quotes and then read them aloud to see if they need to be broken up. Perhaps one brief sentence of your own can create a link more tightly than the speaker did.

What you must do, in short, is to make an arrangement—one that hangs together from beginning to end and that moves with economy and warmth. Such a construction can only be achieved with a fair amount of trial and error, and doing this on a screen beats doing it over and over on a typewriter. Two books that I wrote on a word processor, in which I was working mainly with oral material—one on jazz, the other on baseball— took less than a year to complete. On a typewriter they would have taken two years. The difference was not only in speed and morale; it was also in control. At the end I felt that I had made exactly the arrangement that I had in mind when I started.

These are crucial areas of gain for a writer: time, energy, enthusiasm, output and control. A word processor can cut a year off the writing of a Ph.D. dissertation and probably two—quite a bargain. In the business of writing, time is money. For the dissertation writer, the Ph.D. degree qualifies that man or woman to enter the job market as a professor. For the free-lance writer, every completed article liberates him or her to start the next one.

Nor is the saving limited to writing; it also applies to the publishing of what has been written. Normally when a writer finishes a manuscript the publisher allows six months for it to be copyedited and typeset. In the case of my jazz book *Willie and Dwike* I gave a printout of my manuscript to Harper & Row, where it was copyedited in a week. I made the changes on my screen in a few hours and gave the publisher the two disks that contained my finished book. These were converted directly into phototype and I had page proofs a few weeks later.

I commend one thought to you as you dip your toe in the computer culture: You are more competent than you think you are. All of us liberal arts types have coddled ourselves with the idea that we can't perform mechanical tasks or understand machines. Most of that is self-delusion—people will learn what they need to learn. In my case, as soon as I began to glimpse the countless ways in which a word processor could change my life, I enjoyed thinking of all sorts of uses that would help me in my writing and editing.

Still, resistance is strong. People say, "I'm sure you're right—maybe next year I'll give it a try." They're afraid to give up the crutches they're sure they need to perform the act of writing. I was sure, for instance, that I couldn't write unless I could flick back and forth among several pieces of paper to see what I had written. I needed that continuity and always would. Well, it turns out that I don't need it. On my screen I can see twenty lines at a time, and that's usually enough. If it isn't, I can bring the preceding lines into view. O.K., it's not ideal. But it's not fatal—the mind adjusts and develops new aptitudes.

The best way to start is to learn from another writer. Beginners assume that they have to take a computer course or immerse themselves in the instruction manual. But courses and manuals are meant mainly for office workers, who will use a word processor for office tasks. The manuals are often written by people who aren't writers themselves and don't know the cognitive steps that go into writing, revising and editing. By contrast, any writer who uses a word processor should be able to launch another writer in an hour. When I do this I demonstrate the few functions that a writer needs, point out the keys that govern these functions, and explain the logic that the machine uses to do what it does. Twenty minutes is generally enough. Then I sit my pupil down at the keyboard and tell him or her to write something. At first there is a timidity, as if to avoid striking a key that might blow the machine up. But this quickly dissolves into childlike pleasure. In fifteen minutes the beginner is writing real paragraphs and adding and deleting words. All the fear is seen to have been unreasonable. At the end of an hour the worst is over.

Like many writers, I don't like to write; I like to have written. Now, however, I sit down to write more willingly than ever before, especially if I'm facing a complex problem of organization. It's often said that because writing on a screen comes so easily and looks so neat it will make many people write worse; they will assume that their beautiful-looking words are perfect. True enough: sloppy writers may write even more sloppily. But a certain number of sloppy writers will improve, noticing for the first time the disarray of their thoughts on the screen and knowing that they have a second chance to make their sentences—and themselves—look better. Or a third chance. The machine is forgiving: it invites you to take risks, to try things out, to fly a little. If the flight doesn't work, nobody will know—you can delete it and try something else. But at least you have stretched your sense of possibility. Maybe next time you will soar.

When you see your words on the screen, study them closely. Remember that the two main virtues of writing are clarity and simplicity. Look for clutter and prune it out. Read your sentences aloud. Do they sound like you? If they don't, fiddle with them until they do. Don't say anything in writing that you wouldn't comfortably say in conversation. If you're not a person who says "indeed" or "moreover" or "kindly," or who calls someone an individual ("he's a fine individual"), don't ever write it. Are you drowning in long words? Think of shorter ones. Are your sentences full of abstract nouns like "productivity"? Turn the nouns into active verbs that get real people doing real things. Is a sentence stiff and pompous? Relax and write a new one right after it that expresses the warm and lovable person you really are. Then delete the earlier sentence; the stiff and pompous you will vanish into the electricity. Use the machine, in short, to capture your humanity.

If that's a paradox, don't knock it.

22

Trust Your Material

The longer I work at the craft of writing, the more I realize that there's nothing more interesting than the truth. What people do—and what people say—continues to take me by surprise with its wonderfulness, or its quirkiness, or its drama, or its humor, or its pain. Who could invent all the astonishing things that really happen? I increasingly find myself saying to writers and students: "Trust your material."

Recently I spent some time as a writing coach at a newspaper in a small American city. I noticed that many of the reporters had fallen into the habit—quite common in nonfiction writing today—of trying to make the news more palatable by writing in a feature story style. Their leads consisted of a succession of tiny paragraphs that went something like this:

Whoosh!
It was incredible.
Something was definitely wrong.
Al Potter wondered if he was seeing things.
Or maybe it was just spring fever.
It wasn't as if he hadn't checked his car before leaving the house.
But then again, he hadn't remembered to tell Linda.
Which was odd, because he always remembered to tell Linda.

Ever since they started going together back in junior high.
Was that really twenty years ago?
And now there was also little Jo-Jo to worry about.
Come to think of it, the dog was acting kind of funny.

These articles often began on page 1, and I would read as far
as the line that said "Continued on page 9" and still have no
idea what they were about. Then I would dutifully turn to page
9 and find myself in an interesting story, full of unusual facts and
details. I'd say to the reporter, "That was a good story when I
finally got to it—over here on page 9. Why didn't you put that
stuff in your lead?" The reporter would say, "Well, in the lead
I was writing color." The assumption is that fact and color are
two separate entities. Of course they're not; color is organic to
the fact. The writer's job is to present the colorful fact.

Therefore one question you should ask at the start of every
article or book is: How strong a presence should you be in your
presentation of the facts?

In my own writing I usually like to be strongly present. To
write in the first person—"I," "me," "we," "us"—is the most
natural way of talking to someone else on paper, which is what
writing is, and in books like this one, where my main purpose
is to teach, I want readers to feel that they are hearing from a
writer who has wrestled with the craft himself. That's also true
of such forms as travel writing; a good travel writer must make
himself available.

But in two other books I discovered the opposite lesson: that
a writer can damage his material if he intrudes himself and his
opinions on it. The first book was *Willie and Dwike,* a profile
of two black jazz musicians, Willie Ruff and Dwike Mitchell,
who have played together as the Mitchell-Ruff Duo since 1955.
Mitchell is the pianist; Ruff plays the bass and the French horn.
I met them when I was at Yale, where Ruff teaches, and I loved
their music from the start. But what gave me my affection for

the two men was that teaching is a strong current in their lives. They avoid club dates, preferring to give concerts at schools and colleges where they can also explain jazz and hold workshops. In 1959 they introduced jazz to the Soviet Union, playing and teaching for five weeks in Soviet conservatories. For that trip Ruff taught himself Russian, his seventh language.

I wanted to know where they had acquired this teaching bent—two poor boys growing up in small towns in the South. I started asking them about their boyhoods and found that their lives had been crossed, again and again, by someone who taught them what they needed to know next. I decided that I wanted to write a book about Mitchell and Ruff, which would really be a book about teaching and learning.

But before I got started, Ruff told me that he and Mitchell were going to China to introduce jazz there. (The Chinese had never heard live American jazz.) Ruff said he had been taking intensive courses in Mandarin and felt that he was now fluent enough. I said I'd like to go along, and I asked *The New Yorker* if it would be interested in an article. The editor, William Shawn, said that it sounded like a good story and that I should aim for ten thousand words.

We flew to Shanghai, and there, on June 2, 1981, jazz came to China. Mitchell and Ruff gave a concert at the Shanghai Conservatory of Music for three hundred students and professors. As Ruff began to talk I could hardly contain my excitement over the antitheses that were at play in the room. We were in the oldest conservatory in the oldest literate society in the world, where students pride themselves on being able to play a piece of music exactly the same way over and over again, and they were listening to two black men, one of whom was speaking Chinese, and what he was explaining was an oral tradition that started in West Africa with drum language—a language so refined, Ruff said, that it could be used to tell stories and recite proverbs. "The drum is to West African society what the book is to literate society," he said. He could hardly have said anything more contrary to the culture of China.

Ruff explained how American jazz evolved out of those rhythms. But it took its harmonic elements, he said, from the Protestant hymns that the slaves were encouraged to embrace, and to illustrate the point he and Mitchell played and sang a beautiful old Negro spiritual called "My Lord, What a Morning!" As the only white American in the room, knowing that Mitchell and Ruff were the great-grandsons of slaves, I heard a faraway sadness that none of the Chinese would have heard. It was an extra overlay of emotion on a situation that already had enough. Next Ruff explained that the essence of jazz is improvisation. The Chinese don't even have a word for improvisation; Ruff translated it as "something created during the process of delivery."

Near the end of the concert, the two men played a number that I had never heard but that had an obvious shape: themes that had been stated earlier came back in different form. When it was over, Ruff said, "We call that 'Shanghai Blues'—we just made it up." The Chinese found that unbelievable, and they began to pour out questions about improvisation. Finally one old professor said, "Do you really mean you could improvise on any theme at all—one you had never heard before?" Ruff said, "I would like to invite one of you to come up here and play a Chinese melody, and we will make a piece out of that."

The room erupted in oohs—the kind you hear at the circus—and a young Chinese man came forward and played a very Chinese piece on the piano. It was his own composition, about fourteen bars long—stately and beautiful. Mitchell gave Ruff a look that said, "This time you've gone too far." But then he went to the piano and played the student's piece exactly—in the same key, and with the same chords, and with the same feeling. Then he began to embroider the piece, giving it a series of new lives but never violating its integrity, calling out the chord changes to Ruff on his bass. The Chinese were amazed; they saw that for a jazz musician no point of departure is alien; even their own musical traditions could be adapted with respect. Despite the huge gulf between the two cultures, music was finally the strongest force in the room.

I went back to New York and wrote my ten thousand words. Shawn called from *The New Yorker* to say that he liked the piece but that he would want to cut all the parts where I expressed an opinion about Mitchell and Ruff or their music. I thought, "That kills it—surely the reader needs to know why I admire these men as artists and teachers." But my second thought was to trust Shawn's judgment, and the piece was duly edited. None of my words were changed, but all interpretation or commentary was removed. I remained in the piece as a reporter, but not as a person.

When the article was published it had a stronger emotional impact than anything I had ever written. People said to my wife, "Bill knows those men very well, doesn't he?" That was a revelation to me. I realized that the material was so rich that any attempt to explain *why* it was rich would be patronizing. It would deprive readers of the pleasure of bringing their own emotions to whatever portions of the story happened to touch their own lives. In fact, many readers made connections—with music, with China, with education—that had never occurred to me. I saw that the reader plays a major role in the act of writing and must be given room to play it.

The Shanghai piece became the first chapter in *Willie and Dwike*. Then I started over, made a number of other trips with Mitchell and Ruff, and wrote the rest of the book: one chapter about Mitchell's boyhood in Florida, one about Ruff's boyhood in Alabama, one about the army base in Ohio where they met and were taught by a cadre of brilliant black musicians, one that trailed them through a winter week in the Midwest as they gave workshops in schools, one about Mitchell as a teacher and a pianist, and a final chapter about Ruff's trip to Venice to play Gregorian chants on his French horn in St. Mark's basilica, alone at night, to record its amazing acoustics.

Throughout, I applied the Shawn principle, trusting my material. It's very American material, full of small triumphs over the odds of being born black in America, and I began to take pleasure in it as material and in the task of organizing it: presenting the facts coherently and simply. *I* never made the point that it's hard to be born black in America; the narrative did that for me. The final manuscript doesn't even have any adverbs, like "surprisingly" or "predictably," that put a value on a fact before the reader encounters the fact. The result is a book that readers call "moving." But what makes it moving is its content.

I've recalled this experience because I hope it will help other writers as much as it helped me. It sharpened my awareness of how much writers add that doesn't need to be added, and how annoying this is to the reader. What's missing is what shouldn't be missing in the work of a careful writer: control.

In 1988 I put the same lessons to work when I wrote *Spring Training*. As a baseball book, it combined my lifelong vocation with my lifelong addiction, which is one of the best things that can happen to a writer. Writers of every age will write better and more confidently if they are allowed to write about what they care about. Affection for the subject is a tonic.

I chose spring training as my slice of the larger subject of baseball for several reasons. It's a time of renewal, both for the players and for the fans; American families have been making this annual pilgrimage to small towns in Florida since the early 1920s. It's also a time when the game is given back to us in its original purity: it's played outside, in the sun, on grass, without organ music or electronic scoreboards, by young men who are almost near enough to touch and whose owners, agents, salaries and umbrages are mercifully put aside for six weeks. But above all, spring training is a time of teaching and learning. I chose the

Pittsburgh Pirates as the team I would cover, partly because I liked their old-time ballpark in Bradenton, but mainly because they were a young club just starting to rebuild. Their manager, Jim Leyland, and his coaches were men who were committed to teaching.

One thing I knew was that I didn't want to romanticize the game. I can't stand baseball movies that go into slow motion when the batter hits a home run, to notify me that it's a pregnant moment. I *know* that about home runs—especially if they're hit with two out in the bottom of the ninth to win the game. I resolved not to let my writing go into slow motion—not to nudge the reader with significance—or to claim baseball as a metaphor for life, death, middle age, lost youth or a more innocent America. My premise was that baseball is a job—a form of honorable work—and I wanted to know how that job got learned.

So I went to Jim Leyland and his coaches and I said, "You're teachers. I'm a teacher. Tell me: How do you teach hitting? How do you teach pitching? How do you teach fielding? How do you teach baserunning? How do you keep these young men *up* for such a brutally long schedule?" I had the feeling that no other writer had called them "teacher"; in America the sacred word is "coach." All of them responded to the word and told me in detail how they do what they do. So did the players, and so did all the other people I approached—general managers, scouts, trainers, umpires, ticket sellers, fans—who possessed some kind of information that I wanted.

One day, for instance, I went up into the grandstand behind home plate to try to find a scout. Spring training is baseball's ultimate talent show, and the camps are infested with laconic men who have spent a lifetime looking at talent. I spotted an empty seat next to a man in his sixties who was using a stopwatch and taking extensive notes. When the inning was over I asked him what his name was and what he was timing. He gave me a card that identified him as Nick Kamzic, Northern Scouting Coordinator of the California Angels, and he said he was timing runners on the base paths. I asked what kind of speeds he was looking for.

"Well, it takes a right-handed batter 4.3 seconds to reach first base," he said, "and a left-handed batter 4.1 or 4.2 seconds. Naturally that varies a little—you've got to take the human element into consideration."

"What do those numbers tell you?" I asked.

"Well, of course the average double play takes 4.3 seconds," he said. He said it as if it was common knowledge. I realized that I had never given any thought to the elapsed time of a double play.

"So that means . . ."

"If you see a runner who gets to first base in less than 4.3 seconds you're interested in him."

That kind of information is the substance and strength of the book. As a set of facts it's self-sufficient. There's no need to add a sentence pointing out that 4.3 seconds is remarkably little time to execute a play that involves one batted ball, two thrown balls and three infielders. Given the figure 4.3 seconds, the reader can do his own marveling.

Umpires also need a spring tuneup, and they were another source of lore. One day I went into the umpires' dressing room before a Pirate game and found the home-plate umpire, a genial Iowan named Bob Davidson, sitting on a stool, methodically performing a rite that I didn't know was part of the game: taking the shine off the baseballs that would be used that afternoon.

On one side he had a bag of five dozen new official National League baseballs, duly certified by the signature of A. Bartlett

Giamatti, pres. In front of him on the floor was a tin can filled with a brown substance that looked like axle grease. I asked him what the stuff was.

"It's Delaware River mud," Davidson said. He explained that no other product of man or nature is so uniquely suited to getting the gloss off a new baseball without discoloring it. Because new baseballs are too slippery for a pitcher to fully control, it has long been the duty of the home-plate umpire to give them a rubdown before every major league game.

The procedure calls for an equal application of spit and mud. As we talked, Bob Davidson spat on his hands five dozen times, scooped out a dab of Delaware River mud and rubbed the resulting mixture into the ball. Nothing in his manner suggested that it was a chore or an indignity; they were the motions of a man washing his car or of a cowboy saddling his horse. I said I was surprised that home-plate umpires were stuck with such an inelegant task and couldn't get someone of lesser rank to do it for them. "It's no big deal," Davidson said. "Besides, it's a way to make sure that only the umpire touches the ball before it's put into play." The mud, I later learned, was discovered by Lena Blackburne, a coach of the Philadelphia Athletics, in Pennsauken Creek, a tributary of the Delaware, in 1938. It has been used ever since.

Trust your material. And when you go forth to gather that material, trust yourself. As a nonfiction writer you'll be repeatedly thrown into special worlds that you know almost nothing about, and you'll worry that you're not qualified to bring the story back out. I felt that anxiety when I went to Bradenton to write *Spring Training*. I had never done any sports reporting, never interviewed a professional athlete. Strictly, I had no credentials; any of the people I approached with my notebook could have asked, "What else have you written about baseball?" But nobody did. The reason they didn't is that I had another kind of credential: sincerity. It was obvious that I really wanted to know how those men did their work. Remember this when you enter strange or unfriendly territory and need a shot of confidence. Your best credential is yourself.

In urging you not to intrude on your material I obviously don't mean that that's the only way to write. (Chapter 20, on memoir, makes just the opposite point.) Different subjects call for different approaches. Your job is to present your material in the way that serves it best: to find the right voice and the right framework. Maybe you should be strongly present in your story; maybe not. Usually the material tells you at the start how it wants to be narrated. But after that the writer must be in charge, shaping and organizing. Organizing is the most unsung and untaught of the writing skills, but it's just as important as knowing how to write a clear and pleasing sentence. All your clear and pleasing sentences will add up to chaos if you don't keep remembering that writing is linear and sequential, that logic is the glue that holds it together, that tension must be maintained between every sentence and every paragraph, and that narrative—good old-fashioned storytelling—is what should pull the reader along without his ever noticing the tug. The only thing the reader should notice, subconsciously, is that you have made a sensible plan for the trip and know where you're going. Every step should seem inevitable.

If that sounds like an arduous journey, here's a final thought from spring training to take along. At some point every Pirate coach reminded me that baseball is a negative game: that a hitter who hits .300, which is the mark of greatness, fails seven times out of ten, or that a pitcher can pitch well and still lose because of errors, bad bounces or various other factors beyond his control. Something about the message struck a familiar echo. Then I thought, "Writing is a negative game—we're all .300 writers on our first draft." The good news is that with every revision and repair we're given a chance to raise our average.

23

A Writer's Decisions

This has been a book about decisions—the countless successive decisions that go into every piece of nonfiction writing. Some of the decisions are big ("What should I write about?") and some are as small as the smallest word. But all of them are important. In this next-to-last chapter I thought it might be helpful to show how some of those decisions get made—to provide a laboratory exhibit that illustrates the general points made in earlier chapters, using one of my own articles as the specimen being dissected. It's a travel piece, and I've added comments along the way explaining the decisions I made.

THE NEWS FROM TIMBUKTU

The hardest decision about any article is how to begin it. The lead must grab the reader with a provocative idea and continue with each paragraph to hold him in a tight grip, gradually adding information. The point of the information is to get readers so interested that they will stick around for the whole trip. The lead can be as short as one paragraph and as long as it needs to be. You'll know it's over when all the necessary work has been done and you can take a more relaxed tone and get on with your narrative. Here the first paragraph gives the reader an arresting notion to think about—one that I hope has never crossed his mind before.

What struck me most powerfully when I got to Timbuktu was that the streets were of sand. I suddenly realized that sand is very different from dirt. Every town starts with dirt streets that eventually get paved as the inhabitants prosper and subdue their environment. But sand represents defeat. A city with streets of sand is a city at the edge.

Notice how simple those five sentences are: plain declarative sentences, not a comma in sight. Each sentence contains one thought—and only one. Readers can process only one idea at a time, and they do it in linear sequence. Much of the trouble that writers get into comes from trying to make one sentence do too much work. Never be afraid to break a long sentence into two short ones, or even three.

That, of course, is why I was there: Timbuktu is the ultimate destination for edge-seekers. Of the half-dozen places that have always lured travelers with the mere sound of their name—Bali and Tahiti, Samarkand and Fez, Mombasa and Macao—none can match Timbuktu for the remoteness that it conveys. I was surprised by how many people, hearing of my trip, didn't think Timbuktu was a real place, or, if it was, couldn't think where in the world it might be. They knew it well as a word—the most vivid of all synonyms for the almost-unreachable, a God-given toy for songwriters stuck for an "oo" rhyme and a metaphor for how far a lovestruck boy would go to win the unwinnable girl. But as an actual place— surely Timbuktu was one of those "long-lost" African kingdoms like King Solomon's Mines that turned out not to exist when the Victorian explorers went looking for them.

The first sentence of that paragraph grows out of the last sentence of the previous paragraph; the reader is given no chance to squirm away. After that the paragraph has one purpose: it acknowledges what the reader already knows—or half knows—

about Timbuktu. It thereby welcomes him as a fellow traveler, someone who brings the same emotions to the trip as the writer himself. It also adds a certain kind of information—not hard facts, but enjoyable lore.

The following paragraph gets down to hard work—work that can't be put off any longer. Notice how much information is crammed into these three sentences:

> The long-lost Timbuktu, however, got found, though the men who finally found it after terrible ordeals—the Scotsman Gordon Laing in 1826 and the Frenchman René Caillié in 1828—must have felt cruelly mocked for their efforts. The legendary city of 100,000 people described by the 16th-century traveler Leo Africanus—a center of learning with 20,000 students and 180 Koranic schools—was a desolate settlement of mud buildings, its glory and its population long gone, surviving only because of its unique location as the junction of important camel caravan routes across the Sahara. Much of what got traded in Africa, especially salt from the north and gold from the south, got traded in Timbuktu.

So much for the history of Timbuktu and the reason for its fame. It's all that a magazine reader needs to know about the city's past and its significance. Don't give readers of a magazine piece more information than they require; if you want to tell more, write a book or write for a scholarly journal.

Now: What do your readers want to know next? Ask yourself that question after every sentence. Here what they want to know is: Why did *I* go to Timbuktu? What was the purpose of the trip? The following paragraph gets right to it—again, keeping the thread of the previous sentence taut:

> It was to watch the arrival of one of those caravans that I had come to Timbuktu. I was one of six men and women bright enough or dumb enough—we didn't yet know

which—to sign up for a two-week tour that we had seen
announced in the Sunday *New York Times,* run by a small
travel agency of French origins that specializes in West
Africa. (Timbuktu is in Mali, the former French Sudan.) The
agency's office is in New York, and I had gone there first thing
Monday morning to beat the crowd. I asked the usual questions and got the usual answers—yellow fever shots, cholera
shots, malaria pills, don't drink the water—and was given a
brochure.

Besides explaining the genesis of the trip, that paragraph does
one other job: it establishes the writer's personality and voice.
In travel writing you can never forget that you are the guide.
It's not enough just to take your readers on a trip; you must take
them on *your* trip. Make them identify with you—with your
hopes and apprehensions. This means giving them some idea of
who you are. For instance, the phrase "bright enough or dumb
enough" calls up a familiar figure in travel literature: the tourist
as a possible patsy or buffoon. Another throwaway phrase is the
line about beating the crowd. I put it in just to amuse myself.
Writing is a lonely occupation; if something strikes me as funny
in the act of writing, I assume that a few other people will also
find it funny, and that seems to me to be a good day's work.
Write for yourself.

Strictly, that fourth paragraph is too late to say where Timbuktu is. But I just couldn't find a way to mention it earlier
without pulling apart the tight fabric of the lead. Here's paragraph five:

"It's your opportunity to participate in a once-in-a-lifetime
extravaganza—the annual Azalai Salt Caravan to Timbuktu!"
the brochure began. "Picture this: Hundreds of camels carrying huge slabs of precious salt ('white gold' to the natives of
land-locked West Africa) make their triumphant entry into

Timbuktu, an ancient and mystical part desert/part city of some 7,000 inhabitants. The colorful nomads who drive the caravans have traveled 1,000 miles across the Sahara to celebrate the end of their trek with outdoor feasts and traditional tribal dances. Spend the night in a desert tent as guest of the tribal chief."

That's a typical example of how a writer can get other people to do helpful work for him—in their words, which are usually far more revealing than the writer's words. In this case the brochure not only tells the reader what kind of trip has been promised; its language is an amusement in itself and a window into the grandiosity of the promoters. Always be on the watch for funny or self-serving quotes and use them with gratitude. Here's the last paragraph of the lead:

Well, that's my kind of trip, if not necessarily my kind of prose, and it also turned out to be my wife's kind of trip and four other people's kind of trip. In years we ranged from late middle age to Medicare. Five of us were from mid-Manhattan, one was a widow from Maryland, and all of us had made a lifelong habit of traveling to places on the edge. Names like Venice and Versailles didn't bob up in our accounts of earlier trips, or even Marrakech or Luxor or Chiang Mai. The talk was of Bhutan and Borneo, Tibet and the Yemen and the Moluccas. Now—praise Allah!—we had made it to Timbuktu. Our camel caravan was about to come in.

*

That concludes the lead. Those six paragraphs took as long to write as the entire remainder of the piece. But when I had finally wrestled them into place I felt confidently launched. Maybe somebody else could write a better lead for that story, but *I* couldn't. I felt that readers who were still with me would stay to the end.

No less important than decisions about structure are decisions about individual words. Banality is the enemy of good writing; the challenge is to not write like everybody else. For example, a fact that had to be stated somewhere in the lead was how old the six of us were. Initially I wrote something serviceable like "we were in our fifties and sixties." But the merely serviceable is a drag. Was there any way to state the fact with freshness? There didn't seem to be. At last a merciful muse gave me Medicare—and thus the phrase "from late middle age to Medicare." If you look long enough you can usually find a proper name or a metaphor that will bring those dull but necessary facts to life.

Even more time went into the sentence about Venice and Versailles. Originally I wrote, "Names like London and Paris didn't turn up in our accounts of earlier trips." Not much fun there. I tried to think of other popular capitals. Rome and Cairo? Athens and Bangkok? No better. Maybe alliteration would help—readers enjoy (if only subconsciously) any effort to gratify their sense of rhythm and cadence. Madrid and Moscow? Tel Aviv and Tokyo? Too tricky. I stopped thinking of capitals and tried to think of tourist-infested cities. Venice popped into my head and I was glad to see it; everybody goes to Venice. Did any other cities begin with "V"? Only Vienna, which was too close to Venice in several ways. Finally I shifted my thinking from tourist cities to tourist sites, mentally fanning out from the major capitals, and it was on one of those excursions that I hit Versailles. It made my day.

Next I needed a fresher verb than "turn up." I wanted an active verb that conveyed an image. None of the usual synonyms was quite right. Finally I thought of "bob"—a three-letter word, ludicrously simple. Yet it was the perfect word: it paints a picture of an object periodically rising to the surface of the water. That left just one decision to complete the sentence: What slightly offbeat tourist sites would seem commonplace to six travelers who had signed up for Timbuktu? The three that I finally chose—Luxor, Marrakech and Chiang Mai—were quite exotic in the 1950s, when I first visited them. Today they're not; the age of jet travel has made them almost as popular as London and Paris.

Altogether, the sentence took almost an hour. But I didn't begrudge a minute of it. On the contrary, seeing it fall into place gave me great pleasure. No writing decision is too small to be worth a large expenditure of time. Both you and the reader know it when your finicky labor is rewarded by a sentence coming out right.

Notice that there's an asterisk at the end of the lead. (It could also be a line of blank space.) That asterisk is a signpost. It announces to the reader that you have organized your article in a certain way and that a new phase is about to begin— perhaps a change of chronology, such as a flashback, or a change of subject or emphasis or pace. Here, after a highly compressed lead, the asterisk enables the writer to take a deep breath and start over, this time at the more leisurely gait of a storyteller.

We got to Timbuktu by flying from New York to Abidjan, capital of the Ivory Coast, and taking a plane from there to Bamako, capital of Mali, its neighbor to the north. Unlike the verdant Ivory Coast, Mali is dry, its southern half nourished mainly by the Niger River, its upper half pure desert; Timbuktu is literally the last stop for travelers going north across the Sahara, or the first stop for travelers coming south—a coveted speck on the horizon after weeks of heat and thirst.

None of us on the tour knew much about Mali or what to expect of it—our thoughts were fixed on our rendezvous with the salt caravan at Timbuktu, not on the country we would cross to get there. What we didn't expect was that we would be so instantly taken with it. Mali was an immersion in color: handsome people wearing fabrics of intoxicating design, markets bright with fruits and vegetables, children whose smile was a routine miracle. Desperately poor, Mali was people-rich. The tree-lined city of Bamako delighted us with its energy and confidence.

Up early the next morning, we drove for ten hours in a van that had seen better days, but not much better days, to reach the holy city of Djenné, a medieval center of trade and Islamic scholarship on the Niger that predated Timbuktu and rivaled it in luster. Today Djenné can only be reached by a small ferry, and as we bounced over unspeakable roads, hurrying to arrive before dark, the spires and turrets of its great clay mosque, looking like a distant sandcastle, taunted us by seeming to recede. When we finally got there the mosque still looked like a sandcastle—an elegant fortress that might have been built by children on a beach. Architecturally (I later learned) it was in the Sudanese style; all these years, children on beaches have been building in the Sudanese style. To linger in Djenné's ancient square at dusk was a high moment of our trip.

The next two days were no less rich. One was spent driving into—and back out of—Dogon country. The Dogon, who live on an escarpment not easily reached by outsiders, are prized by anthropologists for their animist culture and cosmology and by art collectors for their masks and statues, and the few hours that we spent climbing around their villages and watching a masked dance gave us too brief a glimpse of a society that was far from simple. The second day was spent in Mopte, a vibrant market town on the Niger that we liked enormously and also left too soon. But we had a date in Timbuktu and a chartered plane to take us there.

Obviously there's far more to say about Mali than is jammed into those four paragraphs—many scholarly books have been written about the Dogon culture and the Niger River peoples. But this wasn't an article about Mali; it was about a quest for a camel caravan. Therefore a decision had to made about the larger shape of the piece. My decision was to get across Mali as fast as possible—to explain in the barest number of sentences what route we took and what was important about the places where we stopped.

At such moments I ask myself one very helpful question: "What is the piece *really* about?" (Not just "What is the piece about?") Fondness for material that you've gone to a lot of trouble to gather isn't a good enough reason to include it if it's not central to the story you've chosen to tell. Self-discipline bordering on masochism is required. The only consolation I can offer for the loss of so much material is that it isn't totally lost. It remains in your writing as an intangible that the reader can sense. Readers should always feel that you know more about your subject than you've put in writing.

Back to "But we had a date in Timbuktu":

The exactness of that date was what had worried me most when I visited the travel agency. I asked the head of the agency how she could be so sure that the salt caravan would arrive on December 2; nomads leading camels aren't my idea of people operating on a timetable. My wife, who isn't cursed with my optimism about such life forces as camels and travel agents, was certain we would be told at Timbuktu that the salt caravan had come and gone, or, more probably, hadn't been heard from at all. The travel agent scoffed at my question.

"We're in close touch with the caravan," she said. "We send scouts into the desert. If they tell us the caravan is going to be a few days late we can juggle your itinerary in Mali." That made sense to me—optimists can make sense of anything— and now I was in a plane not much bigger than Lindbergh's, flying north toward Timbuktu over terrain so barren that I saw no sign of human habitation below. Simultaneously, however, hundreds of camels carrying huge slabs of salt were moving south to meet me. Even now tribal chiefs were turning their thoughts to how to entertain me in their desert tent.

Both of the preceding paragraphs contain touches of humor—tiny jokes. Again, they are efforts to keep myself amused. But they are also a deliberate attempt to maintain a persona. One of the oldest strains in travel writing and humor writing is the eternal credulity of the narrator. Used in moderation, making yourself gullible—or downright stupid—gives the reader the enormous pleasure of feeling superior.

> Our pilot circled over Timbuktu to give us an aerial view of the city we had traveled so far to see. It was a large sprawl of mud buildings that looked long abandoned, as dead as Fort Zinderneuf at the end of *Beau Geste;* surely nobody was alive down there. The Sahara in its steady encroachment, which has created the drought belt across central Africa known as the Sahel, had long since pushed past Timbuktu and left it marooned. I felt a tremor of fear; I didn't want to be put down in such a forsaken place.

The reference to *Beau Geste* is an effort to tap into associations that readers bring to the story. Much of what makes Timbuktu legendary was put there by Hollywood. By invoking the fate of Fort Zinderneuf—Brian Donlevy played a sadistic French Foreign Legion commandant who propped the dead bodies of his soldiers back into the niches of the fort—I'm revealing my own fondness for the genre and striking a bond with fellow movie buffs. What I'm after is resonance; it can do a great deal of emotional work that writers can't achieve on their own.

Two words—"tremor" and "forsaken"—took a while to find. In fact, when I found "forsaken" in my *Roget's Thesaurus* I was quite sure I had never used it before. I was glad to see it there among the synonyms. As one of Jesus' last words (speaking of resonance), it could hardly convey more loneliness and abandonment.

At the airport we were met by our local guide, a Tuareg named Mohammed Ali. For a travel buff he was a consoling sight—if anybody can be said to own this part of the Sahara, it is the Tuareg, a race of proud Berbers who wouldn't submit to the Arabs or the later French colonials who swept into North Africa, withdrawing instead into the desert and making it their preserve. Mohammed Ali, who was wearing the traditional blue robe of Tuareg men, had a dark, intelligent face, somewhat Arabic in the angularity of its features, and he moved with an assurance that was obviously part of his character. As a teen-ager, it turned out, he had gone with his father on the *haj* to Mecca (many Tuareg eventually converted to Islam) and had stayed for seven years in Arabia and Egypt to study English, French and Arabic. The Tuareg have a language of their own, with a complex written alphabet, called Tamashek.

Mohammed Ali said he had to take us first to the police station in Timbuktu to have our passports checked. I've seen too many movies to feel comfortable in this kind of interview situation, and as we sat in a dungeon-like room being interrogated by two armed policemen, not far from a jail cell where we could see a man and a boy sleeping, I had another flashback—this one to *The Four Feathers* and the scene of the British soldiers long imprisoned at Omdurman. The oppressiveness stayed with me when we got back out and Mohammed Ali walked us through the forlorn city, dutifully showing us its few "points of interest": the Grand Mosque, the market, and three dilapidated houses, commemorated by

plaques, where Laing, Caillié and the German explorer Hein-
rich Barth lived. We didn't see any other tourists.

*

Again, the *Four Feathers* allusion, like the mention of *Beau
Geste,* will bring a chill of recognition to anyone who knows the
movie. The fact that the movie was based on a real campaign—
Kitchener's expedition up the Nile to avenge the Mahdi's defeat
of General Gordon—gives the sentence an edge of real fear.
Obviously Arab justice in outposts of the Sahara is still far from
merciful.

Once more the asterisk announces a change of mood. It says,
in effect: "So much for Timbuktu itself. Now we're going to get
down to the real business of the story: looking for the camel
caravan." Making these divisions in a long and complex article
not only helps the reader to follow your road map. It also takes
some of the fear out of the act of writing, enabling you to break
your material into manageable chunks and to take one chunk
at a time. The total task seems less formidable, and panic is
staved off.

At the Azalai Hotel, where we appeared to be the only
guests, we asked Mohammed Ali how many tourists were in
Timbuktu to greet the salt caravan.

"Six," he said. "The six of you."

"But . . ." Something in me didn't want to finish the sentence. I took a different approach. "I don't quite understand
what this word 'Azalai' means. Why is it called the Azalai Salt
Caravan?"

"That's the word the French used," he said, "when they
organized the caravan and all the camels made the trip together once a year, around the beginning of December."

"What do they do now?" several voices asked.

"Well, when Mali got its independence they decided to let the traders bring their salt caravans to Timbuktu whenever they wanted to."

Mali got its independence in 1960. We were in Timbuktu for an event that hadn't been held in 27 years.

The last sentence is a small bomb dropped into the middle of the story. But it's allowed to speak for itself—just the facts, please—without comment. I didn't add an exclamation point to notify readers that it was an amazing moment. That would have spoiled the pleasure of realizing it on their own. Trust your material.

My wife, among others, was not surprised. We took the news calmly: old travel hands who have faith that they will find their camel caravan one way or another. Mainly our reaction was one of amazement that the canons of truth-in-advertising had been so brazenly disregarded. Mohammed Ali knew nothing about the gaudy promises tendered by the brochure. He only knew he had been hired to take us to meet a salt caravan, and he told us that in the morning we would go looking for one and would spend the night in the Sahara. Early December, he said, was the usual time for caravans to start arriving. He didn't say anything about a chieftain's tent.

More carefully chosen words: "canons," "brazenly," "gaudy," "tendered." They're vivid and precise. Best of all, they are words that readers probably weren't expecting and that they therefore welcome.

The sentence about the chieftain's tent, referring back to a phrase in the brochure, is another tiny joke. These "snappers" at the end of a paragraph propel the reader into the next paragraph and keep him in a good mood.

In the morning my wife—a voice of reason at the edge of infinity—said she wouldn't go into the Sahara unless we went in two vehicles. I was therefore glad to see two Land Rovers awaiting us outside the hotel. One of them was having its front tire pumped up by a boy with a bicycle pump. Four of us squeezed into the back seat of one Land Rover; Mohammed Ali sat in front, next to the driver. The second Land Rover took our other two tour members and two boys who were described as "apprentices." Nobody said what they were apprenticing for.

Another startling fact that needs no embellishment—the tire-pumping—and another small joke at the end.

We drove straight out into the Sahara. The desert was a brown blanket without any end and with no tracks of any kind; the next big town was Algiers. That was the moment when I felt most at the edge, when a small voice said, "This is crazy. Why are you doing this?" But I knew why; I was on a quest that I could trace back to my first encounters with the books of Britain's "desert eccentrics"—solitaries such as Charles Doughty, Richard Burton, T. E. Lawrence and Wilfred Thesiger, who lived among the Bedouin. I had always wondered what that austere existence was like. What was its hold over those obsessed Englishmen?

More resonance. The reference to Doughty and his compatriots makes the point that the desert has a written literature no less powerful than its movie literature. It adds one more item to the emotional baggage that I was carrying and that the reader is entitled to know about.

The following sentence answers the question that ended the previous paragraph:

Now I was starting to find out. As we drove over the sand, Mohammed Ali gave the driver an occasional gesture: a little more to the right, a little more to the left. We asked how he knew where he was going. He said he could tell by the dunes. The dunes, however, all looked alike. We asked how long we would have to drive to find a salt caravan. Mohammed Ali said he hoped it wouldn't be more than three or four hours. We kept driving. To my object-oriented eye there was almost nothing to see. But after a while the almost-nothingness became an object in itself—the entire point of the desert. I tried to get that fact into my metabolism. It lulled me into a certain acceptance and I totally forgot why we were out there.

Suddenly the driver made a sharp left and came to a stop. "Camels," he said. I strained my urban eyes and didn't see anything. Then it came into focus, far away: a caravan of forty camels moving at a stately gait toward Timbuktu, as camel caravans had for a thousand years, bringing salt from the mines at Taoudenni, twenty days to the north. We drove to within a hundred yards of the caravan—no nearer, Mohammed Ali explained, because camels are nervous creatures, easily panicked by anything "strange." (We were undeniably strange.) He said that the camels are always brought into Timbuktu to unload the salt late at night, when the city is empty of people. So much for the "triumphant entry."

It was a thrilling sight, far more dramatic than the organized march would have been. The aloneness of the caravan was the aloneness of every caravan that had ever crossed the Sahara. The camels were hitched to each other and seemed to be walking in unison, as precise as Rockettes in their undulating rhythm. Each camel had two slabs of salt roped to each side. The salt looked like dirty white marble. The slabs (which I subsequently measured in the Timbuktu market) are 3½ feet long, 1½ feet wide, and ¾ inch thick—the maximum size and weight, presumably, that can be loaded onto a camel.

We sat on the sand and watched the caravan until the last
camel disappeared over a dune.

The tone has now settled into straight narrative—one declarative sentence after another. The only troublesome decision involved "aloneness," which is not my kind of word—it's too
"poetic." But I finally decided that there was no other word that
could do the same job, and I reluctantly stayed with it.

By now it was midday and the sun was fiercely hot. We
climbed back in our Land Rovers and drove farther into the
desert until Mohammed Ali found a tree that cast a shadow
just big enough for five New Yorkers and a widow from Maryland, and there we stayed until about 4, having a picnic lunch,
gazing at the bleached-out landscape, dozing, moving our
blanket periodically as our shadow moved with the sun. The
two drivers spent the entire siesta tinkering with and seeming to dismantle the engine of one of the Land Rovers. A
nomad appeared from nowhere and stopped to ask if we had
any quinine. Another nomad appeared from nowhere and
stopped briefly to talk. Later we saw two men walking toward
us across the desert and beyond them . . . was it our first
mirage? It was another salt caravan, this one fifty camels long,
silhouetted against the sky. Spotting us from God knows how
far away, the two men had left the caravan to come over for
a visit. One of them was an old man, full of laughter. They sat
down with Mohammed Ali and got the latest news of Timbuktu.

The hardest sentence in that paragraph was the one about the
drivers tinkering with the Land Rovers. I wanted it to be as
simple as all the other sentences and yet to have a small surprise
tucked into it—a wry touch of humor. Otherwise, my purpose

at this point was to tell the remainder of the story as simply and directly as possible:

So the four hours passed before we knew they were gone, as if we had slipped into a different time zone, Sahara time, and in the late afternoon, when the sun's heat had begun to ebb, we got back into our Land Rovers, which, to my surprise, still worked, and set out across the Sahara for what Mohammed Ali called our "encampment." I pictured, if not a chieftain's tent, at least a tent—something that announced itself as an encampment. When we finally did stop, it was at a spot that looked strikingly similar to what we had been driving over all day. It did, however, have one small tree. Some Bedouin women were crouched under it—black-garbed figures, their faces veiled—and Mohammed Ali put us down on the desert next to them.

The women shrank back at the sight of us—white aliens dumped abruptly in their midst. They were huddled so close together that they looked like a frieze. Obviously Mohammed Ali had just stopped at the first sight of "local color" that he happened to find for his tourists, counting on us to manage for ourselves after that. We could only sit and try to look friendly. But we were very conscious of being intruders, and we probably looked as uncomfortable as we felt. Only after we had sat there for a while did the black frieze slowly come apart and turn into four women, three children and two naked babies. Mohammed Ali had gone off somewhere, seemingly not wanting to have anything to do with the Bedouins; perhaps as a Tuareg he considered them desert riffraff.

But it was the Bedouins who had the grace to put us at ease. One of the women, lowering her veil and revealing a movie star's smile—white teeth and shining black eyes in a beautiful face—rummaged in her belongings, pulled out a blanket and a straw mat, and brought them over for us to sit on. I remembered from all those books that in the desert there's no such thing as an intruder; anyone who turns up is somehow expected. Soon after that, two Bedouin men came in from the desert, completing the family unit, which, we now saw, consisted of two men, two wives for each man, and their various children. The older husband, who had a strong and handsome face, greeted both of his wives with a gentle tap on the head, somewhat like a blessing, and then sat down not far from me. One of the women brought him his dinner—some millet in a bowl. He immediately offered the bowl to me. I declined, but the offer is one that I won't forget. We sat in companionable silence while he ate. The children came over to get acquainted. The sun went down and a full moon came up over the Sahara.

Meanwhile our drivers had spread some blankets next to the two Land Rovers and started a fire with desert wood. We regrouped on our own blankets, watched the stars coming out in the desert sky, had some kind of chicken for dinner, and got ready to turn in. Bathroom facilities were ad hoc—to each his own. We had been warned that Sahara nights were cold and had brought sweaters along. I put on my sweater, rolled up in a blanket, which slightly softened the hardness of the desert, and fell asleep surrounded by an immense stillness. An hour later I was awakened by an equally immense racket—our Bedouins had brought their herd of goats and their camels in for the night; Times Square doesn't get any noisier. Then all was quiet again.

In the morning I noticed paw prints in the sand next to my blanket. Mohammed Ali said that a jackal had come by to clean up the leftovers from our dinner—of which, as I recalled the chicken, there must have been quite a few. But I didn't hear a thing. I was too busy dreaming that I was Lawrence of Arabia.

[END]

One of the most important decisions about a piece of writing is where to end it. Often the story will tell you where it wants to end. In this case my ending was not the one I had in mind. Because the goal of our trip was to find a salt caravan, I assumed that in my article I would have to complete the ancient cycle of trade: to describe how we returned to Timbuktu and saw the salt being unloaded in the market and bought and sold. But the nearer I got to writing that final section, the more I didn't want to write it. It loomed as drudgery, no fun either for me or for the reader.

Suddenly I realized that I was under no obligation to the actual shape of our trip. I didn't have to reconstruct *everything*. The real climax of my story was not finding the salt caravan; it was finding the timeless hospitality of the people who lived in the Sahara. Not many moments in my life have matched the one when a family of nomads with almost no possessions offered me their dinner. Nor could any other moment distill more vividly what I had come to the desert to find and what all those Englishmen had written about—the nobility of living on the edge.

When you get such a message from your material—when your story tells you that it's over, regardless of what subsequently happened—look for the door. I got out fast, pausing only long enough to make sure that the unities were still intact: that the writer-guide who started the trip was the same person who was ending it. The playful reference to Lawrence preserves the persona, wraps up a multitude of associations and brings the journey full circle. The realization that I could just stop was a terrific feeling, not only because my labors were over but because the ending felt right. It was the correct decision.

As a postscript, there's one last decision I'd like to mention. It has to do with the nonfiction writer's need to make his own luck. An exhortation that I often use to keep myself going is "Get on the plane." When Willie Ruff told me he was going to

Shanghai and to Venice (pp. 237–240), he had no assurance that he would be allowed to play music in either of those cities; I might have wasted my time and money by deciding to go along. But I got on the plane, and the two experiences that Ruff gave me—one in the Shanghai Conservatory, the other in St. Mark's basilica at night—were two of the most intense moments of my life. By no coincidence, the articles I wrote about those two trips are my two best articles. I got on the plane to Timbuktu to look for a camel caravan that was an even bet not to materialize, and I got on the plane to Bradenton for spring training not knowing if I would be welcomed or rebuffed. My book *Writing to Learn* was born because of one phone call from a stranger: it raised an idea so interesting that I got on the plane to Minnesota to pursue it. Getting on the plane has taken me to unusual stories all over the world, and every year it takes me all over America. That isn't to say I'm not nervous when I leave for the airport; I always am—that's part of the deal. (A little nervousness gives writing an edge.) But I'm always replenished when I get back home.

As a nonfiction writer you must get on the plane. If a subject interests you, go after it, even if it's in the next county or the next state or the next country. It's not going to come looking for you. Decide what you want to do. Then decide to do it. Then do it.

24

Write as Well as You Can

I'm occasionally asked if I can recall the moment when I knew I wanted to be a writer. No such blinding flash occurred; I only knew that I thought I'd like to work for a newspaper. But I can point to a set of attitudes that I inherited early in life and that have guided me ever since. They came from both sides of my family, by totally different routes.

My mother loved good writing, and she found it as often in newspapers as she did in books. She regularly clipped columns and articles out of the paper that delighted her with their graceful use of language, or their wit, or their original vision of life. Because of her I knew at an early age that good writing can appear anywhere, even in the lowly newspaper, and that what matters is the writing itself, not the medium in which it is published. Therefore I've always tried to write as well as I could by my own standards; I've never changed my style to fit the size or the presumed education of the audience I was writing for. My mother was also a person of tremendous humor and optimism. These are lubricants in writing, as they are in life, and a writer lucky enough to have them in his baggage will start the day with an extra round of confidence.

Originally I wasn't meant to be a writer. My father was a businessman. His grandfather had come from Germany in the great immigration of 1848 with a formula for making shellac.

He built a small house and factory in a rocky field far uptown in Manhattan—at what is now Fifty-ninth Street and Tenth Avenue—and started a business called William Zinsser & Company. I still have a photograph of that pastoral scene; the land slopes down toward the Hudson River, and the only living creature is a goat. The firm stayed at that location until 1973, when it moved to New Jersey.

For a business to remain in the same family on the same Manhattan block for more than a century is rare, and as a boy I couldn't escape the naggings of continuity, for I was the fourth William Zinsser and the only son; my father's fate was to have three daughters first. In those Dark Ages the idea that daughters could run a business as well as sons, or better, was still twenty years off. My father was a man who loved his business. When he talked about it I never felt that he regarded it as a venture for making money, but as an art, to be practiced with imagination and only the best materials. He had a passion for quality and had no patience with the second-rate. As far as I know, he never went into a store looking for a bargain. He charged more for his product because he made it with the best ingredients, and his company prospered. It was a ready-made future for me, and my father looked forward to the day when I would join him.

But inevitably a different day arrived, and not long after I came home from the army I got a job on the *New York Herald Tribune* and had to tell my father that I wasn't going to carry on the family business. He accepted the news with his usual generosity and wished me well in my chosen field. I couldn't have received a finer gift. I was liberated from having to fulfill somebody else's expectations, which were not the right ones for me. I was free to succeed or fail on my own terms.

Only later did I realize that I took along on my journey another gift from my father: a bone-deep belief that quality is its own reward. I, too, have never gone into a store looking for a bargain. Ironically, though my mother was the literary one in our family—magpie collector of books, lover of the English language, writer of dazzling letters—it was from the world of business that I absorbed my craftsman's ethic, and over the years, when I found myself endlessly rewriting what I had endlessly rewritten, determined to write better than everybody else who was competing for the same space, the inner voice that I was hearing was the voice of my father talking about shellac.

Besides wanting to write as well as possible, I wanted to write as entertainingly as possible. When I tell aspiring writers that they should think of themselves as part entertainer, they don't like to hear it—the word smacks of carnivals and jugglers and clowns. But to succeed you must make your piece jump out of a newspaper or a magazine by being more diverting than everyone else's piece. You must find some way to elevate your act of writing into an entertainment. Usually this means giving the reader an enjoyable surprise. Any number of methods will do the job: humor, anecdote, paradox, an unexpected quotation, a powerful fact, an outlandish detail, a circuitous approach, an elegant arrangement of words. These seeming amusements in fact become your "style." When we say that we like a writer's style, what we mean is that we like his personality as he expresses it on paper. Given a choice between two traveling companions—and a writer is someone who asks us to travel with him—we usually choose the one who we think will make an effort to brighten the trip.

Unlike medicine or the other sciences, writing has no new discoveries to spring on us. We're in no danger of reading in our morning newspaper that a breakthrough has been made in how to write a clear English sentence—that information has been around since the King James Bible. We know, for instance, that verbs have more vigor than nouns, that active verbs are better than passive verbs, that short words and sentences are easier to read than long ones, that concrete details are easier to picture than vague abstractions.

Obviously the rules have often been bent. Victorian writers had a taste for the ornate and didn't consider brevity a virtue, and many modern writers—like Tom Wolfe and Norman Mailer today—have broken out of the cage, turning a headlong exuberance of language into a source of positive energy. Such skillful acrobats, however, are rare; most nonfiction writers will do well to cling to the ropes of simplicity and clarity. We may be given new technologies like the word processor to ease the burdens of composition, but on the whole we know what we need to know. We're all working with the same words and the same principles.

Where, then, is the edge? Ninety percent of the answer lies in the hard work of mastering the tools discussed in this book. Add a few percentage points for such natural gifts as a good ear, a sense of rhythm and a feeling for words. But the final advantage is the same one that applies in every other competitive venture. If you would like to write better than everybody else, you have to *want* to write better than everybody else. You must take an obsessive pride in the smallest details of your craft. And you must be willing to defend what you've written against the various middlemen—editors, agents and publishers—whose sights may be different from yours, or whose standards may not be as high. Too many writers are browbeaten into settling for less than their best.

I've always felt that my "style"—the careful projection onto paper of who I think I am—was my only marketable asset, the only possession that might set me apart from other writers. Therefore I've never wanted anyone to fiddle with it, and after I submit an article I protect it fiercely. Several magazine editors have told me that I'm the only writer they know who cares what happens to his piece after he gets paid for it. Most writers won't argue with an editor because they don't want to annoy him;

they're so grateful to be published that they agree to having their style—in other words, their personality—violated in public.

But to defend what you've written is a sign that you are alive. I'm a known crank on this issue—I fight over every semicolon—but editors put up with me because they can see that I'm serious. In fact, my crankiness has brought me more work than it has driven away. Editors with an unusual assignment often thought of me because they knew I would do it with unusual care. They also knew, incidentally, that they would get it on time and that it would be accurate. Remember that the craft of nonfiction writing involves more than writing; it also means being reliable. Editors will properly drop a writer they can't count on.

Which brings us to editors. Are they friends or enemies—gods who save us from our sins or bums who trample on our poetic souls? Like the rest of creation, they come in all varieties. I think with gratitude of a half-dozen editors who sharpened my writing by changing its focus or its emphasis, or questioning its tone, or detecting weaknesses of logic or structure, or suggesting a different lead, or letting me talk a problem through with them when I couldn't decide between several possible routes, or cutting various forms of excess. Twice I threw out an entire chapter of a book because editors told me the chapter was unnecessary—and in both cases they were right. But above all I remember those good editors for their generosity. They had an enthusiasm for whatever project we were trying to bring off together as writer and editor. Their confidence that I could make it work kept me going.

What a good editor brings to a piece of writing is an objective eye that the writer has long since lost, and there is no end of ways in which an editor can improve a manuscript: pruning, shaping, clarifying, tidying a hundred inconsistencies of tense and pronoun and location and tone, noticing all the sentences that could be read in two different ways, dividing awkward long sentences into short ones, putting the writer back on the main road if he has strayed down a side path, building bridges where the writer has lost the reader by not paying attention to his transitions. An editor's hand must also be invisible. Whatever he adds in his own words shouldn't sound like his own words; they should sound like the writer's words.

For all these acts of salvation, editors can't be thanked fervently enough. Unfortunately, they can also do considerable harm. In general the damage takes two forms: altering style and altering content. Let's look at style first.

A good editor likes nothing better than a piece of copy he hardly has to touch. A bad editor has a compulsion to tinker, proving with busywork that he hasn't forgotten the minutiae of grammar and usage. He is a literal fellow, catching cracks in the road but not enjoying the scenery. Very often, for instance, it simply doesn't occur to him that a writer is writing by ear, trying to achieve a particular sound or cadence, or playing with words just for the pleasures of wordplay. One of the bleakest moments for writers is the one when they realize that their editor has missed the point of what they are trying to do.

I remember many such dismal revelations. A minor one that comes to mind involved an article I wrote about a program called Visiting Artists, which brought artists and musicians to a group of Midwestern cities that were economically depressed. Describing them, I wrote: "They don't look like cities that get visited by many visiting artists." When the galleys came back the sentence said: "They don't look like cities that are on the itinerary of many visiting artists." A small point? Not to me. I had used repetition because it's a device I like—it takes the reader by surprise and refreshes him in midsentence. But the editor remembered the rule about substituting synonyms for words that are repeated, and he corrected my error. When I called to protest, he was amazed. We argued for a long time, neither of us yielding. Finally he said, "You really feel strongly about this, don't you?" I feel strongly that one such erosion leads to another and that the writer must take a stand. I've even bought articles back from magazines that made changes I wouldn't accept. If you allow your distinctiveness to be edited out you will lose one of your main advantages.

Ideally the relationship between a writer and an editor should be one of negotiation and trust. Frequently, for example, an editor will make a change to clarify a muddy sentence and will inadvertently lose an important point—a fact or a nuance that the writer included for reasons the editor didn't know about. In such cases the writer should ask to have his point back. The editor, if he agrees, should oblige. But he should also insist on his right to fix whatever had been unclear. Clarity is what every editor owes the reader. An editor should never allow something to get into print that he doesn't understand himself. If he doesn't understand it, at least one other person won't understand it, and that's one too many. The process, in short, is one in which the writer and the editor proceed through the manuscript together, finding for every problem the solution that best serves the finished article.

It's a process, incidentally, that can be done just as well over the phone as in person. Don't let editors use distance or their own disarray as an excuse for altering your work without your consent. "We were on deadline," "we were already late," "the person who usually deals with you was out sick," "we had a big shake-up here last week, "it got put in the wrong pile," "the editor's on vacation"—these dreary phrases cloak a multitude of inefficiencies and sins. One startling change in the publishing profession has been the erosion of courtesies that were once routine. Magazine editors, especially, have become cavalier about a whole series of actions that should be automatic: notifying the writer that the piece has arrived, reading it with reasonable speed, telling the writer whether it's O.K., returning it immediately if it's not, working supportively with the writer if the piece needs changes, sending the writer galley proofs, seeing that the writer gets paid promptly. Writers are vulnerable enough without being put through the repeated indignities of writing or calling to learn the status of their article and to beg for their money. The prevailing notion seems to be that "courtesies" are merely frills and can therefore be forgotten. On the contrary, they are organic to the craft. They are the code of honor that anchors the whole enterprise, and editors who forget them are toying with nothing less than the writer's fundamental rights.

This arrogance is at its most injurious when an editor goes beyond changes of style or structure and enters the sacred realm of content. I often hear free-lance writers say something like this: "When I got the magazine I looked for my article and I didn't even recognize it. They had written a whole new lead and had me saying a lot of things that aren't what I believe at all."

That's the cardinal sin—tampering with a writer's opinions. But editors will do what writers let them do, especially if time is short. Writers acquiesce in their own humiliation. With every surrender they remind editors that they can be treated like hired help. In part this treatment grows out of the rise of the special-interest magazine. A generation ago America had many magazines that took the whole world as their domain, like the old *Life* and *Saturday Evening Post,* and their writers were generalists who brought individuality to their articles. Today there are far more magazines, but most of them were created to provide information about one specialized field. The result is a nation of magazines that are being edited by formula. The editors feel secure with their formula and don't want—God forbid—a fresh approach. A writer who tries something novel will often find his piece rewritten by the editors to serve their own purposes.

But finally the purposes that writers serve must be their own. What you write is yours and nobody else's. Take your talent as far as you can and guard it with your life. Only you know how far that is; no editor knows. Writing well means believing in your writing and believing in yourself, taking risks, daring to be different, pushing yourself to excel. You will only write as well as you make yourself write.

My favorite definition of a careful writer comes from Joe DiMaggio, though he didn't know that that's what he was defining. DiMaggio was the greatest player I ever saw, and nobody looked more relaxed. He covered vast distances in the outfield, moving in graceful strides, always arriving ahead of the ball, making the hardest catch look routine, and even when he was at bat, hitting the ball with tremendous power, he didn't appear to be exerting himself. I marveled at how effortless he looked because what he did could only be achieved by great effort. A reporter once asked him how he managed to play so well so consistently, and he said: "I always thought that there was at least one person in the stands who had never seen me play, and I didn't want to let him down."

Sources

Most of the material that I have quoted in these pages was first written for a magazine or a newspaper and was subsequently reprinted in a book. In general the source cited below is for the original hardcover edition of the book. Many of these editions are now out of print but are available in public libraries. In many other cases the book has been reprinted in paperback and is quite easy to obtain.

P 29–30. Preface by E. B. White to *A Basic Chicken Guide* by Roy E. Jones. Copyright 1944 by Roy E. Jones. Reprinted by permission of William Morrow & Co. Also appears in *The Second Tree from the Corner.* Harper & Bros., 1954.

P 30–31. "The Hills of Zion," by H. L. Mencken, from *The Vintage Mencken,* gathered by Alistair Cooke. Vintage Books (paper), 1955.

P 32–33. *How to Survive in Your Native Land,* by James Herndon. Simon & Schuster, 1971. Reprinted by permission of Simon & Schuster, a division of Gulf & Western Corporation.

P 66–68. *The Lunacy Boom,* by William Zinsser. Harper & Row, 1970.

P 70–71. *Slouching Toward Bethlehem,* by Joan Didion. Farrar, Straus & Giroux, 1968. Copyright © 1966 Joan Didion. Reprinted by permission of the publisher.

P 72–73. *The Dead Sea Scrolls 1947–1969,* by Edmund Wilson. Copyright © 1955 by Edmund Wilson. Renewal copyright © 1983 by Helen Miranda Wilson. Reprinted by permission of Farrar, Straus & Giroux, Inc.

P 73–74. "The Last Time I Played Rugby," by Richard Burton. From *The Observer* (London), Oct. 4, 1970.

P 77. *Nixon Agonistes,* by Gary Wills. Houghton Mifflin, 1970. Reprinted by permission of the publisher.

P 78. "Coolidge," by H. L. Mencken, from *The Vintage Mencken.*

P 78–79. *Iron and Silk,* by Mark Salzman. Copyright © 1986 by Mark Salzman. Reprinted by permission of Random House, Inc.

P 80. *Pop Goes America,* by William Zinsser. Harper & Row, 1966.

P 92–93. *The Bottom of the Harbor,* by Joseph Mitchell. Little, Brown and Company, 1960. Reprinted by permission of Harold Ober Associates, Inc. © 1960 by Joseph Mitchell.

P 97–98. *Slouching Toward Bethlehem.*

P 98–99. *Coming into the Country,* by John McPhee. Farrar, Straus & Giroux, 1977.

P 100. *Fierce Attachments,* by Vivian Gornick. Simon & Schuster (Touchstone paperback), 1988.

P 101. "The South of East Texas," by Prudence Mackintosh. From *Texas Monthly,* October 1989.

P 101–2. *The Right Stuff,* by Tom Wolfe. Copyright © 1979 by Tom Wolfe. Reprinted by permission of Farrar, Straus & Giroux, Inc.

P 103–4. *The Offensive Traveler,* by V. S. Pritchett. Alfred A. Knopf, 1964.

P 106–7. *The White Nile,* by Alan Moorehead. Copyright © 1961 by the author. Reprinted by permission of Harper & Row, Publishers, Inc.

P 134–36. "Brain Signals in Test Foretell Action," Feb. 13, 1971, by Harold M. Schmeck, Jr. © 1971 by The New York Times Company. Reprinted by permission.

P 136–37. "The Mystery of Memory," by Will Bradbury. *Life,* Nov. 12, 1971. © 1971, Time Inc. Reprinted by permission.

P 138. *Eleven Blue Men and Other Narratives of Medical Detection,* by Berton Rouché. Little, Brown and Company, 1954.

P 139–40. *Beyond Habitat,* by Moshe Safdie. The M.I.T. Press, 1970.

P 140–41. "Bats," by Diane Ackerman. From *The New Yorker,* Feb. 28, 1988.

P 142. *The Immense Journey,* by Loren Eiseley. Random House, 1957.

P 142–43. *The Lives of a Cell: Notes of a Biology Watcher,* by Lewis Thomas. Viking Press, 1974.

P 143–44. "A Normal River Doesn't Have a Waterfall," by Dava Sobel. From *Harvard Magazine,* March–April 1980.

P 145–46. *The Adventures of a Mathematician,* by S. M. Ulam. Copyright © 1976, 1983 by S. M. Ulam. Reprinted by permission of Charles Scribner's Sons, an imprint of Macmillan Publishing Company.

P 148. From George Orwell's essay "Politics and the English Language."

P 164. "Hub Fans Bid Kid Adieu," by John Updike. From *Assorted Prose*, by John Updike. Alfred A. Knopf, 1965.

P 166–67. *Life on the Run*, by Bill Bradley. Quadrangle/The New York Times Book Co., 1976.

P 167–68. "Breaking Away," by Janice Kaplan. From *Vogue*, January 1984.

P 169. "Cliffhanger," by Trip Gabriel. New York Times Magazine, Dec. 31, 1989. Copyright © 1989 by the New York Times Company. Reprinted by permission.

P 169–70. "Politics of Sports," by Janice Kaplan. From *Vogue*, July 1984.

P 170–71. "In Indiana, The Roar of the Motor Is the Sweetest Sound," by Jean Shepherd, © 1974 by the New York Times Company. Reprinted by permission.

P 177. "Peter Pantheism," by Molly Haskell. © 1988 by Molly Haskell. From *Vogue*, September 1988.

P 178–79. "Deep Streep," by Molly Haskell. © 1988 by Molly Haskell. From *Ms.*, December 1988.

P 179–80. "Rebel With a Shrine," by Molly Haskell. © 1988 by Molly Haskell. From *Vogue*, September 1988.

P 180–81. *Living-Room War*, by Michael J. Arlen. Viking Press, 1969.

P 182–83. *The Musical Scene*, by Virgil Thomson. Alfred A. Knopf, 1945.

P 183–84. "T. S. Eliot at 101," by Cynthia Ozick. Copyright © 1989 by Cynthia Ozick. Originally in *The New Yorker*, Nov. 20, 1989. Reprinted by permission of Cynthia Ozick and her agents, Raines & Raines, 71 Park Ave., New York, N.Y. 10016.

P 189–90. *The Haircurl Papers*, by William Zinsser. Harper & Row, 1964.

P 196. *The America of George Ade*, edited, with an introduction by Jean Shepherd. G. P. Putnam's Sons, 1961.

P 197–98. *Shut Up, He Explained*, a Ring Lardner Selection. Charles Scribner's Sons, 1962.

P 198–99. *Archy and Mehitabel*, by Don Marquis. Doubleday & Co., 1927.

P 199–200. *The Owl in the Attic and Other Perplexities*, by James Thurber. Harper & Bros., 1931.

P 200. *Benchley—or Else!*, by Robert Benchley. Harper & Bros., 1947.

P 202. *Strictly from Hunger*, by S. J. Perelman. Random House, 1937. Also in *The Most of S. J. Perelman*, Simon & Schuster, 1958.

P 203. *Getting Even*, by Woody Allen. Random House, 1971.

P 204. "End of the Trail," by Garrison Keillor. Reprinted by permission of Garrison Keillor. © 1984. Originally in *The New Yorker*. Published in *We Are Still Married*, by Garrison Keillor, Viking Penguin, Inc., 1989.

P 204–05. "How the Savings and Loans Were Saved," by Garrison Keillor. Reprinted by permission of Garrison Keillor. © 1989. Originally in *The New Yorker*. Published in *We Are Still Married*.

P 212–14. *One Writer's Beginnings*, by Eudora Welty. Copyright © 1983, 1984 by Eudora Welty. Reprinted by permission of the publishers, Harvard University Press, Cambridge, Mass.

P 214–15. *A Walker in the City*, by Alfred Kazin. Harcourt, Brace, 1951.

P 216. *A Romantic Education*, by Patricia Hampl. Houghton Mifflin Co. 1981.

P 217. *Clinging to the Wreckage*, by John Mortimer. Penguin Books, 1984.

P 218–19. *Growing*, by Leonard Woolf. Harcourt Brace Jovanovich (Harvest paperback), 1975.

P 219–20. "Ornament and Silence," by Kennedy Fraser. Reprinted by permission; © 1989 Kennedy Fraser. Originally in *The New Yorker*, Nov. 6, 1989.

P 242–43. *Spring Training*, by William Zinsser. Harper & Row, 1989. Prentice-Hall paperback, 1990.

P 245–262. "The News From Timbuktu," by William Zinsser. From *Condé Nast Traveler*, October 1988.

Index